Muslim Travellers

Comparative Studies on Muslim Societies
General Editor, Barbara D. Metcalf

Muslim Travellers
Pilgrimage, migration, and the religious imagination

Edited by
Dale F. Eickelman *and*
James Piscatori

University of California Press
Berkeley · Los Angeles

Published by the University of California Press
Berkeley and Los Angeles, California

First published 1990
by Routledge
11 New Fetter Lane, London EC4P 4EE

Library of Congress Cataloging in Publication Data

Muslim travellers: pilgrimage, migration, and the religious
imagination / edited by Dale Eickelman and James
Piscatori.
    p.   cm.
Includes bibliographical references.
ISBN 0-520-07019-4
1. Travel − Religious aspects − Islam.   2. Muslim
pilgrims and pilgrimages.   3. Islamic countries −
Emigration and immigration.   4. Emigration and
immigration − Religious aspects − Islam.
I. Eickelman, Dale F., 1942−   .   II. Piscatori, James P.
BP190.5.T73M87   1990
297'.446−dc20   90-33657
                                                                              CIP

Comparative Studies on Muslim Societies, 9

ISBN 0-520-07019-4 cloth
ISBN 0-520-07252-9 paper

Printed in Great Britain
1 2 3 4 5 6 7 8 9

Contents

Illustrations

Notes on contributors

Julia A. Clancy-Smith is Assistant Professor of Middle Eastern and North African History at the University of Virginia, Charlottesville. She received a PhD from the University of California at Los Angeles in 1988. She also holds a BSFS and an MA from Georgetown University. She is the author of 'Saints, mahdis and arms: religion and resistance in nineteenth-century North Africa', in Edmund Burke III and Ira Lapidus (eds) *Islam, Politics and Social Movements* (University of California Press, Berkeley, Calif., 1988) and 'In the eye of the beholder: the North African Sufi orders and colonial production of knowledge, 1830–1900', *African Journal*, 16, 1988.

Dale F. Eickelman is the Ralph and Richard Lazarus Professor of Anthropology and Human Relations at Dartmouth College, Hanover. His field research in the Middle East includes extensive studies of religion and politics in Morocco, the Sultanate of Oman, and elsewhere. His publications include: *Moroccan Islam* (University of Texas Press, Austin and London, 1976; Arabic translation 1988); *The Middle East: An Anthropological Approach* (Prentice-Hall, Englewood Cliffs and London, 1981; 2nd edn, 1989); *Knowledge and Power in Morocco* (Princeton University Press, Princeton and London, 1985); and numerous scholarly articles and contributions to edited books. He is currently completing a study on changing perceptions of religious and political authority in the Arabian Gulf.

Sam I. Gellens teaches history at the Ramaz School in New York City. A specialist in Islamic social history, his Columbia University dissertation was awarded the Malcolm H. Kerr Dissertation Prize in Humanities in 1986 by the Middle East Studies Association of North America. He is the author of a forthcoming monograph, *Learning and Local Identity in Medieval Islam: Egypt, 218–487/ 833–1094* (Institut Français d'Archéologie Orientale, Cairo).

Kemal H. Karpat is Professor of History at the University of Wisconsin, Madison. He is author of *The Gecekondu: Rural Migration and Urbanization in Turkey* (Cambridge University Press, Cambridge, 1976); and *Turkey's Politics: the Transition to a Multi-Party System* (Princeton University Press, Princeton, 1959), and editor of *Political and Social Thought in the Contemporary Middle East* (Pall Mall, London, 1968; Praeger, New York, 1982); and *The Ottoman State and its Place in World History* (Brill, Leiden, 1974).

Robert Launay is Associate Professor of Anthropology at Northwestern University. He has published an ethnography of the Dyula of the northern Ivory Coast, *Traders Without Trade: Responses to Change in Two Dyula Communities* (Cambridge University Press, Cambridge, 1982), and is currently completing a second book, *Silamaya: Controversy, Change and Identity in Islam Among the Dyula*.

Mary Byrne McDonnell is a Program Associate at the Social Science Research Council in New York. She completed her studies at Columbia University in 1986, where she specialized in South-east Asian and Middle Eastern social history. From 1981–4 she conducted fieldwork in Malaysia on the socio-economic impact of the *hajj* on Malay society over the past century at both the national and the local levels. She was particularly interested in comparing the role of the *hajj* in the urban and rural environments.

Ruth Mandel received her PhD in Anthropology from the University of Chicago. She has conducted fieldwork among migrant workers in West Berlin and Paris, and with repatriated workers in Turkey and Greece. She is a Lecturer in Social Anthropology at the University of London, continuing her studies on the *Gastarbeiter* (guestworker) community. She has contributed to several journals and edited volumes.

Muhammad Khalid Masud is editor of *Islamic Studies*, a quarterly journal of the Islamic Research Institute, Islamabad. He has taught Islamic Law at the Institute of Administration, Ahmadu Bello University, Zaria, Nigeria, at the Qaid-i-Azam University, Islamabad, and at the International Islamic University, Islamabad. He is author of *Islamic Legal Philosophy* (Islamic Research Institute, Islamabad, 1977), and *Iqbal and the Concept of Ijtihad* (in Urdu) and several articles on law and social change in Islam.

Barbara D. Metcalf is Professor of History at the University of California, Davis. She is author of *Islamic Revival in British India* (Princeton University Press, Princeton, 1982), and editor of *Moral*

Conduct and Authority: The Place of Adab in South Asian Islam (University of California Press, Berkeley, 1984).

Abderrahmane El Moudden is Assistant Professor of History at Mohammed V University, Rabat, where he received his Doctorat de Troisième Cycle on 'The relations between rural society and the central government in 18th and 19th century Morocco' (1984). He is currently at Princeton University, studying Moroccan–Ottoman relations in the sixteenth through nineteenth centuries.

James Piscatori is Senior Lecturer in Middle East Politics at the University College of Wales, Aberystwyth. Among his publications are *Islam in a World of Nation-States* (Cambridge University Press, Cambridge, 1986) and an edited book, *Islam in the Political Process* (Cambridge University Press, Cambridge, 1983).

Nancy Tapper is Lecturer in the Anthropology of the Arab World at the School of Oriental and African Studies, University of London. She has conducted fieldwork among pastoral nomads in Iran and Afghanistan and has published numerous articles on women, marriage, and politics in these societies. Her most recent fieldwork has been on women and religion in a provincial town in Turkey.

Alex Weingrod is Professor of Anthropology at The Ben Gurion University of The Negev. He is author of *Reluctant Pioneers: Village Development in Israel* (Cornell University Press, Ithaca, 1966) and editor of *Studies in Israeli Ethnicity: After the Ingathering* (Gordon & Breach, New York, 1985).

Note on transliteration

Any book that draws upon materials in Arabic, Persian, Urdu, Malay, Turkish, Dyula, and Hebrew poses considerable problems of transliteration, especially as many contributors stress colloquial rather than literary usages. The system employed here, with as much consistency as possible, has been to use the system adopted by the *International Journal of Middle East Studies* for Arabic, Persian, Turkish, and Hebrew, with additions to represent other languages as necessary. Diacritics have been omitted, except in the glossary, where they are given in full. As suggested by Judith Butcher's *Copy-Editing: The Cambridge Handbook*, the plural of words has been formed by the addition of an "s" to the singular, except in such cases as *'ulama'* in which the transliterated plural form has become standard.

Preface

The subject of Muslim travel is unexpectedly complex. One might assume that religious doctrine prescribes certain kinds of travel, and that the ritual movement of Muslims leads to a heightened identification with Islam and with fellow Muslims. But the chapters of this book question such conventional wisdom. In looking for the answers to the basic questions that underlie this discussion – What does travel mean to Muslims? What are its motivations? What are its effects – we are struck by a pervasive intricacy and even ambiguity.

When the first question on the nature of Muslim travel is considered, it seems judicious to infer that, like all travel, it is principally a journey of the mind. Travel is pre-eminently an act of imagination, and, as our contributors amply demonstrate, a literal reading of *hajj* (pilgrimage), *hijra* (emigration), *rihla* (travel for learning and other purposes), *ziyara* (visits to shrines), and even labour migration, is inappropriate. These obviously constitute physical movement from one place to another, but, owing to the power of the religious imagination, they involve spiritual or temporal movement at the same time. Muhammad Khalid Masud indicates that one sense of *hijra* is movement of the soul from a state of corruption to one of purity, and Julia Clancy-Smith shows that for Rahmaniyya adepts in North Africa, *ziyara* to the tomb of their founder guarantees movement from unhappiness to happiness in this world, and from damnation to salvation in the next.

There may also be imagined movement across gender or ethnic lines. Nancy Tapper points out that for Turkish women, participation in the *hajj*, *ziyarets* to local shrines and religious festivals becomes an act of affirmation that, before God, they are equal to men, and that they too can attain salvation. Referring to a non-Muslim but parallel context, Alex Weingrod shows how visits to saint shrines in Israel are, for Moroccan and Tunisian Jews, a sign of their passage from hesitant, socially and politically distinct

xii

immigrants to self-confident, equal citizens. Finally, Muslims may envision travel across time as a substitute for physical travel, as when, in the case of the pre-twentieth-century Dyula whom Robert Launay describes, travel to the Hijaz was unnecessary to trace one's line of intellectual descent (*isnad*) back to illustrious Muslims of the early Islamic period.

Yet the very idea of travel, however much it may project the believer across spiritual space and time, and overcome barriers of gender and politics, cannot be separated from the anticipation of return to home. Here, too, travel is an inventive journey. Whether home is the place of departure, as in the case of the *hajjis* whom Barbara Metcalf and Mary McDonnell describe, or a new place of settlement, as in the case of the Turkish *Gastarbeiter* in Germany whom Ruth Mandel details, or the Balkan *muhajirs* on whom Kemal Karpat writes, travel has inevitably invested it with new meanings. Travellers may, as the labour migrants generally do, long for the old home; or, like the children of those migrants, increasingly regard the old as incomprehensible and in any case irrelevant; or, like the Balkan *muhajirs* to Turkey, believe that they have at last gone home. What seems clear is that travel and home – motion and place – constitute one process, and that in travelling beyond one's local time and space, one enters a mythical realm where home, the "fixed point" of departure and return, is re-imagined and further travel inspired. In the *Enigma of Arrival*, V.S. Naipul (1987: 318) testifies to the power of this process when he speaks of:

> Places doubly and trebly sacred to me because far away in England I had lived them imaginatively over many books and had in my fantasy set in those places the very beginning of things, had constructed of them a fantasy of home.

When we turn to the second question – the motivations for travel – we confront head on the role that religion, and specifically Islam, has to play. It is tempting to take the view that religion, as a set of universal and authoritative beliefs and practices, enjoins certain conduct upon Muslims everywhere. But the contributors to this volume illuminate inherent tensions that belie such a decided view. The presumed constancy of dogma competes with the actual shift in meanings that dogma acquires in differing contexts, and the presumed universality of the Islamic community competes with the local communities in which Muslims actually live. But what also emerges is that the co-existence of these contrasting tendencies, however forced it may seem in the abstract, is largely unremarked upon by Muslims themselves.

Ideas such as *hijra* and *rihla* do change over time and in various places, but, as Masud observes, there is also a "semantics of expectation" that makes such key terms instantly recognisable, and valued in themselves, as signposts on a changing landscape. In a similar manner, Muslims seem effortlessly to juggle local and multiple identities – villager, tribesman, woman, citizen – with the broader identity of believer and to legitimise them all by reference to the idiom of the cosmopolitan community of believers (*umma*). This is not to suggest, however, that the modes of Islamic belief are uniform. Rather, as Launay points out, a greater sensitivity to the tenets of the law among the Dyula – "*shari'a*-mindedness", to use Hodgson's evocative phrase – is related to economic liberalisation and the rise of a more pronounced social hierarchy. In addition, Tapper notes that the emphasis which Turkish women place upon travel for religious purposes depends to a considerable extent upon their general attitude towards the role of men and women in society.

The image of a flexible Islam in thought and practice thus emerges in this book, and we see that the motives for action in general, as for travel in particular, are inevitably mixed – a combination of holy reason and social, economic, and political concerns. As the introduction points out, ideas are unquestionably important spurs to social action, but they are not the sole determinants. Our contributors show that such factors as status, self-affirmation, and economic interest are equally as important as the sense of obligation, and that such categories as class, ethnicity, gender, and historical memory are as relevant as doctrine.

Sam Gellens, for example, observes that *rihla* in the tenth and eleventh centuries was often intimately connected with trade and associated with a certain class structure – traders, commercial middle-men, and intellectuals – and both Metcalf and McDonnell demonstrate that the hope of enhanced social standing accounts, in part, for why people of varying social backgrounds undertake the pilgrimage to the holy places. The attractions of the "centre" may be several, therefore, but what also emerges in these pages is a questioning of the received wisdom that there is but one validating centre in Islam. To use Tapper's expression, a more complex "sacred geography" appears, as does a more subtle sense of location, of where Muslims stand in relationship to each other and to religiously defined space. The need to travel to saintly shrines or, as Mandel shows, the need of Turkish workers in Europe to travel back to Turkey, may be as compelling as the doctrinally enjoined pilgrimage to Mecca and Medina.

In turning to the third basic question, concerning the effects of travel, we find that a heightened identification with Islam may result. However, as Abderrahmane El Moudden says of Moroccan travellers in the sixteenth to the eighteenth centuries, an ambivalence of identity is also as likely, if not more likely, to result. Cornell Fleischer (personal communication) suggests that the consciousness of locality and difference appears to have intensified in the seventeenth and eighteenth centuries throughout the Middle Eastern Muslim world in general. This intensification allows one to infer that the transition to territorially-based plural communities preceded the advent of western powers in the region, the normally accepted bench-mark for the emergence of the "modern" era.

From this transitional period suggested by Fleischer and El Moudden to the present, the travellers for religious purposes have, as in earlier periods, been aware of the community of faith and goals that ties them to fellow travellers. But at the same time, they have come into direct contact with the real differences of language, sect, race, and customs that unavoidably make up the *umma*. Contrary to the conventional wisdom of western social scientists, therefore, the encounter with the Muslim "other" has been at least as important for self-definition as the confrontation with the European "other".

Indeed, even as travellers sense participation in a great enterprise, they become aware of the lack of commonalities and are sometimes overwhelmed by them. Whether it is the sixteenth-century Arab traveller to Istanbul whom El Moudden describes; or Kemal Karpat, the Romanian-born ethnic Turk who migrated to Turkey in the 1940s; or the Europeanised Turkish worker returning to Turkey whom Mandel describes, each has the unsettling experience of feeling different within a Muslim community when only familiarity, even solace, was anticipated. The ironic counterpoint to travel broadening one's consciouness of the spiritual unity of the *umma* is that travel may define frontiers between Muslims and thus narrow their horizons.

Travel can also be politically subversive. Launay explains how the Dyula, who travelled to Mecca and Medina for pilgrimage or religious learning, returned to advocate greater orthodoxy – thus undermining the established order based upon local notions of scholarly and political legitimacy. Mandel shows how the Turkish Alevi *Gastarbeiter* who are marginalised twice over – Turkish in Germany, Alevi in Sunni Turkey – reshape their Islamic and political identities in their new environment and, in the process, seek to reverse the pattern of Sunni domination and even to create an Alevi nationalism. Weingrod demonstrates that travel to saint shrines and proximity to saintly *baraka* (grace) have served as a focal point for Sephardic Israelis who take pride in their recent assimilation into the society, and have thus helped to encourage the growth of rightist-nationalist political ideologies among them.

But governments, always mindful of the political potential of Islam, have sought to co-opt religious practice. The Turkish government has promoted the identification of "modern" Islam with republicanism and, as McDonnell documents in the case of Malaysia, the *hajj* has to a considerable extent been nationalised. Pilgrims travel in national delegations under the auspices of the national bureaucracy and spend the brief time in Arabia in minimal contact with other pilgrims. Popular identification of the nation with Islam is in the government's interest, and a probable result. Yet political identities, like religious ones, are constantly re-imagined, and the effects of travel are as ambiguous as the motives for it.

In the preparation of this book, we have become acutely aware that the role of travel in Muslim societies and in Islamic doctrine is not a topic which has been systematically explored by historians or social scientists. Moreover, we have tried to encourage thinking on a common topic among scholars concerned with historical periods ranging from the first centuries of Islam to the present, and with Muslims in societies ranging from Malaysia and West Africa to Western Europe, and from different traditions of scholarly enquiry. This has posed particular challenges. As we suggest above, at an abstract level, travel for pilgrimage, scholarly learning, proselytisation, visits to saints' shrines, commerce and migration, both forced and voluntary, has contributed significantly to shaping the religious imagination in both the past and the present. More-over, travel for these various purposes is not mutually exclusive. None the less, there appears to have been an implicit scholarly division of labour among disciplines, with historians and scholars in the history of religions focusing upon various aspects of the pilgrimage and the religious imagination, while social scientists have for the most part concentrated upon migration, particularly labour migration, to the exclusion of considering its impact upon religious expression and thought.

As we suggest in the bibliographic essay at the end of this volume, until the mid-1980s, few studies crossed this line. We find it encouraging that this implicit disciplinary division of labour has become increasingly blurred in recent years. Anthropological studies of pilgrimage and other forms of travel have now become much more common. Indeed, some of the most significant recent contributions are studies of Muslims who have migrated to or settled in Europe. Likewise, most of the chapters in this volume derive from recent field research or historical inquiry, or, as in the case of Masud, represent new directions of research by senior scholars.

As in any collective enterprise intended to represent cross-disciplinary approaches, we have faced a more substantial editorial challenge than would be the case with an endeavour in which most contributors share the same disciplinary training or are at comparable levels in their scholarly careers. Whereas some contributions represent single-case studies, the comparisons built into many of the papers – across region (e.g. Gellens), time (e.g. El Moudden, McDonnell, and Metcalf), or both (e.g. Masud) – suggest a surprising level of linkages. Other contributions, including the introductory chapter by the editors, are intended to set a framework for wide-ranging comparison and to elicit the conceptual issues, both implicit and explicit, underlying this book.

Not the least of the challenges in creating this book has been to encourage contributors from varying disciplines and national scholarly traditions to speak to one another in a mutually intelligible language. The conceptual language invoked by participants in one discipline as practised in, say, North America, might adequately convey in shorthand form the lineage of an idea or a particular theoretical orientation, but may appear as impenetrable jargon to other scholars. Indeed, as an anthropologist and a political scientist respectively, we acknowledge that the contributions from social scientists, including ourselves, have often verged upon the semi-private vocabularies of our respective trades, while the early drafts of other contributions often unrealistically assumed prior knowledge of specific historical periods and places. As editors and contributors, we have made an effort in good faith to avoid the private languages of disciplinary specialists.

Chapters 2 and 3 provide complementary discussions of doctrines of travel in Muslim societies. We begin with a discussion of doctrine because it has often been argued that Muslims share more explicit doctrinal tenets enjoining movement than do the followers of other major religious traditions. The originality of Muhammad Khalid Masud's analysis of doctrinal issues is twofold. First, in contrast to many accounts of Muslim jurisprudence, he stresses the necessity of considering the *contexts* in which doctrines are developed and propagated. Second, he considers how the rise of "new intellectuals" in the Muslim world – i.e. those who have graduated from western-style schools and universities – affects the interpretation and justification of "traditional" doctrine. He argues that one consequence of not being tied to the interpretive styles of the traditional schools of jurisprudence is to create an

Muslim travellers

opening for extremism, although the impact of such radical interpretations is often "partial and ephemeral".

Sam Gellens's chapter complements Masud's in indicating the importance accorded to travel in the *hadith* literature, and the practical importance of travel in the forms of pilgrimage, trade, and, in particular, scholarship. Gellens argues that doctrines of travel and travel for the sake of religious learning framed issues of locality, universality, and identity in the medieval Muslim world from the ninth through the eleventh centuries. Through comparing three contemporary Muslim societies in communication with one another – Andalusia, Egypt, and Khurasan – Gellens suggests why travel for learning shaped a cosmopolitan sense of identity in all cases, but was particularly important in shaping a sense of local identity for Andalusia, which sought intellectual succor from more secure centres of learning. Indeed, one of Gellens's major points is that the changing military and political conditions – particularly as Andalusia's relations with its Christian neighbours to the north steadily deteriorated – led to shifts in notions of centre and periphery. Although he only briefly considers the importance of scholarly travel in shaping the sense of identity of Jewish communities in the medieval Muslim world, he points out important parallels with Muslim senses of centre. For both communities, Andalusia became increasingly peripheral, and Iraq, Egypt (and, in the Jewish case, Tunisia) became increasingly "central".

Chapters 4 and 5 deal with travel accounts, particularly those related to the *hajj*, in different historical periods. Abderrahmane El Moudden's account compares the importance of travel – in particular, for commerce, diplomacy, and learning – to Moroccans from the sixteenth through the eighteenth centuries, the subtle ways in which practice and perceptions varied over time and place, and the importance of travel accounts for those unable to undertake such arduous journeys. If, as with the accounts analysed by Gellens, travel offered the opportunity to imagine the wider, encompassing horizons of Muslim community, it also progressively contributed to an emerging awareness of being at the frontier of the Islamic world and of a sense of distinctive political identity.

Barbara Metcalf similarly deals with differences in travel accounts from the Indian sub-continent from the late eighteenth century to the present. As she points out, the pace at which this genre of narratives is produced accelerates with the onset of British colonial rule, in part because the new technology of the printing press accelerates their dissemination. Indeed, by the late nineteenth century many accounts began to be produced in English. She notes in particular the changing sense of person which emerges over time

xviii

from these accounts, and the growing importance of individual, internalised experience. Yet even if many of these accounts internalise European notions of governance and some imitate European travel writing, they do not simply mirror European individualism.

The section on pilgrimage and migration emphasises how these experiences complement one another and shape religious experience. In Chapter 6, Mary McDonnell discusses patterns of pilgrimage from Malaysia over the past century, assessing how changing economic, political, and social contexts have affected its conduct and significance. In the latter part of the nineteenth century, the typical pilgrim was a member of the elite. Increasingly since the 1930s, however, pilgrims have come from the middle classes and, since the 1970s, from the wealthier rural areas. In earlier periods, almost no women participated in the *hajj*, but their participation has steadily increased since the 1930s to the point where nearly half of all Malaysian pilgrims today are women. Parallel to trends described by Metcalf, McDonnell shows how the pilgrimage has both a communal and an individual importance and how "external" considerations of status blend with "internal" considerations of state of mind. Moreover, she shows that enhanced state supervision of the *hajj* is one of the most important developments of the postcolonial period. Contrary to the general trend established in this book, however, McDonnell argues that Malaysians have an undifferentiated concept of centre – modern-day Saudi Arabia – and are drawn to it because of the perception of their own "peripheral" position. The result, she argues, is a suffusion of the periphery with the "central" values of a non-revivalist, politically accommodationist Islam that the Saudis espouse and the Malaysian government favours.

In Chapter 7, Kemal Karpat deals primarily with Muslim identity in the Balkans from the mid-nineteenth century to 1914, and the ways in which forced migrations during this period – an all too common occurrence – served as catalysts for re-imagining complex national, ethnic, and religious identities. If, unlike Metcalf, Karpat emphasises changes in collective, communal identities, we find particularly fascinating the juxtaposition of his historical narrative with a postscript in which he describes his personal experience of migration from Romania in the 1940s.

Karpat's argument echoes what might be called the "Turkish–Islamic synthesis". In his view, an apolitical sense of Muslim identity, which obtained in the pre-nineteenth century Ottoman Empire, was transformed into a politicised one largely because of the new immigrants to Turkey. This transformation, in turn, is made to account for the emergence of the Turkish nation-state.

The assumptions underlying the "Turkish–Islamic" synthesis are admittedly controversial. But Karpat's narrative, representing a distinct school of thought, becomes all the more useful because of its admixture of "objective" and "personal" histories, with the one informing the other. Karpat's essay, like all historical representations, may be read as an ethnographic text.

In Chapter 8, Ruth Mandel traces how the sense of centre becomes transformed over time for Turkish workers in Europe, so that West Germany itself becomes "central" for the second generation while Turkey becomes peripheral. Turkish Alevi Muslims, often perceived as a "fifth column" in the Ottoman Empire and identified with the political left by Sunni Muslims in contemporary Turkey, have emerged in West Germany as the dominant group instead of Sunni Muslims. The Alevis consider themselves to be more "democratic, tolerant, and progressive" than their Sunni Turkish counterparts and feel less threatened by German society. In Turkey, Alevi identity is constructed primarily in contrast to that of Sunni Turks; in Germany, both Germans and Sunni Turks become the "other".

The final section, "Saints, Scholars, and Travel", concerns more particularistic forms of travel for religious purposes. In scholarship on Islam and in the history of religions in general, there is often a tendency to assume that the more encompassing formulations of belief and practice shared by the community of believers inevitably overshadow more particularistic and locally oriented ones in importance. In Chapter 9, Robert Launay's account of scholarly credentials among the Dyula indicates the links between travel, commerce, and religious learning, but cautions against the *a priori* assumption that travel and study in the Arabic-speaking Middle East were more prestigious than access to local knowledge. However, local controls over knowledge were challenged by revivalist movements from the mid-nineteenth century. Their adherents had gone to the Arab East in search of superior knowledge. Upon returning, they questioned the social distinctions of the religious and political status quo, based upon both heredity and a monopoly of Islamic knowledge. This tension between locally derived answers to what is Islam and "being Muslim", and answers inspired by contact with the wider community of the believers, continues to the present period.

In Chapter 10, Julia Clancy-Smith's essay on the Rahmaniyya religious order in Algeria during the late eighteenth century also concerns the shifting balance between local, regional, and wider bases for religious authority. Her account combines attention to the biography of the movement's founder, regional politics, and social history to explain why new networks of religious authority arose during the late eighteenth century. She demonstrates the way in which the founder gained adherents during his travels at a time of political uncertainty, and the importance subsequently attached to visits to his shrines. The individual act of self-assertation that such visits represented also enhanced a sense of solidarity which sustained the new brotherhood.

In Chapter 11, Alex Weingrod's study of visits to saints' shrines in Israel since the early 1960s amplifies this connection between individual movement and collective religious experience. For the newly arrived Moroccan and Tunisian Jews, or for those who have long settled but who have not socially or politically "arrived", the hope of acquiring saintly blessings can be comforting, and even transforming. The sense of being part of a great movement results, and in fact the shrine visits often take on institutional form through the establishment of associated educational and social centres and through their explicit politicisation. Although obviously not directly concerned with the Muslim world, Weingrod's essay provides an instructive comparison with it. The Israeli Sephardic experience points to a larger Maghribi culture shared by both Muslims and Jews and which leads to the linking of spiritual fulfilment with periodic visits to saints' shrines and even to the need for "living saints".

In Chapter 12, Nancy Tapper demonstrates that visits to saints' shrines, often thought to be especially pronounced in the Maghrib, are significant in Turkey. She also confirms that travel associated with religious purposes has more to do with spiritual and social compensations than with doctrine, and shows that visits to shrines are officially discouraged, but that women especially undertake them. The opportunity to travel and visit together, without men present on these occasions, provides companionship and a network of support, and when men and women do travel together, as on the *hajj* or to visit family members at the end of the month of fasting, women are afforded the opportunity to assert their equality.

With these examples of travel provided by Tapper and the other contributors, we have juxtaposed ideas and activities whose generic diversity is vast. Defenders of comparative studies would acknowledge that these studies are difficult to elaborate in cases such as the wider Muslim community in which the existence of a presumed cultural whole may render its independent units virtually indistinguishable. In the search for common elements, it is also possible that we may force comparisons. Furthermore, to the extent that common elements are found, there is the danger of unintentionally generating an essentialist view of Islam or of being Muslim. We believe, however, that the comparative nature of this volume has its uses. It specifically helps us to avoid what Skocpol (1984: 376) calls "the interpretive tendency to attribute self-contained significance" to each form of travel in the Muslim world that either is initiated for religious purposes or comes to assume religious significance.

Our comparative focus has been facilitated by the collaborative quality of this project. With one exception, the contributions to this book were initially presented in a workshop on "Movement and Exchange in Muslim Societies", New York, 24–26 April 1986, and in a conference on the same topic held in Princeton, 17–19 September 1987. Both were sponsored by the Joint Committee for the Comparative Study of Muslim Societies of the Social Science Research Council and American Council of Learned Societies, of which the co-editors were members. The committee also generously provided support for the preparation of this volume, the first to result from projects initiated directly by the committee since its formal inception. The editors thank David L. Szanton, Executive Associate, for support rendered at critical stages; Cornell Fleischer, Ladislav Holy, and William R. Roff for reading the typescript in its entirety in an earlier version; Carol Delaney for valuable insights along the way; and Barbara D. Metcalf for ideas towards an appropriate title.

References

Naipul, V.S. (1987) *The Enigma of Arrival*, Penguin, London.
Skocpol, Theda (1984) "Emerging agendas and recurrent strategies in historical sociology", in Theda Skocpol (ed.) *Vision and Method in Historical Sociology*, Cambridge University Press, New York, pp. 356–91.

Introduction

Chapter one

Social theory in the study of Muslim societies

Dale F. Eickelman and James Piscatori

Pilgrimage and migration in Muslim societies are forms of political and social action. These forms of action, like others, raise basic questions for the contemporary social scientific study of Islam. The most basic issue is how to understand such action – in this case, the actions of Muslims and the thoughts presumed to guide them – in various places and times.

This problem is especially acute because it brings us into the opaque realm, on the one hand, of reasons for action (i.e. why is it undertaken) and, on the other, of the meanings that various actors impute to action (i.e. what impact or change is generated by it). This is to say nothing of the ability of actors to accomplish an action (Giddens 1984: 5–13).

Our argument takes the following course in explaining travel as specific forms of social action within Muslim religious traditions. First, we consider what is meant by "Islam" itself as a social phenomenon in which these actions take place. Second, we indicate the specific importance of travel and its significance as a process of social action in understanding "Islam" and ideas of Muslim community. Third, we consider the idea of motives and "interests", those culturally and materially informed incentives to travel. In doing so, we seek to clarify key concepts which are relevant in general to social thought in religious contexts and in particular to the issue at hand: doctrine in context; the relationship between centre and periphery; and scale. Fourth, we turn to the complementary issue of effects and identities, those specific social and religious meanings created through travel which inspire changes in how Muslims conceive of and experience "Islam" and the communities in which they live.

"Islam" as a social phenomenon

Muslim communities, like all religious communities, are *imagined* (Anderson 1983: 14–16). They are created – and knowable – through the vision, faith, and practices of their adherents. Faith is accepted and sustained through symbol and metaphor, the very stuff of imagination which not only enlarges adherents' perceptions but reorders them so that the validity and rationality of religious faith and practice seem only natural (Coulson 1981: 3–8). However, the senses of community which derive from faith and practice are necessarily interpreted and shaped in distinct ways in differing places, times, and societies. Participants may assert that their representations of practice and tradition are stable, uniform, and derive from the distant past, yet an examination of the history of these communities indicates both the diversity of these practices and traditions, and their transformations over time.

The paradoxes encountered by theorists of nationalism apply equally to scholars concerned with religious traditions. Historians, writes Anderson (1983: 14), see ideas of nationalism and nation as "objectively modern", although nationalists consider these notions to possess a "subjective antiquity"; nationality is formally enshrined in international law but irremediably particular in its concrete manifestations; nationalisms carry political force yet often reflect a "philosophical poverty or even incoherence. . . . Like Gertrude Stein in the face of Oakland, one can rather quickly conclude that there is 'no there there' ".

In a similar manner, the concept of "religion" is paradoxically consistent and clear to most carriers of particular religious traditions, yet unsettled, and perhaps even inherently ambiguous, in content and form to others – including many committed to these traditions. Religious adherents often assert that their beliefs and practices have been fixed over time, and scholars who have argued for placing religious thought and practice into their different historical contexts have often encountered stiff opposition. In the particular case of Islam, advocates of such studies, including the late Fazlur Rahman (1982, 1985), have often faced criticisms similar to those levied earlier against W. Robertson Smith (1956 [orig. 1889]), who argued for the historical study of biblical texts and institutions. But, as Coulson (1981: 3) says: "When the vital connection between religion and imagination is either overlooked or denied, it is not merely theology or the theologian that suffers. The very life of religion ebbs and becomes infertile". Indeed, the reality is that religious communities, like all "imagined" communities, change over time. Their boundaries are shifted by, and shift,

4

the political, economic, and social contexts in which these participants find themselves.

Muslim travel as social action

As in other civilisations and traditions, travel is particularly important when considering changes in Muslim imagined communities past and present. Travel creates boundaries and distinctions, even as travellers believe that they are transcending them. In the hope of creating new horizons, travellers set off from home, encounter "others" and return with a sharpened awareness of difference and similarity.

Muslim doctrine explicitly enjoins or encourages certain forms of travel. One is the express obligation to undertake the pilgrimage to Mecca (*hajj*). Another, *hijra*, is the obligation to migrate from lands where the practice of Islam is constrained to those where in principle no such constraints exist. Visits to local or regional shrines (*ziyaras*) and travel in search of knowledge (*rihla*) provide further examples of religiously inspired travel. Yet other forms of travel unrecognised in doctrine can have equal or even greater significance. For example, Muslims have often mixed travel for trade purposes with religiously motivated travel. Moroccan travellers from the sixteenth through the eighteenth century (see El Moudden, Chapter 4 of this volume) and Dyula ones in the nineteenth and twentieth centuries (see Launay, Chapter 9 of this volume) combined travel and *rihla*. To take another example, contemporary labour migration within the Muslim world, but also in Europe – called Islam's new "frontier" in one recent study (Dassetto and Bastenier 1988) and its "suburbs" in another (Kepel 1987) – has facilitated changes in religious institutions and practices at least as important as those inspired by earlier generations of elite Muslim intellectuals in the Middle East and the Indian subcontinent.

Travel of several kinds is therefore significant for Muslim self-expression, and travel is of course informed by the cultural and social contexts in which Muslims are located. None the less, such phenomena need not be seen as unique to the Muslim world in order for their significance to be affirmed. The argument can be made that pilgrimage as a form of movement is significant in both Hindu and Christian traditions, as it is in Judaism in the Middle East (see Weingrod, Chapter 11 of this volume). Moreover, just as the *hijra*, the migration of the Prophet and his followers from Mecca to Medina in 622, became a dominant theme in Islamic political thought (see Masud, Chapter 2 of this volume), Walzer

(1985: 142) argues that the biblical story of Exodus has served as a key metaphor − the flight from bondage to freedom − in western political thought over the centuries.

Motives and interests

It would be helpful if, with some confidence, we could understand why certain types of persons or social categories in Muslim societies are disposed to undertake pilgrimage, other travel for religious reasons, or economic migration. The difficulty of imputing motives and interests to individuals or peoples is now commonly recognised. The literature of the social sciences offers two suggestive yet incomplete approaches to dealing with this issue.

The first is to examine social status and class position and to presume that the "interests" associated with them inform conduct. It might be assumed, for example, that the educated or intellectual elites are more likely to be influenced by doctrinal considerations, or at least to say that they are. It might also be assumed that those deemed by the upper strata of their own society to constitute the "lower" orders − in terms of birth, gender, ethnicity, education, wealth, or authority − are motivated primarily by social, political, and economic deprivation. The "middle" orders, or the bourgeoisie, would then be assumed to be particularly sensitive to questions of status, both to enhance their image in the eyes of those whom they consider to be above them and to differentiate themselves clearly from those below. Some nineteenth- and twentieth-century pilgrims to Mecca from the Indian sub-continent, for example, wrote accounts of their travels in English (see Metcalf, Chapter 5 of this volume). These accounts were accessible only to the British and British-educated Indian elite. Their authors thereby distanced themselves from both the traditional Muslim elite and other Muslims, and implicitly fulfilled the British image of the good and loyal Muslim.

Tempting though such generalisations may be, however, studies of specific Muslim societies provide contrary interpretations of the relationship between styles of Islamic belief and social origins. The case of Islamic activism in Egypt is instructive. One observer (Ibrahim 1980: 438−9) suggests that most of the Islamic activists responsible for violent acts against the Egyptian state were from modest, but not poor, backgrounds and were first-generation city dwellers. Another (Kepel 1986: 221) implies that a significant number had professional middle or upper class backgrounds. Still another (Ansari 1984) argues that the most successful activist groups contained persons of varying social backgrounds and that it was this mixture that accounted for their success.

In the case of northern Nigeria, the official report (Federal Government of Nigeria 1981: 79) on the Kano disturbances in 1980 attributed them to rural migrants who had been "brought up in extreme poverty [and] generally had a grudge against privileged people in the society". A recent study (Lubeck 1987) suggests a more complex relationship to social origins. Both industrial workers and marginalised "lumpen" labourers in northern Nigeria are predominantly of rural origin. The industrial workers generally seem to remain active in Qur'anic school networks, and use Islamic symbols and slogans in the effort to negotiate improved working conditions with their employers. The more marginal workers, including seasonal labourers and street peddlers, seem to be more inclined to adhere to itinerant Muslim preachers. It was only this group that was attracted to the millenarian violence of Alhaji Mohammed Marwa, known as Maitatsine ("the one who damns"), instigator of the Kano riots. The distinction between factory and "marginal" workers may partly be explained by the differences in their capability to effect changes in their living conditions.

Yet the specific case of northern Nigeria also suggests that explanations based upon social class or the relationship to specific modes of production cannot in themselves account for motives and interests. It is important, for example, to recall that millenarianism in Africa antedates Islam and that, in present-day northern Nigeria, there is a division between an "establishment" claiming descent from the eighteenth-century religious reformer 'Uthman dan Fodio and those Muslims who, for whatever reason, are not part of it. Thus explanations based upon social class or background must be supplemented by an appreciation of the larger historical circumstances.

The second approach offered by the social sciences focuses upon the rational choice of actors. This approach, in assuming that individuals or groups discern and choose among their interests according to a code of rationality, leaves the disquieting impression that they will reach the same decisions given similar circumstances. In this sense, both interests and rational choice become overly abstract. Apart from the inherent philosophical problem of the relationship between choice and rationality, this kind of conclusion fails to acknowledge that rationality needs to be interpreted and put into context.

The manifestly political example of the 1956 Suez crisis illustrates this. The Shuckburgh diaries (1986: 341) confirm that Anthony Eden, who incidentally had read Persian and Arabic at

Cambridge, thought of 'Abd al-Nasir as an Arab Mussolini. 'Abd al-Nasir could proclaim that the time of the Arab nation had come, and that moral power had shifted in favour of the non-aligned movement. Yet in Eden's view, the Egyptian leader could not fail to see that he still had to accommodate the military and economic might of the great powers. Heikal's (1986) account of Suez shows that 'Abd al-Nasir, for his part, believed that Eden could not fail to recognise that the great powers were no longer able to exercise their military options without incurring unacceptable political risks. Both leaders thought that the other was acting irrationally and therefore against his own interests.

This discussion of rationality reminds us of how difficult it is to establish the relationship between motives and social action with precision. None the less, this relationship can be more clearly discerned by elaborating upon its complexity, and that, in turn, suggests, in the case of action in religious contexts – specifically Muslim travel – the need to place doctrine in context, reconsider the centre–periphery dichotomy, and take into account the scale of Muslim societies and communities.

Doctrine

Many studies of doctrine imply or assume that it has an independent existence and is invariable across time and place. Committed believers make this assumption, but so do many scholarly observers who may be either sympathetic to Islam or not. Qur'anic injunctions, although almost self-evidently applicable to all Muslims, are none the less necessarily subject to differing social and political interpretations. The injunction to undertake the *hajj* is not necessarily invested with the same meaning for all Muslims, as those who write devotional literature on the pilgrimage sometimes assert. For Iranian Muslims in recent years, the pilgrimage to Mecca has had a political significance and intent certainly not shared by the keepers of the holy places. Moreover, Muhammad Ilyas, the founder of the transnational reform movement Jama' at Tabligh, suggested that *tabligh*, or proselytisation, is as important as, if not more important than, the *hajj* itself (Nadwi 1983: 44).

The Islamic notion of almsgiving (*zakat*) also illustrates the variability of doctrine according to circumstances. Some Muslims contend that *zakat* is a voluntary act of piety; others maintain that it is obligatory – to be collected and disbursed by the central government. There is also debate as to what percentage of income should be collected and how often. In the particular case of Shi'i Islam, the relationship between *zakat* and *khums*, that portion of

Figure 1.1 The cover art and title of this book, *The Slaughter at Mecca*, represent a contemporary, Iranian-influenced attempt to invest the *hajj* with political significance. Needless to say, the Saudi view of their management of the pilgrimage would be radically different from the one presented here. (Used by permission of the Committee for the Liberation of the Arabian Peninsula, London.)

income that the Shi'a give to their leading religious scholars (*'ulama'*), is a matter of active debate. The obligatory collection of *zakat* from bank accounts in Zia's Pakistan, part of an effort to impose an Islamic order, stimulated Shi'i opposition. Opposition to the mandatory collection of the *zakat* also appeared in Saudi Arabia (Piscatori 1986: 179) in the early 1950s and among peasants in Malaysia (Scott 1985).

Another example is the interpretation of the well-known Qur'anic phrase referring to the "oppressed" (*mustad'afun*) of the earth (Sura 4: 97), juxtaposed with the "oppressors" (*mustakbarun*) (Sura 16: 22–3). These terms have obviously had different meanings throughout history, and possess a special significance for contemporary Iranian Shi'a. The late Ayatollah Khomeini's use of these terms ironically evoked for some of his Iranian audience the secular discourse of the 1950s and 1960s on the dispossessed and the wretched of the earth.

Yet one must do more than acknowledge that the interpretation of doctrine changes according to prevailing economic, social, and political contexts. What is also required is a more nuanced consideration of time. Attempts to distinguish between classical and modern doctrines, for example, inadvertently create crude typologies that obscure the social and political forces which render certain doctrines more acceptable than others at any given time. Take the conventional assumption that the "gate of independent reasoning" (*bab al-ijtihad*) of Sunni Islamic jurisprudence was effectively closed by the beginning of the tenth century. It is generally accepted that the initial inspiration for this was the decision by the early 'Abbasid court that the interdiction on interpretive licence would support the political status quo. Independent reasoning, so the argument runs, was only re-allowed in the eighteenth and nineteenth centuries with the disruption of Muslim political authority that accompanied growing European hegemony. Liberal reformers such as Jamal al-Din al-Afghani (1893–97) assumed a causal link between the supposed stagnation of Muslim society and the prohibition on independent reasoning. It was presumed that, between the tenth and the eighteenth centuries, legal interpretations somehow went politically unchallenged.

This view belies the reality of both an almost continuous process of interpretation over the centuries and a complex relationship between legal and political authorities (Halleq 1984). Such conventional wisdom is also misleading when applied to the Shi'a. Their supposed continuous reliance on *ijtihad*, in contrast to Sunni Muslims, simplifies a complex situation in which various factions of Imami Shi'a struggled from the eleventh to the seventeenth centuries over whether the traditions of the Imams should take precedence over the reasoning of contemporary religious leaders (*mujtahids*).

A layer-cake form of historical periods, or even the separation of Islamic history into "pre-modern" and "modern" eras, is predicated on a sequential view of history – one authoritative act of domination following another. There are indeed discernible historical shifts in ideas as well as practices – as, for example, in the distinct appearance of *rihla* texts and their association with the *hajj* beginning in the twelfth century (see Gellens, Chapter 3 of this volume), and the emergence of an explicit notion of "Morocco" in the sixteenth (see El Moudden, Chapter 4 of this volume). Although less dramatic, generational changes are also important, as testified by the differences between Turkish migrant workers in Germany and their German-born children (see Mandel, Chapter 8 of this volume) or ritual offerings and sacrifices performed by various generations of Pakistani labour migrants in Manchester (Werbner 1988).

The division of history into sharply delineated periods, however, may encourage the assumption that there are dominant doctrines in any given time, unchallenged by competing doctrines and their carriers. An alternative view of time accepts the simultaneity, and the continuity, of ideas which are fundamentally dependent upon the groups, social institutions, and status of those who use and select them.

It is tempting, for example, to make the symmetrical argument that *hijra* in the classical period meant the obligation to migrate from non-Muslim lands (*dar al-kufr*) to Muslim ones (*dar al-Islam*), and that today the notion is principally metaphorical, implying only a spiritual migration. But as this century demonstrates, various ideas of *hijra* co-exist with each other (see Masud, Chapter 2 of this volume). For some Muslims, *hijra* means the transition from accommodating state authority to resisting it because of a growing realisation of its illegitimacy. For others, it means the transition from poverty to a better life through affiliation with specific Islamic movements. For the Wahhabiyya of Saudi Arabia, it meant the transition from nomadic to settled life.[1] The Muridiyya of Senegal stand the presumed classical notion on its head. *Hijra* in their case means emigration from a land where Muslims are in a majority but face poverty, to places such as New York and Paris, where, under the direction of their spiritual leaders and largely perhaps for their benefit, they find economic opportunity (Diop 1985).

Centre and periphery

The concept of centre is important in understanding motives and interests because of the appeal the centre, as sacred space, has for Muslims. Proximity to the centre is assumed to invest persons or institutions with greater sanctity and thus, religious or political legitimacy. Muslims pray towards Mecca, and if possible culminate their lives by making the pilgrimage to it. Visits to regional shrines complement the pilgrimage, and such key institutions of learning as al-Azhar in Cairo, the Qarawiyyin in Fez, and the religious colleges of Qum have regularly attracted students and scholars from across the Muslim world.

Sociologists and political scientists who have predicated the success of development upon secularisation find the idea of centre and periphery as the key to their analysis of national and state authority. Indeed, the prevailing orthodoxy of the social sciences from the 1950s through the 1970s was modernisation theory (Binder 1986). It presupposed that a prerequisite of political development, and sometimes of political liberty, was the integration of outlying regions to national and international, political and economic networks through a common educational, economic, and communications system.[2] These ideas have percolated into the study of Islam within both the social sciences and the humanities in such forms as the dichotomy of "great tradition" and "little tradition" (Eickelman 1982: 10–11), the division between "central" and outlying lands, as in the *Cambridge History of Islam* (Holt *et al.* 1970), and the idea of *l'Islam périphérique* among some French scholars.[3]

The first difficulty with such organising schemes is that they presuppose only one centre rather than multiple ones. Can it be said of Shi'i Muslims that Mecca is more their spiritual centre than Karbala, Najaf, or indeed Qum? Or that Mecca is "central" for an Alevi, for whom the genuine pilgrimage is one of the heart? (See Yalman 1969: 61–2.) Conceptualising the centre in a more institutional or political fashion leads to similar difficulties. When the Turkish Grand National Assembly abolished the caliphate in March 1924, several competitors unhesitatingly claimed the mantle: Egypt's King Fu'ad, 'Abd al-'Aziz ibn Sa'ud, Sharif Husayn of Mecca, and even the French-dominated Sultan of Morocco.[4] More recently, the elites of Egypt, Saudi Arabia, Pakistan, and, of course, Iran have competed – probably for political reasons – for leadership of the international Islamic movement.

The idea of centrality can be modified to presume an agreed hierarchy (or, indeed, hierarchies) of centres. In this view, the key to the integration of the community, whether it is the nation-state of modernisation theories or the Islamic community (*umma*) of pan-Islamic literature, involves the projection of hierarchical order upon the periphery. Yet the problem with this conceptualisation is that it is possible to conceive of forms of integration which do not presuppose such an order. In many parts of the world, and certainly within the Muslim world, there exist multiple linkages among the various ethnic, kinship-based, regional, and religious communities which do not arrange themselves into an agreed ranking or which do not allow the emergence of a code for such ranking. The relations and even alliances among these groups often shift, frequently in ways that block or thwart bureaucracies of the modern state. Terrorist networks in Lebanon and Iran may be extreme examples, but such networks illustrate the fragility of modern state authority and the way in which modern politics may not be so much the struggle of the centre to dominate the periphery, as the struggle of multiple centres to retain their autonomy.

Our basic point is that although there doubtless is a powerful tendency in modern societies towards the establishment and maintenance of central authority, there is a persistence of other networks of value and authority which are independent, or at least partially independent, of that authority, and do not appear to be on the wane. Thus, the straightforward distinction between centre and periphery is called into question, and the image of the Chinese puzzle may not be entirely inappropriate.[5]

The notion of centrality also becomes problematic if we think in terms of transnational movements. By definition, transnational institutions range across national borders and involve "non-state" actors, although they are not exclusively limited to them. An obvious example is the Catholic Church, and another, clearly, is Islam. But the example of the Catholic Church may be misleading if it leads us to assert that transnational movements require an organisational centre. A specific example in the Muslim world is the Barelwi movement. Although its ideas have spread from the Indian sub-continent, they have done so without the benefit of a clear, authoritative ideological centre such as the Deobandis possessed with their educational institutions (Metcalf 1982; Gaborieau 1986).

Terrorism can be another form of transnational movement. In the context of the contemporary Muslim world, it has become common currency to accuse Tehran, and also Tripoli and Damascus, of masterminding or directing a vast terrorist network whose aim is to intimidate other regimes and eliminate opponents. While these centres have provided political inspiration and material support, it would be incorrect to conclude that local groups committed to violent political action, such as Hizb Allah in southern Lebanon, are merely extensions of these centres. They have agendas, political leadership, and multiple – if shifting – lines of support of their own (Raufer 1987: 213–28).

Finally, in the study of Muslim societies, there has been the almost unquestioned assumption that written texts are more central than oral traditions or other cultural forms of authority. The Qur'an is at the apex of formal sources of jurisprudence, followed by the examples of the Prophet (*sunna*) and sayings attributed to him (*hadith*). Legal scholars say that those who practise the subsidiary sources of law, consensus (*ijma'*) and independent reasoning (*ijtihad*), must rely upon the Qur'an, the *sunna* and the *hadith* literature to inform their judgement. Yet there are times when the *sunna* seems to take precedence over the Qur'an in the formation of consensus and the exercise of independent reasoning. In any case, as we have discussed earlier, there is no reason to assume that a standard interpretation of either exists. The significance of texts derives not from their inherent centrality but from the contingent political, social, and economic circumstances of those intepreting them. It is precisely for this reason that a recent re-examination of the origins of the early Muslim caliphate (Crone and Hinds 1986) places as much emphasis, if not more, upon the evidence supplied by coins and Umayyid poetry as upon chronicles and juridical texts.

Scale

Most scholars acknowledge the need to place Islamic thought and practice into some sort of context, but do so without sufficient attention to the *scale* of what they describe. We regard the issue of scale as particularly important (see Eickelman 1987: 23–5). Devout Muslim writers tend to focus upon the universality of the *umma*, whereas social scientists usually look at less comprehensive entities, whether they are the nations of the political scientists or the local communities of the anthropologists. Each approach has its strengths and drawbacks in examining a phenomenon such as the pilgrimage to Mecca.

Muslim writers emphasise that the pilgrimage is a communal and personal experience shared by Muslims across the world, but overlook many aspects of its impact upon the individual pilgrim returning to his or her local community (see, for example, Esin 1963). Anthropologists have explored its impact at the local level and remind us that in small-scale, face-to-face communities, many facets of religious experience are inherently parochial and intensely personal, deriving their strength from this depth of shared local experience (Appardurai 1986; Turner 1973).[6] They are perhaps less sensitively attuned to pilgrimage as a national event and political act. Political scientists rarely study the pilgrimage – itself a telling commentary – but when they do consider it, it is briefly to make the point that it is an aspect of colonial, national, or international politics (e.g. Piscatori 1983; Kramer 1988). Similarly, studies of contemporary migration focus upon its political and economic implications, but often neglect its important consequences for religious beliefs and practice (e.g. Owen 1985). Colonial scholarship, by way of contrast, took the political potential of the pilgrimage seriously but commonly neglected its local and personal characteristics.[7] Social scientists have until recently tended to downplay the transnational dimensions.

Ideally, analysis of the pilgrimage, and indeed of all travel, requires dealing simultaneously with these several levels of experience and the linkages among them. For the Turkish or Malay *hajji*, for instance, the pilgrimage is often simultaneously a village, national and international phenomenon (see McDonnell, Chapter 6 of this volume). The problem is all the more challenging because the relationships among these levels are not necessarily arranged in a nesting order. Nor should they imply a preferred order. There is no reason to presume that the more universal or encompassing community is inherently more attractive than the small-scale particularistic one. Launay (Chapter 9 of this volume) stresses that in the realm of religious learning, locally-oriented regional networks of scholarship in West Africa were for long regarded as superior in authority to those based upon links with the more externally oriented centres of learning such as Mecca. In the later clash between a Wahhabi-influenced vision of Islamic community and the locally inspired vision, the Dyula tended to choose the latter, even as they continued to feel the pull of the former. Of course, the constraints on achieving a sustained awareness of multiple levels and perspectives such as this are substantial: limitations of time and scholarly access, and the continuing hold of disciplinary traditions in spite of the "blurring" of genres that may have occurred.

Effects and identities

Up to this point we have been concerned with the complex issue of what motivates social action in the religious environment. We consider now the complementary issue of effect – that is, the specific social and religious meanings that Muslims, or groups of

15

Muslims, attach to various forms of travel and the changes that travel induces in imagining their communities.

The most perplexing question to ask is whether there is a direct causal relationship between the act of travel and a heightened sense of being Muslim. We initially assumed that there was such a causal relationship in the discussions that led to this book. In time, however, it became clear that the disadvantage of such an assumption is that it implies that Muslim identity is an object whose contours can be specified. As it is impossible to say with certainty at any given moment precisely what Islam is, so is it impossible to specify the contours of Muslim identity. After the Ahmadi riots in Pakistan in 1953, when the Pakistani government asked the Munir Commission to define what a Muslim was, it admitted an inability of religious scholars to agree on such a definition: "[I]f considerable confusion exists in the minds of *'ulama'* on such a simple matter, one can easily imagine what the differences on more complicated matters will be" (Punjab Government 1954: 215). After twenty years of debate, all that the writers of the Pakistani constitution could agree upon was belief in the oneness of God and the finality of Muhammad's prophethood (Rahman 1981: 13), but, it should be noted, in the political context of excluding the Ahmadis and thereby making them second-class citizens.

It would also be misleading to assume a uniformity of Muslim identity. The Shi'a, the Alevis, the Muwahhidun (the Wahhabiyya) of Saudi Arabia, the Ibadiyya, the Isma'iliyya, the Zaydis, the Sunnis, and so on, all possess – at least on the basis of self-assertion – a Muslim identity. Individual believers or groups of believers may at times more strongly identify, or be identified, with the concrete sect or rite than with the abstract community of Islam. Indeed, political circumstances often compel individuals and sects to emphasise and act in terms of their more parochial identities. This has been the case with the 'Alawis in Syria and their Turkish counterparts. The Sunni majority of Syria has, until fairly recently, questioned whether the 'Alawis are Muslim. The issue has also arisen in Turkey (see Mandel, Chapter 8 of this volume), even as both the questioners and those questioned fervently maintain that there are no divisions within the house of Islam.

In the earlier discussion of centre and periphery, we have seen some of the difficulties in presuming that values and institutional loyalties are hierarchically arranged. The creation of a hierarchy of identities is also misleading. There is an almost infinitely diverse literature on the concept of identities and little agreement on how they are formed and change over time. One way of ordering this complex debate is to distinguish between the "primordialist" and "instrumentalist" perspectives (Bentley 1987). The primordialist view holds that identity flows from shared cultural or symbolic values; the instrumentalist perspective maintains that individuals or groups assert or emphasise particular identities because they provide a means to maximise their individual or collective interests.

Both views are suggestive but neither is satisfactory. The fundamental difficulty with them is that they predicate the formulation of identity upon a reality that appears abstract and somehow independent of those persons or groups who perceive and participate in it. The specific difficulty with the instrumentalist approach is that it imputes to actors an ordering and clarity of goals, but these goals are necessarily dependent upon ever-shifting cultural and social contexts and are often ambiguous as a consequence (Laitin 1986: 10–11). Moreover, social action, as Weingrod (Chapter 11, this volume) shows, may well generate unforeseen consequences. The growing attachment of Sephardic Israeli Jews to saints and shrines, for example, has reinforced the emergence of radical, right-wing nationalism. As for the primordialist perspective, it leaves the impression that shared cultural and symbolic values are fixed, or at least change only in the long run.[8]

Identities change over time, as studies of migration amply demonstrate. Some migrants continue to regard their land of birth as "home", while others come to identify primarily with their land of settlement (see Karpat, Chapter 7 of this volume). Others, such as Turkish workers in Germany (see Mandel, Chapter 8 of this volume), or indeed such intellectuals as Salman Rushdie (1988), may feel at home in neither place, at ease in neither their land of settlement nor their land of origin. There may also be multiple, co-existing identities. For instance, Moroccan travel accounts (see Moudden, Chapter 4 of this volume) suggest that travellers identified at various times with their region of origin within Morocco; Morocco itself; the cosmopolitan centres such as Cairo, Medina, or Istanbul to which they journeyed; and (with some ambivalence) the *umma*. At various times – and perhaps simultaneously – class, ethnicity, nation, and Islam itself have been defining characteristics for Malay pilgrims (see McDonnell, Chapter 6 of this volume).

There is no reason to assume that multiple identities such as those described by McDonnell exist necessarily in a hierarchical order. For instance, Turkish women sometimes identify first with their families and then with other Muslims – men and women – as during the *hajj* and major religious festivals. At other times, however – as during visits to saint shrines – they identify primarily with other women (see Tapper, Chapter 12 of this volume). That no fixed hierarchical order exists is also demonstrated by another example from South-east Asia. In parts of the Tengger highlands of eastern Java in the nineteenth century, some villages consisted of both Muslim and non-Muslim (*Buda*) hamlets. The introduction of coffee as a cash crop by the early years of the century led to subtle changes of political and economic balance both between and within these hamlets. In addition, Dutch colonial policies in central Java stimulated labour migration to the eastern highlands, and links to cities were developed because of the need to market the coffee crop. Questions of identity were intensified and complicated by changes in wealth, status, and regular contact with central Java. Islam was one factor among many, and did not appear to be particularly "central", as is demonstrated by the example of the first Muslim chief in one of these villages, Besuki.

> A wealthy entrepreneur and the first villager ever to make the *hajj* pilgrimage, he was none the less Javanese and a native son of Besuki, from one of the first local families to break into the coffee industry previously monopolized by the [immigrant] Madurese.
>
> (Hefner 1987: 61–2)

Conclusion

We have been concerned with discerning how instances of social action can be understood and illuminated within religious traditions, and, specifically, within Muslim religious traditions. The deliberate use of "traditions" in the plural suggests the view that historical "Islam" does not neatly coincide with doctrinal "Islam" and that the practice and significance of Islamic faith in any given historical setting cannot readily be predicted from first principles of dogma or belief. It is difficult to assess motive and effect in the general realm of social action, but it would seem all the more difficult in the case of religious traditions such as Islam, whose adherents assert that Islamic directives are universal and clear and yet whose manifestations in thought and practice are so varied and indeterminate.

As iconoclastic as it may seem, even the basics of faith are not as luminous or lucid as one might hope for the purpose of eliciting the contours of the religious imagination of the Muslim community past and present. Of the "five" pillars of faith – ritual prayer, pilgrimage to Mecca, almsgiving, fasting, and the profession of faith – four have been subject to dispute and different interpretation at various times, and continue to be so today (Eickelman 1989:

262–73). Similar difficulties adhere to substituting the search for explicitly shared fixed beliefs transcending time and place with one for authoritative uniform practice, or orthopraxy, since again there are significant divergences among Muslims. Alternatively, it is possible to say, as indeed one Muslim scholar has, that there is no Islam but "islams" (Zein 1977). This approach, intended to displace "essentialist" views, ironically creates a new essentialism by assuming that all the various "islams" are composed of common structural elements. The "islams" approach also under-plays the "rather unique" insistence by most Muslims that Islam is "a coherent and closed system" (Smith 1963: 84).

An alternative to the "essentialist" approach of discerning the religious imagination within Muslim traditions is to acknowledge that many Muslims share a common vocabulary of key terms which shape their experience and perceptions of it. These terms, not necessarily Qur'anic or doctrinal, such as the Arabic *'aql* ("reason") and *nafs* ("passions" or the "lower" human instincts), appear throughout the non-Arab Muslim world. Such terms were, indeed, often introduced with the spread of Islam. Yet one must exercise caution in assuming that common items of vocabulary constitute a shared language through which ideas of self, society, responsibility, justice and so on shape and express social experi-ence. After all, in any given context there are a number of non-Islamic terms and concepts used by Muslims which equally shape and express ideas such as these. As indicated earlier, the Qur'anic verse referring to the "oppressed of the earth" resonated pro-foundly in the 1960s with Fanon's "wretched of the earth" and became consciously (and brilliantly) fused in the speeches and writings of such figures as Ali Shari'ati (d. 1977). For some of the audience for such writings, the Qur'anic language was undoubtedly "central", but for others it was not. The appeal of the phrase related largely to its bridging of Islamic and non-Islamic concepts. To assume that the concepts and vocabulary identified as "Islamic" carry greater authority than any others may distort how Muslims themselves address these issues.

A more effective first step towards depicting Islam is to acknow-ledge that there are particular difficulties in understanding action within "religious" fields because, by their very nature, "religions", or at least world religions, are proposed to various degrees by their adherents to be universal, unaffected by human vicissitudes, and unambiguous. None the less, as Wilfred Cantwell Smith (1963: 85) argues:

the various religious traditions of the world do in fact differ among themselves in the degree to which each presents itself as an organized and systematized entity. If this be so, then one of them may well be the most entity-like. One could suggest that Islam, it so happens, is that one.

We cite Smith at length because, among historians of religion concerned with comparative religious traditions, he recognizes the potential for misleading reification. He argues (1963: 84) that "the various religious traditions *are* different . . . not only in detail but in basic orientation. Each is unique." If the term "religion" has any utility at all, it is in the family resemblances between and within various world religious traditions. Smith's caution against reifying religious forms of social action coincides with that of the social sciences. Max Weber (1968: 399) despaired of defining "religion" and confined himself, as we do, to studying "the conditions and effects of a particular type of social action". Likewise, in characterising religion as a "cultural system", the anthropologist Clifford Geertz (1973 [orig. 1966]: 90) self-consciously sought to delineate a paradigm for certain types of social action rather than provide a definition. Smith (1963: 194–5) goes so far as to suggest that "religion" as a noun is distractingly ambiguous and is best retained only in its adjectival form.

Even if it is accepted that Islam is the most "entity-like" of the world religions, its internal diversity is compelling. To acknowledge this, however, is not to detract from the claim of transcendental unity. Eternal religious truths, like other beliefs, are perceived, understood, and transmitted by persons historically situated in "imagined" communities, who knowingly or inadvertently contribute to the reconfiguration or reinterpretation of these verities, even as their fixed and unchanging natures are affirmed. In fact, when Muslim discourse and practice are considered in the social contexts in which they are produced, the problem of reification is avoided, as is, at the same time, the inadvertent propensity to render representations of Muslim belief and experience parochial. Islam can be seen as the lives of its adherents at the same time as it is divine revelation; and it can be seen as doctrinally complex and evolutionary at the same time that it is seen as a discernibly unique tradition of discourse.

Some social scientists seek to avoid the problem of how to study Islam altogether by asserting that the very act of studying it creates a spurious "object" of study and deflects attention from underlying social, economic, and political processes. Yet the study of religion remains critically important for the modern social sciences. Even Marxism can be shown to have profound roots in the Judaeo−Christian tradition (West 1987: 240−2). It would make as much sense to avoid studying nationalism and ideas of "nation" because to do so would be to make of them an object, as do carriers of particular senses of national identity. In both cases, the "subjective experiences, ideas, and purposes of the individuals concerned" (Weber 1968: 399) form the necessary point of departure for understanding the underlying senses of imagined community.

The examination of travel in Muslim communities offers the opportunity to address the complexity of issues such as these. Acknowledging a debt to Smith's writing on religious traditions in general, we suggest that posing smaller questions of religious traditions is in order. Instead of asking "What is Islam?" or "What is Christianity?", it would be more useful to look at specific kinds of practice and action, such as travel, which constitute religious traditions and inform the religious imagination. The "smaller" questions that we have posed aim at assessing the motives and interests imputed to travel and to its effects and resultant identities. These questions include enquiry into how "authoritative" doctrine emerges, and indeed into how ideas of "authority" and "domination" shift over time and across cultures; a sharper focus upon what is meant by "centre" and "periphery"; and an awareness both that the idea of Muslim community varies according to scale and that these varying communities interact with one another. As a corollary, clearly what is required is collaborative and cross-disciplinary research of a kind that has been all too rare in the study of Islam and which this volume strives to offer.

Acknowledgements

The authors wish to thank Jon Anderson, Christine Eickelman, and Michael Schatzberg for comments on an earlier version of this chapter.

Notes

1 A settlement of the *ikhwan*, or "brotherhood", in the Najd of central Arabia was specifically called a *hijra* (Habib 1978).
2 The popularity of the centre and periphery idea owes much to the sociology of Shils (1975), whose influential articles in the 1950s and 1960s on the subject are most readily available in the collection cited here. For an influential political science perspective, see Deutsch (1966: 188).
3 See, for example, the entire issue of *Archipel*, 29 (1985).
4 On the issue of the caliphate, see, *inter alia*, Public Record Office

(London), FO371/10015, EN214/7624/91; FO371/10016, E9975/7624/91; FO371/11920, W3227/2249/28; FO371/15283, E6046/1205/65; and the *Manchester Guardian*, 13 March 1924.

5 This image was suggested to us by Michael Schatzberg.

6 In a later book-length study, Turner (1978) was one of the first anthropologists to explore the broader significance of pilgrimage as a general phenomenon. But even this work primarily emphasises the presumed psychological effects upon the individual pilgrims connected to and changed by "the center out there" and their relation to local societies, and pays less attention to their altered sense of "home" when they return to their society of origin. Roff (1985: 86) offers a similar critique.

7 For examples of earlier colonial scholarship, generally see the *Revue du Monde Musulmane* and the *Revue Indigène*.

8 Consider, for example, the influential characterisation of culture as:

> an historically transmitted pattern of meanings embodied in symbols, a system of inherited conceptions expressed in symbolic forms by means of which men communicate, perpetuate, and develop their knowledge about and attitudes toward life.
>
> (Geertz 1973 [orig. 1966]: 89)

References

Anderson, Benedict (1983) *Imagined Communities: Reflections on the Origin and Spread of Nationalism*, Verso, London and New York.

Ansari, Hamied N. (1984) 'The Islamic militants in Egyptian politics', *International Journal of Middle East Studies*, 16, no. 1, pp. 123–44.

Appardurai, Arjun (1986) 'Theory in anthropology: center and periphery', *Comparative Studies in Society and History*, 28, no. 2, pp. 356–61.

Bentley, G. Carter (1987) 'Ethnicity and Practice', *Comparative Studies in Society and History*, 29, no. 1, pp. 24–55.

Binder, Leonard (1986) 'The natural history of development theory', *Comparative Studies in Society and History*, 28, no. 1, 3–33.

Coulson, John (1981) *Religion and Imagination: In Aid of a Grammar of Assent*, Clarendon Press, Oxford.

Crone, Patricia, and Hinds, Martin (1986) *God's Caliph: Religious Authority in the First Centuries of Islam*, Cambridge University Press, Cambridge.

Dassetto, Felice and Bastenier, Albert (1988) *Europa: Nuova frontiera dell'Islam*, Edizioni Lavoro, Louvain.

Deutsch, Karl (1966) *Nationalism and Social Communication: An Inquiry Into the Foundations of Nationality*, 2nd edn, MIT Press, Cambridge, Mass.

Diop, Moustapha (1985) 'Les associations murid en France', *Esprit*, no. 102, pp. 197–206.

Eickelman, Dale F. (1982) 'The study of Islam in local contexts', *Contributions to Asian Studies*, 17, pp. 1–16.

——— (1987) 'Changing interpretations of Islamic movements', in William R. Roff (ed.) *Islam and the Political Economy of Meaning: Comparative Studies of Muslim Discourse*, Croom Helm, London; University of California Press, Berkeley and Los Angeles, pp. 13–30.
——— (1989) *The Middle East: An Anthropological Approach*, 2nd edn, Prentice-Hall, Englewood Cliffs, N.J.
Esin, Emel (1963) *Mecca the Blessed, Madinah the Radiant*, Elek Books, London.
Federal Government of Nigeria (1981) *Report of Tribunal of Inquiry on Kano Disturbances*, Federal Government Press, Lagos.
Gaborieau, Marc (1986) 'Les ordres mystiques dans le sous-continent indien: un point de vue ethnologique', in *Les ordres mystiques dans l'Islam: cheminements et situation actuelle*, EHESS, Paris, pp. 105–34.
Geertz, Clifford (1973 [orig. 1966]) 'Religion as a cultural system', in *The Interpretation of Cultures*, Basic Books, New York, pp. 87–125.
Giddens, Anthony (1984) *The Constitution of Society*, University of California Press, Berkeley and Los Angeles.
Habib, John S. (1978) *Ibn Sa'ud's Warriors of Islam: The Ikhwan of Najd and Their Role in the Creation of the Sa'udi Kingdom, 1910–1930*, E.J. Brill, Leiden.
Halleq, Wael B. (1984) 'Was the gate of ijtihad closed?', *International Journal of Middle East Studies*, 16, no. 1, pp. 3–41.
Hefner, Robert W. (1987) 'The political economy of Islamic conversion in modern East Java', in William R. Roff (ed.) *Islam and the Political Economy of Meaning*, Croom Helm, London; University of California Press, Berkeley and Los Angeles, pp. 53–78.
Heikal, Mohamed H. (1986) *Cutting the Lion's Tail: Suez Through Egyptian Eyes*, André Deutsch, London.
Holt, P.M., Lambton, Ann K.S., and Lewis, Bernard (eds) (1970) *The Cambridge History of Islam*, Cambridge University Press, Cambridge.
Ibrahim, Saad Eddin (1980) 'Anatomy of Egypt's militant Islamic groups: methodological note and preliminary findings', *International Journal of Middle East Studies*, 12, no. 4, pp. 423–53.
Kepel, Gilles (1986 [orig. 1984]) *Muslim Extremism in Egypt: The Prophet and Pharaoh*, translated by Jon Rothschild, University of California Press, Berkeley and Los Angeles.
——— (1987) *Les banlieues de l'Islam*, Editions du Seuil, Paris.
Kramer, Martin (1988) 'Tragedy in Mecca', *Orbis*, 32, no. 2, pp. 231–47.
Laitin, David (1986) *Hegemony and Culture: Politics and Religious Change Among the Yoruba*, University of Chicago Press, Chicago.
Lubeck, Paul M. (1987) 'Structural determinants of urban protest in northern Nigeria', in William R. Roff (ed.) *Islam and the Political Economy of Meaning: Comparative Studies of Muslim Discourse*, Croom Helm, London; University of California Press, Berkeley and Los Angeles, pp. 79–107.
Metcalf, Barbara Daly (1982) *Islamic Revival in British India: Deoband, 1860–1900*, Princeton University Press, Princeton, N.J.
Nadwi, S. Abul Hasan Ali (1983) *Life and Mission of Maulana Mohammad*

Ilyas, 2nd edn, trans. by Mohammad Asif Kidwai, Academy of Islamic Research and Publications, Lucknow.

Owen, Roger (1985) *Migrant Workers in the Gulf*, Minority Rights Group, 68, The Minority Rights Group, London.

Piscatori, James P. (1983) 'Interests and values in foreign policy: the case of Saudi Arabia', in Adeed Dawisha (ed.) *Islam in Foreign Policy*, Cambridge University Press, Cambridge, pp. 33–53.

—— (1986) *Islam in a World of Nation States*, Cambridge University Press, Cambridge.

Punjab Government (1954) *Report of the Court of Inquiry*, Government Printing Office, Lahore.

Rahman, Fazlur (1981) *Implementation of Shari'ah in Pakistan*, Council of Islamic Ideology, Islamabad.

—— (1982) *Islam and Modernity: Transformation of an Intellectual Tradition*, University of Chicago Press, Chicago.

—— (1985) 'Approaches to Islam in religious studies', in Richard C. Martin (ed.) *Approaches to Islam in Religious Studies*, University of Arizona Press, Tucson, pp. 189–202.

Raufer, Xavier (1987) *La nébuleuse: Le terrorisme du moyen-orient*, Fayard, Paris.

Roff, William R. (1985) 'Pilgrimage and the history of religions: theoretical approaches to the hajj', in Richard C. Martin (ed.) *Approaches to Islam in Religious Studies*, University of Arizona Press, Tucson, pp. 78–86.

Rushdie, Salman (1988) *The Satanic Verses*, Viking, New York.

Scott, James C. (1985) 'Resistance without protest and without organization: peasant opposition to the Islamic zakat and Christian tithe', *Kajian Malaysia*, 3, no. 1, pp. 58–100.

Shils, Edward (1975) *Center and Periphery*, University of Chicago Press, Chicago.

Shuckburgh, Evelyn (1986) *Descent to Suez: Diaries, 1951–56*, Weidenfeld and Nicolson, London.

Smith, W. Robertson (1956 [orig. 1889]) *The Religion of the Semites*, 2nd edn, Meridian Books, New York.

Smith, Wilfred Cantwell (1963) *The Meaning and End of Religion*, The Macmillan Company, New York.

Turner, Victor W. (1973) 'The center out there: pilgrim's goal', *History of Religions*, 12, no. 3, pp. 191–230.

—— with Edith Turner (1978) *Image and Pilgrimage in Christian Culture: Anthropological Perspectives*, Columbia University Press, New York.

Walzer, Michael (1985) *Exodus and Revolution*, Basic Books, New York.

Weber, Max (1968) *Economy and Society*, Guenther Roth and Claus Wittich (eds), Bedminster Press, New York.

Werbner, Pnina (1988) ' "Sealing" the Koran: offering and sacrifice among Pakistani labour migrants', *Cultural Dynamics*, 1, no. 1, pp. 77–97.

West, Charles C. (1987) 'Marxism', in Mircea Eliade (ed.) *The Encyclopedia of Religion*, vol. 9, Macmillan, New York, pp. 240–49.

Yalman, Nur (1969) 'Islamic reform and the mystic tradition in eastern Turkey', *European Journal of Sociology*, 10, no. 1, pp. 41–60.

el-Zein, Abdel Hamid (1977) 'Beyond ideology and theology: the search for an anthropology of Islam', *Annual Review of Anthropology*, 6, pp. 227–54.

Part one
Doctrines of travel

Chapter two

The obligation to migrate: the doctrine of *hijra* in Islamic law

Muhammad Khalid Masud

Introduction

On 22 March 1987 three young men approached Allama Ihsan Ilahi Zaheer.[1] They wanted to discuss with him the meaning of a Qur'anic verse about *hijra*,[2] and argued that the situation in Pakistan was worsening. They specifically argued that the Family Laws Ordinance governed the personal lives of Muslims instead of *Shari'a* law,[3] so that the political environment was not conducive to the practice and propagation of Islam. The youths argued that under these circumstances, according to the Qur'anic verse, there were only two options available to Pakistani Muslims: either to declare Pakistan *dar al-harb* (an enemy territory) and wage *jihad* against it until it is restored to *dar al-Islam*; or to leave Pakistan altogether.

The Allama disagreed with them and explained that they held an extremist view. He emphatically refuted their arguments, but the young men kept arguing and departed unsatisfied. The Allama was very much perturbed and expressed his anxiety over rising extremism among the Muslim youth (Najmi 1987: a). On 23 March, a day later, a bomb exploded at a public meeting which Allama Zaheer was addressing. He received serious injuries and later died of his wounds.

There may not be any connection between the bomb explosion and the three youths, and their extremist views are not typical of Pakistani youth. None the less, I cite the incidents to illustrate that some Muslim youth, albeit extremists, still believe that *hijra* (the physical movement away from unbelief) is an essential expression of Muslim identity. Similar trends are apparent in other parts of the Muslim world: for example, *Jama'at al-Muslimin* (The League of Muslims) in Egypt were nicknamed by their opponents *Jama'at al-Takfir wa-l-Hijra* (The Society of Excommunication and Emigration) because of their emphasis on *hijra* (Kepel 1985: 77).

This chapter traces how the doctrine of *hijra* took shape. Any generalisation about the historical development of this doctrine is difficult because no systematic studies of it exist. Moreover, although references to *hijra* are quite frequent in the *fatawa* literature, which consists of responses to specific questions, they are scattered throughout the regular books of Islamic law rather than grouped together under the heading of emigration.

In view of these difficulties I propose first to present an account of *context*, describing the particular events in the history of Islam which gave rise to thinking on *hijra*. Next, I deal with *doctrinal foundations* – i.e. the written texts on which doctrinal discussions about *hijra* are based. Finally, I consider *challenges and responses* to the doctrine occasioned by historical developments that have encouraged the doctrine's reinterpretation or reconstruction by Muslim jurists. These developments include the revolt of the Khawarij (AD 657),[4] the occupation by non-Muslims of Muslim lands and western colonialism, Muslim migration to non-Muslim countries, and the rise of Muslim nation-states.

After an analysis of the period of civil wars (the first *fitna*, AD 656–61, and the second *fitna*, AD 683–92), this chapter discusses developments in Indo-Pakistani and Nigerian Muslim societies, two Muslim societies with which the present writer has been professionally concerned. Moreover, this choice provides an opportunity to study the formulation and development of the doctrine of *hijra* in two different legal contexts and interpretive frameworks – Hanafi in the case of Pakistan and Maliki in the case of Nigeria.

Context

Hijra, an Arabic term which literally means "to abandon", "to break ties with someone" (such as a bond of kinship or other personal association), or "to migrate" (Watt 1971: 366), refers primarily to the Prophet Muhammad's migration from Mecca to Medina in AD 622. It is also discussed with reference to the migration of a group of Muslims from Mecca to Abyssinia in AD 615–22. Although the *hijra* to Abyssinia was voluntary and limited in scope, the *hijra* to Medina was obligatory and involved almost the entire Muslim community. No Muslim was supposed to stay behind in Mecca. Exemption was allowed only to the "weak" – women, children, and the sick – and those who could not afford to migrate. Staying behind in Mecca was also allowed after the pact of Hudaybiyya (AD 628–30). While there was no pact between the king of Abyssinia and Muslims, the migration to Medina was preceded by pacts (*bay'at al-harb/hijra*, the pact of war or emigration) between the Prophet and the people of Medina who swore allegiance to protect Muslims and to wage *jihad* against their enemies (Ibn Hisham 1963: II, 303).

A significant fact in the events of the *hijra* to Abyssinia in AD 615–22 was that women's participation in migration was equally prominent. The two group migrations to Abyssinia were family migrations, including both women and children. The migration to Medina was preceded by two pacts concluded in AD 620 and AD 621 between Muslims of Mecca and Medina. As already mentioned, the second pact was called "the pact of war". The first was named "the pact of women" not only because women took part in this pact, but also because the first person to swear allegiance to this pact was a woman named 'Afra' (Ibn Hisham 1963: II, 293). The Qur'an refers to this pact in 60: 12 (*sura* 60, verse 12).[5]

The second pact was a pact of protection and war and included among its signatories Umm 'Amara and Umm Mani', who participated in it along with men. There are stories of families moving together during the actual migration from Mecca to Medina (Ibn Hisham 1963: II, 319–20). The first person to migrate was Abu Salma, whom the Meccans did not allow to migrate with his family. His wife later travelled alone to join him. The second migrant, 'Amir b. Rabi'a, succeeded in migrating to Medina along with his wife (Ibn Hisham 1963: II, 321–4).

After the migration all ties, including "blood" relationships, were broken with both non-Muslims and Muslims who refused to migrate. Instead, a new bond of brotherhood (*mu'akhat*) between *muhajirs* (migrants) and *ansars* (inhabitants of Medina – generally supporters or local hosts) was established, which entitled them even to inherit from one another (al-Tabari 1958: 199). *Hijra* thus meant to abandon one's property and relations in order to support the nascent community of Muslims in Medina. Refusal to perform *hijra* meant to weaken the Muslim cause and to lend support (*wala'* or *muwalat*) to their enemies. Hence in early Islam, non-migrants were not allowed to inherit from Muslims in Medina, not were they entitled to any share in the spoils of war (*ghanima*). The right of inheritance between blood relations among Muslims was later restored, although non-Muslim relations were still disallowed from inheritance (Qur'an, 8: 75).

Doctrinal foundations

The textual sources, the Qur'an and *hadith* (pl. *ahadith*; texts relating to the sayings of the Prophet), abound with references to the events of the original *hijra* and to injunctions given in its context.

The word *hijra* has been used in the Qur'an to mean "to reject" (23: 69), "to shun" (74: 5), "to depart" (19: 46) and "to banish" (4: 34). The shared meaning in all these usages may be deduced to be a distancing – physical or otherwise – usually from evil and disbelief. The derivative forms *hajara* (59: 9; 2: 218; 3: 195) and *muhajir* (9: 100, 117; 33: 6; 59: 8; 60: 10; 8: 72) mean "to migrate". Most verses employing the derivative form *hajaru* ("they migrated") are often paired with *jahadu* ("they waged war") and thus imply a close association of *hijra* with *jihad*.

It is not possible here to survey the implications of all the Qur'anic passages. For the purpose of our discussion we refer only to the two verses most often cited in debates concerning *hijra*:

Those who believed and left their homes [*hajaru*] and strove [*jahadu*] with their wealth and their lives for the cause of Allah, and those who took them in and helped them [*nasaru*], these are protecting friends of one another. And those who believed but did not leave their homes, you have no bond [*walaya*] with them till they leave their homes, but, if they seek help from you in the matter of religion, then it is your duty to help them except against a people with whom you have a treaty [*mithaq*].

(Qur'an, 8: 72)

Lo! as for those whom the angels take [in death] while they wrong [*zalimi*] themselves, the angels will ask: "In what were ye engaged?" They will say: "We were oppressed [*mustad'afin*] in the land". [The angels] will say: "Was not Allah's earth spacious that you could have migrated therein?" As for such, their habitation will be hell, an evil journey's end. Except the feeble [*mustad'afin*] among men, and the women and the children, who are unable to devise a plan and are not shown a way. As for such, it may be that Allah will pardon them – Who so migrateth for the cause of Allah will find much refuge and abundance [of bounties] in the earth.

(Qur'an, 4: 97–100)

From the Qur'anic texts the following significant points about *hijra* can be inferred: (1) It was an obligation of physical movement towards self-definition in the nascent Muslim society. Refusal to migrate meant exclusion from the society; (2) *hijra* was closely associated with *jihad*; and (3) *hijra* established a bond of relationship among Muslims, particularly with the *ansar*.

Among several *hadiths* on the subject of *hijra*, the following offers parallels to the famous five pillars of Islam:

I convey the following five commandments given me by God: attention (*sam'*), obedience (*ta'a*), migration (*hijra*), struggle (*jihad*), and organisation (*jama'a*).

(Ibn Hanbal, n.d.: 130)

There are numerous *hadiths* prescribing *hijra* as an obligation. However, the *hadith* literature adds a new dimension to the Qur'anic injunction. It also refers to situations where *hijra* is no longer obligatory. For example, the Prophet is reported to have said: *la hijrata ba'd al-fathi*, "no migration was required after the conquest" (al-Bukhari 1971: 190). None the less, there are *hadith* texts according to which *hijra* continues to be an obligation (Abu Da'ud 1933: 234).

Abu Sulayman Hamid b. Muhammad Khattabi al-Busti (AD 931–96/8), a scholar of *hadith*, reconciled this difference of opinion and argued that *hijra* was actually meant to support and strengthen *dar al-Islam* in its nascent days. After the conquests *dar al-Islam* was so strong and established that migration was no longer required. The *hijra* would be required again only and whenever the conditions so demanded (Ibn Hajar 1959: vi, 378).

Ibn Khaldun (AD 1332–1406) explained these texts by saying that *hijra* meant migration to join the Prophet Muhammad. *Hijra* might have continued to be an obligation after the conquest of Mecca, but it was definitely not required after the death of the Prophet (Ibn Khaldun 1958: i, 256).

Abu'l-Fadl Ahmad b. 'Ali Ibn Hajar [al-'Asqalani] (d. AD 1449), a later *hadith* scholar, analysed in detail this debate and showed that a number of the companions of the Prophet, including Ibn 'Abbas (d. AD 687), and his contemporaries Ta'us, Mujashi', Ibn Jurayj, 'Ata' and 'A'isha, perceived *hijra* only as migration from Mecca to Medina. Hence, after Mecca was conquered no *hijra* was required (Ibn Hajar 1959: vi, 378).

Thus, even as early as the formative period, we see a refinement in the formulation of the doctrine. During AD 622–8, the *hijra* from Mecca to Medina was obligatory in terms of expressing one's Muslim identity. Migration also meant weakening Mecca and strengthening Medina. Only persons unable to migrate (*al-mustad'afin*) were allowed to stay in Mecca. The situation changed in AD 630 when Mecca joined *dar al-Islam*. After AD 630, the statement that *hijra* was no longer required from Mecca raised the question of whether *hijra* only meant migration from Mecca to Medina. Could it be generalised to state that migration from the outside to *dar al-Islam* was obligatory?

The answer is not simple, because the *hijra* to Abyssinia was not

33

to *dar al-Islam*. The Hudaybiyya pact allowed Muslims to stay in Mecca, and the Prophet did not require the bedouin to migrate to Medina. A general rule was therefore derived that even after the conquest of Mecca, such situations as the following could make *hijra* relevant again: (1) *dar al-Islam* turns into *dar al-kufr*; or (2) a resident of a territory outside *dar al-Islam* embraces Islam.

Is *hijra* obligatory in these situations? An answer to this question also involves other issues, such as (i) how *dar al-Islam* turns into *dar al-kufr*, and (ii) the legal status of a Muslim who does not migrate. Indeed, these and other questions helped refine the doctrine. It should be emphasised that even the early textual formulations of doctrine are closely related to the actual political and social contexts. Subsequent interpretations similarly demonstrate a dynamic interaction between text and social, economic, and political conditions.

Challenges and responses

The revolt of the Khawarij

Civil wars among Muslims erupted quite early during the period of the first caliphs (AD 632–61). The rebels defined their position within the Islamic framework and hence had to justify their war with opposing Muslim groups – most often the ruling groups in the centre – in terms of *jihad*. It was therefore necessary to strengthen their camp by asking their followers to migrate from enemy territories.

Foremost among these dissenters were the Khawarij,[6] who considered the commission of major sins as *kufr* (unbelief). They rebelled against the Caliph 'Ali and subsequently against the Umayyids (AD 661–750). Their support was largely among the nomads. The Khawarij were probably the first Muslim group to define political dissent in theological terms, thus generating scholarly controversies on different issues.

In order to justify their *jihad* and *hijra*, the Khawarij raised the question of the original status of territory. According to them, all territories were *dar al-kufr* until they were brought into the fold of Islam. A territory could turn again into *dar al-kufr* if its rulers denied the sovereignty of Allah, or committed a major sin, whereby they became *kafirs*. In these circumstances, *hijra* from such a territory and *jihad* against it become obligatory. The Khawarij, Azariqa,[7] and Sufriyya[8] all held these general views. Yet, whereas most of the Khawarij declared their opponents *mushriks* (polytheists), the Ibadiyya[9] adopted a more moderate view. They believed that their enemies among the people who prayed in the same direction were *kafirs*, and that marriage and inheritance with them were allowed.

The Ibadiyya did not term all the territories outside their own camps as *dar al-kufr*, but the camp of the sultan was certainly so. According to the Ibadiyya, inability to migrate was not an excuse but a condition that one should strive to remove. The 'Awniyya[10] explained that when the ruler committed *kufr*, his subjects also became unbelievers. They believed that *hijra* and *jihad* were inter-related, and broke ties with those who migrated in order to avoid *jihad* (al-Ash'ari 1950: I, 162–79; al-Shahristani 1899: I, 170–84).

The responses

The views of the Mu'tazila oscillated between the positions of the Khawarij and the Ibadiyya. Jubba'i (d. AD 916), a Mu'tazili leader, expounded the view that as long as it was possible to stay in a territory without being forced to agree or to commit acts of unbelief, the territory was *dar al-iman* (the land of faith). However, according to him, this condition did not prevail in Baghdad (al-Ash'ari 1950: II, 137).

The Shi'a, who opposed the Umayyid and 'Abbasid (AD 750–1258) regimes, did not take the extreme position of the Khawarij. Their position varied according to circumstances. Some Shi'a took a middle position and defined the territory as *dar al-hudna* (the land of peace), from which migration was not obligatory. Others, particularly the Zaydis, called it *dar al-kufr* (the land of unbelief) (al-Ash'ari 1950: II, 137).

The majority of the Muslims who favoured the status quo disagreed with these extreme views of *kufr* and *hijra*. They took a moderate position and referred to a *hadith* which explained the various levels of *iman*. The *hadith* recommended that one should strive to remove evil with hand or tongue depending upon his ability. If one is unable to do either, one should at least distance oneself from evil in one's heart. This, however, was the weakest level of *iman* (Muslim 1954: I, 69). The majority view was that the higher levels called for *jihad* and that *jihad* was a *fard kifaya* (a collective duty) not required of each and every Muslim, and not to be undertaken individually. *Hijra*, according to this majority view, was a *jihad*-related obligation. The only *hijra* that could be performed individually was withdrawal in the heart. Such interiorisation of *hijra* in the esoteric sense was popularised by the Sufis.

Abu'l-Qasim al-Qushayri (d. AD 1074) defined *hijra* as "extracting oneself from the desires of the soul to the shade of His

35

closeness" (al-Qushayri n.d.: I, 51). He explained that complete *hijra* meant "abandoning the soul by not attending to its desires and then migrating from the land of rights to the land of submission to God's will" (al-Qushayri n.d.: II, 335).

The Sufi commentators of the Qur'an usually explain that the obligation of physical migration was repealed. The only *hijra* required was spiritual. Maybudi (d. AD 1125) pointed out that there were three types of *hijra*: (1) that of *ahl al-dunya*, migration of "people of the world" for the purpose of trade; (2) that of the *zahidin*, the ascetics' migration towards the hereafter by performing all religious rituals and spiritual contemplations; and (3) that of the *'arifin*, the mystics' migration from the veils of self to the heart, and from the heart to the soul, and, ultimately, to the Beloved (Maybudi AH 1338: II, 662). The Sufi Najm al-Din Kubra (d. AD 1225) defined *hijra* as migration from the land of human beings to the presence of Allah (al-Bursawi 1911: II, 272).

The Sufi interiorisation of the doctrine was a reaction to adverse social and political conditions. They faced a stark choice: either support an unjust ruling group or, like the Khawarij, revolt against it. In these circumstances, the Sufis took the position of withdrawal. The jurists also did not collectively adopt the extreme position. They perceived that the supremacy of the *shari'a* could be maintained only if there was less interference by the rulers in the interpretation of law. They were not in favour of the *shari'a* being interpreted by governmental institutions.

This view of law developing independently of government started to take shape during the Umayyid period and crystallised during the early 'Abbasid period when attempts were made by the caliphs to take the right of legislation into their own hands (Schacht 1966: 55). The jurists, however, did not want to challenge the political supremacy of the rulers because that would create disunity and political chaos. Hence, they generally supported the political status quo and favoured allegiance to rulers as long as they did not interfere in their right to interpret the *shari'a*.

Jurists therefore defined *dar al-kufr* as a vague and amorphous category. Usually all the territories bordering *dar al-Islam* were *dar al-kufr*, against which the rulers were urged to wage *jihad* at least once a year (Khalil 1916: 73). Such a definition, however, did not operate during the Prophet's period.

The bedouin around Medina and Mecca were never obliged to migrate to Medina. Instead of the *bay'at al-hijra* (pledge to migrate), they pledged to join *jihad* against the unbelievers. The Muslim population in this early period was divided into three categories: *muhajir*, *ansar* and *a'rab* (bedouin) (al-Tabari 1958: 14–78).

In those days the *a'rab* and *muhajir* were opposite terms. The *a'rab* were allowed a share in the spoils of war but not in other revenues. Donner (1981: 79) explains that early Muslims adopted *hijra* as a policy of "sedentarisation" in order to gain dominance by subordinating nomadic groups to a sedentary elite. It is difficult to say if there was a uniform policy for all the nomads, but we do know that it was during the Umayyid period, largely because the Khawarij were supported by nomads, that nomadism was considered the equivalent of returning to the pre-Islamic order. In view of the civil wars during this period, settlement was naturally stressed: the nomads, not under direct control of the centre, could provide refuge and protection to rebels. This Umayyid policy differed from preceding and later policies towards nomadism.[11]

Muhammad Idris al-Shafi'i (d. AD 820), the founder of the Shafi'i school of law, particularly referred to the case of the bedouin to argue that *hijra* was not obligatory for all because the Prophet permitted the bedouin not to migrate if they did not so desire. Shafi'i argued further that *hijra* became an obligation only after the declaration of *jihad*, and then only upon those who had the ability to do so (al-Shafi'i 1903: IV, 84). According to al-Shafi'i, therefore, a Muslim could stay in *dar al-kufr*, even in *dar al-harb*, as long as he was free to practise his religion.

The Maliki formulation and jihadist challenge

The majority of the Maliki jurists agreed with Shafi'i that *hijra* was not an obligation after Mecca was conquered. Al-Maziri (d. AD 1141) argued that staying behind in *dar al-kufr* with a legitimate excuse generally, or for the propagation of Islam specifically, was allowed and did not affect the rights of a Muslim. Even the judgements by a *qadi* appointed by a non-Muslim were valid and executable (Wansharisi 1981: I, 100). Abu'l Hasan al-Manufi al-Maliki (d. AD 1531) similarly held that the *hijra* was not required after Hudaybiyya (al-Maliki n.d.: II, 5). Ibn al-'Arabi (d. AD 1148) argued for the continuity of obligation but subjected *hijra* to a detailed analysis none the less. He argued that there were six situations of migration. *Hijra* was obligatory from territories of unbelief, heresy and injustice, or where unlawfulness prevails. *Hijra* was allowed but not obligatory from lands of physical persecution, lands of disease, and lands of financial insecurity (Ibn al-'Arabi 1972: I, 486).

The Jihadist movement in the eighteenth century criticised the popular definition of *dar al-Islam* as a country ruled by Muslims. Shehu 'Uthman dan Fodio (AD 1754–1817) was the foremost among those leaders who developed a detailed restatement of this doctrine. His formulation is discussed elsewhere in detail (Masud 1986), but can be summarised as it relates to the present argument.

Shehu's restatement of the doctrine of *hijra* was prompted by the actual historical circumstances in which he was forced to fight against the syncretism, injustice, and corruption of the Hebe Muslim rulers. He had to justify his *jihad* and migration against the criticism of Muslim jurists who supported the ruling regimes and who challenged Shehu's *jihad* against Muslim rulers.

Shehu's restatement rested on his argument from the original tradition of the Qur'an, *hadith*, and Maliki *fiqh*. The main points of his doctrine were the continuity of the obligation of migration, the close relationship of *jihad* with *hijra*, and the need for a redefinition of *dar al-Islam*.

Shehu agreed with the Khawarij on most questions of *hijra*, but he disagreed with their considering the commission of a major sin as *kufr*. He did not, however, accept the rulers' nominal adherence to Islam. In fact, he defined *kufr* as, first, their observance of pagan practices, and, second, their support of pagans against Muslims. Shehu succeeded in establishing a *dar al-Islam* in Nigeria that continued to flourish until the British occupied it in 1903.

Shehu's formulation had a far-reaching impact on other *jihadist* movements in West Africa. For example, his doctrine was cited as authority by the *amir* of Massina in his debate with Shaykh 'Umar al-Futi in 1855–64 (Willis 1979: 179). His doctrine also influenced the formulation of doctrines by Amir 'Abd al-Qadir in Algeria, Ma' al-'Aynayn al-Qalqami in Mauritania and Muhammad 'Abdullah Hasan in Somalia (Martin 1976: 33), and it continued to influence the Nigerian response to British hegemony.

Non-Muslim occupation and colonial rule

The questions of *dar al-Islam* and *hijra* arose again after the British occupation of India and Nigeria. Attahiru, the last sultan of the Sokoto Caliphate, resorted to Shehu's formulation of *hijra* when faced with the British invasion from 1900 onward. When Kano was also taken, Attahiru chose to perform *hijra* in order to rally his forces against the British. He called his followers to *hijra* and, in the words of a British journalist:

> each time he passed through the people were told to follow him to Mecca, otherwise they would become Kaffiri and as a result half of the population of every town tied up their bundles and joined in his train.
>
> (cited in Clarke 1982: 195)

Attahiru finally encamped at Burmi where he and his followers valiantly fought their battle against the British. Attahiru was killed and thus the British conquest of Nigeria was complete by 1903. After Attahiru's death, Maliki scholars returned to the formulation that *hijra* was not required. They accepted British rule, arguing that so long as Muslims had freedom to practise their religious duties, the land continued to be *dar al-Islam* (Savi 1971: II, 291).

The situation was different in India, where the Hanafi formulation prevailed. The Hanafi formulation of the doctrine of *hijra* differs from the Maliki formulation on two points. First, Hanafis argue that it is not correct to claim that succession among migrants to Medina in AD 622 was practised on the basis of *hijra*, nor that this Qur'anic injunction was abrogated later in order to restore succession on the basis of "blood" affinity. They maintain that succession was always based on "blood" relationships. Migration was important only to the extent that those "blood" relations who did not migrate did not qualify for succession. Brotherhood between *muhajirs* and *ansars* had economic advantages, but it was not the only ground for inheritance (Jassas 1916: II, 241).

Second, Hanafis stress the territorial factor of *dar al-Islam*. Their disagreement with claims of succession on the basis of migration is in fact also based on consideration of territory. A Muslim who did not migrate to *dar al-Islam* was disallowed from inheriting property there because it would mean transfer of property from *dar al-Islam* to *dar al-harb*. Similarly, even the spoils of war were not granted legal title until they were actually transferred to *dar al-Islam*.

Thus Hanafi doctrine is largely based on ideas of territory. A person is treated according to the territory where he is ('Alamgiri 1932: III, 423). Consequently, a Muslim who does not migrate from *dar al-harb*, although a Muslim, is to be governed by the rules of *dar al-harb*. This is why the Hanafis allow transactions by Muslims in *dar al-harb* that are not allowed in *dar al-Islam*.

Due to these considerations, according to Hanafis, *dar al-Islam* changes into *dar al-harb* if the following three conditions obtain: (1) the laws of disbelievers gain supremacy and no law of Islam can be executed; (2) the Muslim and non-Muslim populations are no longer governed by the original pacts that they enjoyed before the non-Muslim occupation; and (3) the land in question is adjacent to the territory of *dar al-harb* such that there is no land of Islam between them ('Alamgiri 1932: III, 415). Analysing these views in detail, Wahba al-Zuhayli, a modern Muslim jurist, concludes that Hanafis believe in the application of law on a territorial basis, while Malikis and others apply it on a personal basis (al-Zuhayli 1962[?]: 175).

Shah 'Abd al-'Aziz (1904: 16–17) was asked frequently whether British India was *dar al-harb*. He said that it was, but disallowed all of the implications of his declaration. India was *dar al-harb* because the laws of the *shari'a* were not supreme. He did not, however, allow the usury transactions that Hanafis allow in *dar al-harb*. He dismissed as political expediences the freedom allowed by the British to observe Friday services, religious feasts, and the calls to prayer, and the permission to slaughter cows and observe other personal laws. When Shah 'Abd al-'Aziz was asked why he did not call for *hijra* from *dar al-harb*, he replied that the *hijra* required, as a necessary condition, possession of the means to migrate; it was allowed only if the means were available (al-Qannuji 1985: 238). Yet Sayyid Ahmad Barelwi organised *hijra* and *jihad* to restore India's status of *dar al-Islam*. According to William Hunter, the 1857 Muslim revolt against the British was a continuation of Sayyid Ahmad's movement of *hijra* (Hunter 1964: 3).

However, the Hanafi majority view has been that if Friday and the religious holidays can be observed, the land is *dar al-Islam*. The non-Muslim rulers can appoint Muslim governors and judges whose orders would be Islamically valid (Isma'il 1985: 231). Other scholars – such as Karamat 'Ali Jawnpuri, Sayyid Ahmad Khan, and Nadhir Husayn Muhaddith al-Dihlawi – similarly termed British India *dar al-Islam*.

An important event was the 1920 *hijra* from India to Afghanistan after the declaration of India as *dar al-harb*. From a recent analysis of this movement (Qureshi 1979), it is clear that the movement did not possess a traditional doctrinal basis. It was based on the *fatawa* of Mawlana 'Abd al-Bari Farangi Mahli (1828) and Shah 'Abd al-'Aziz (1824). As I have explained, Shah 'Abd al-'Aziz did not call for *hijra*, and 'Abd al-Bari maintained that he did not consider *hijra* mandatory. Scholars belonging to the Deoband and Barelwi schools – such as Ashraf 'Ali Thanawi, 'Abdur Ra'uf Danapuri, Ahmad Riza Khan Barelwi, and Pir Mihr 'Ali Shah – advocated the refrain from *hijra* (Mahmud 1986: 72, 258–69). It was mainly Abu'l Kalam Azad's writings that provided the theoretical and intellectual basis for this movement (Azad n.d.: 31–2). His was in fact a restatement of the doctrine similar to that made by Shehu 'Uthman dan Fodio.

Abu'l Kalam Azad was joined by Muhammad and Shawkat 'Ali, leaders of the Khilafat movement, and many other public leaders. Thousands of Muslims, in fact, responded to the call for *hijra* and many thousands actually began their journey of migration to Afghanistan. Qureshi points out that the Afghani elite also encouraged the movement but only for their own political ends

(Qureshi 1979: 45). The result proved disastrous for Muslims. Afghanistan did not prove to be *dar al-Islam* for these *muhajirin* who had volunteered to move there after disposing of all their possessions. Hundreds died on the way to and back from Afghanistan; others returned to India destitute and frustrated.

It is clear that the *hijra* movement of 1920 was not supported by the established *'ulama'*, who had traditional training. The movement, on the contrary, was led and supported by scholars who were not traditionally trained. In fact, they were scholars like Abu'l Kalam Azad whom the traditional men of learning never recognised as religious scholars (Mushir 1974: 25). Other scholars in the movement came from the Ahl al-Hadith school, which refused adherence to the traditional four Muslim legal schools. Further, the leaders of the movement came from the western-educated class, such as the Ali brothers. It is important to note that whereas the traditionally trained *'ulama'*, whether in Nigeria, India, Pakistan, or Indonesia (Van Dijk 1981), generally favoured the status quo, self-trained scholars led the new Islamic political movements.

It seems that the people who raised the question of *dar al-harb* and asked opinions of scholars like Shah 'Abd al-'Aziz were probably interested in this issue in order to avail themselves of the exemptions from the application of Islamic law that Hanafis allow to Muslims in *dar al-harb*. This is probably why the questions referred mainly to money transactions based on *riba* (usury). Muslims were discouraged from military *jihad* against the British by the military superiority of the colonial powers, Muslim defeat at their hands in Plessey (1757) and Burmi (1903), and the subsequent ruthless repression. The only form of *jihad* available to them was *tark mawalat* (withdrawal or non-cooperation). *Jihad* and *hijra* both required means which the Muslims lacked. Moreover, the general British policy of non-interference in religious matters suited the conception of *dar al-Islam* of traditional *'ulama'*.

During the late nineteenth and twentieth century, the spread of education, growth of political consciousness, and increase in the means of communication made it easier for Muslim religious leaders to learn more about political conditions in developed countries. They compared these conditions with the restrictions prevalent in colonised territories, so that dissatisfaction grew with the status quo. At the same time, leadership came not from traditional scholars and landowners, but from Muslims who had been educated in the west and from reformers.

Traditional scholars and landowners favoured the status quo, however, and the new leadership therefore looked to the masses for support against the British. The most powerful medium against the

41

colonial power was religion, which could eliminate fear and inspire commitment. Religion was not the only factor that could unite the masses against the colonial rulers, but it was the weakest point of the colonial system. The new leadership, although not deeply entrenched in the traditional religious sciences, revived and invoked such religious issues as *hijra* as a rallying point for political advantage.

Hijra to non-Muslim countries

A new dimension of *hijra* emerged during the nineteenth century. For reasons of higher education, training, and employment, Muslims travelled to non-Muslim lands and stayed there for longer periods. In some cases they migrated in order to settle. This was altogether a new type of *hijra*; its motives and objectives were different.

As mentioned earlier, scholars like Ibn al-'Arabi permitted *hijra* from a land of disease and financial insecurity to a better place (Ibn al-'Arabi 1972: I, 486), and based their argument on Qur'anic verse (4: 100). Others allowed *hijra* to non-Muslim lands for the purpose of propagation of Islam. They based their argument on the legal view that Muslims must remain in *dar al-kufr* in order to propagate its reconversion. An illustration is the discussion contained in a recent treatise, *Hukm al-iqama bi-bilad kufr wa-bayan wujubiha fi-ba'd al-ahwal* [*Legal View of Staying in the Lands of Unbelief and the Explanation of Why It Has Been Obligatory in Certain Circumstances*], relating the question of whether residence in non-Muslim countries can be said to be obligatory.[12] The author states that in 1985 some Algerian students met him in Mecca and asked whether staying in European countries and America was allowed. The students claimed that the position of scholars was not clear, and they particularly referred to a recent *fatwa* which prohibited such a stay ('Abd al-'Aziz al-Siddiq 1985: 6).

The author of the treatise discusses the problem at length and concludes that remaining in Europe and America for the purposes of education and employment is not only allowed but is often obligatory. His main arguments include the following: education and training in modern science and technology are obligatory for the progress of Muslim societies, since otherwise they would remain dependent on developed countries ('Abd al-'Aziz al-Siddiq 1985: 12–13); the Qur'an and *hadith* enjoin Muslims to seek knowledge and livelihood all over the globe; and the reason for migration from *dar al-kufr* and for the prohibition from entering it, as given in Islamic law, is the apprehension that the person, property, and/or religion of a Muslim are not safe in these territories, yet today there is no such fear. Indeed, the conditions for the practice and propagation of one's religion are better in Europe and America than in most Muslim countries ('Abd al-'Aziz al-Siddiq 1985: 30, 45–50). He argues, finally, that western countries which have made pacts and treaties with Muslim ones are no longer *dar al-kufr* ('Abd al-'Aziz al-Siddiq 1985: 51). The most distinguished scholars of Islamic law in the Middle East – such as Muhammad b. Ahmad Abu Zahra (1898–1974), 'Abd al-Qadir 'Awda (d. AD 1954), and Wahba al-Zuhayli – have offered similar interpretations of the doctrine of *hijra* (Abu Zahra n.d.: 55; 'Awda 1959: I, 275; al-Zuhayli 1962[?]: 149).

Nation states

Muslims re-emerged after independence from colonial rule divided into a number of nation-states. During the colonial period Muslim romanticism visualised the Muslim world as a single, monolithic and sovereign polity. Now there are a large number of Muslim communities without sovereignty. Are they part of the Muslim world? Should the Muslim world regard them as distant enclaves in foreign lands and therefore help them? Or should they be considered permanently situated under non-Muslim jurisdiction?

What should these Muslim communities do? Should they migrate to Muslim countries? Should they continue struggling to achieve liberation and sovereignty? Should their objectives be the achievement of civil and cultural rights within a non-Muslim polity?

It is clear that the emerging Muslim world is not the *dar al-Islam* of medieval times. It consists of nation-states looking after their own national interests. Unlike the situation that prevailed in the medieval *dar al-Islam*, a Muslim cannot freely travel, migrate, or settle in any Muslim country today. Some of these countries are secular; others have reformed religious and personal laws along western lines. The non-Muslim populations in these Muslim countries have been participating equally in the struggle for freedom, independence, and progress, and thus are not conquered people to be forced to accept the status of a protected minority (*dhimmis*). The doctrine of *hijra* consequently faces new challenges.

In early Islamic history, the formulation of the doctrines of *hijra* was interconnected with the definition of *dar al-Islam* and *kufr*. However, the issues posed by the framing of these doctrines varied. In the early period, the question was: from where to where must one migrate? Although this question had a different meaning for dissident political groups, it continued to be asked during the medieval period about Muslims not living in *dar al-Islam*. For Muslims living within *dar al-Islam* the question was: from where must Muslims not migrate? Whereas in the early period *dar al-kufr* defined *hijra*, in the medieval period *hijra* defined *dar al-Islam*. Any movement of migration from a certain territory meant that it was no longer considered *dar al-Islam* – at least, not by the migrants.

The question of *hijra* became prominent again during the thirteenth century when Christians in the west and Tartars in the east occupied Muslim lands. The question was now posed differently: must one migrate from a territory that once was *dar al-Islam*? Categories between *dar al-Islam* and *dar al-kufr* were developed to answer the question, and these categories proved to be useful during the colonial period between the eighteenth and nineteenth centuries.

With the rise of nation-states and a secular world-view, the definition of *dar al-Islam* has become increasingly problematic. In this context, the definition of *hijra* in terms of movement from *dar al-kufr* becomes irrelevant. One must ask not only *from* where must one migrate, but also *to* where? Several modern scholars (e.g. al-Zuhayli 1962: 159; Abu Zahra n.d.: 55) seem to have redefined *dar al-Islam* and searched for new categories of territory (*dar*) from the point of view of *hijra*.

Dar al-Islam and related *dar* categories are now being defined more frequently with reference to the question: from where does one not need to migrate? Answers to this question have produced categories such as *dar al-'ahd* (the land of pact), *dar al-sulh* (the land of truce), and *dar al-aman* (the land of peace), in which a Muslim's freedom to practise his religion is protected by covenant. It is significant that the frame of reference for this apparently new interpretation is still the early tradition of *hijra*. This particular movement of *hijra* – migration to a non-Muslim land – is alluded to as the Abyssinian model, referring to the earliest *hijra* by Muslims to Abyssinia, a Christian country. It is also justified with reference to the Hudaybiyya model, whereby Muslims were not required to migrate from Mecca – at that time still a non-Muslim land – because of a pact between it and Medina. These interpretations seem appropriate to the world of nation-states because citizens are protected by pacts between them.

Conclusion

This discussion is intended to be exploratory rather than definitive, but several points emerge. First, it should be noted that *hijra*, which appears as one of the essential obligations in early Islam and is often discussed at length in *hadith*, *tafsir*, *fiqh*, *fatawa*, and Sufi literature, did not earn sufficient prominence in the later classification of *fiqh* or *kalam* subjects to deserve treatment as a subject in itself.

Second there is a distinction, although often blurred, between the Hanafi and other schools in the debates about *hijra*. While the Hanafis tend to define the status of a person living in *dar al-harb* and the transformation of *dar al-Islam* into *dar al-harb* in terms of territory, the other legal schools do not. It can be argued that among the Hanafis there was a trend towards a territorial definition of law, in contradistinction to others who adhered to a personal definition. Other legal schools considered a Muslim living in *dar al-harb* to be still subject to Islamic law, but, in contrast, the Hanafis were not in favour of applying Islamic law to Muslims in enemy territories. This distinction would have developed had it not been for the exemption from the application of certain Islamic laws to non-Muslims living in *dar al-Islam* – an exception that probably grew out of the principle of freedom of religion.

Third, the formulation of the doctrine at various historical junctures shows the discursive nature of intellectual arguments in the Muslim tradition. Jurists constantly go back to texts – often the same ones – interpreting and reinterpreting them in order to justify the opinions shaped by earlier social, economic, and political conditions. The extreme views, which in the case of *hijra* invariably rely on Khawarij interpretations, are taken by political dissenters.

Finally, it should be noted that although one might expect a written text as a frame of reference to prove restrictive on subsequent interpretations, the doctrine of *hijra* has, on the contrary, been quite adaptable to varying political contexts. The same texts have been interpreted to justify widely different views.

The reason for this flexibility lies perhaps in the acceptability of these interpretations more than in the interpretability of the doctrine itself. There is something which we may call a "semantics of expectation" on the part of society. Words acquire new meanings according to these expectations. The shifts of meaning of *hijra* – from movement itself to settlement, from physical movement to spiritual and mental withdrawal, and from movement to Muslim territory to residence in Western countries for the purpose of propagating Islam – are examples of this semantics of expectation.

The calls for the establishment of *dar al-Islam*, sometimes without call for physical *hijra*, have curiously been made not by the traditional scholars, but by a new type of Muslim intellectual, self-trained and lacking formal education in the traditional schools of jurisprudence. These new intellectuals have either graduated from western-style schools and universities or have been intellectually nourished on western literature. Because of their modern world views, these intellectuals are more acceptable to urban, educated Muslims than their traditional counterparts, who still attract a primarily rural and "superstitious" clientele. These new intellectuals, for the simple reason that they are not hindered by the complexities of traditional legal thought, have the freedom of selecting more eclectically from tradition and justifying their views directly from the Qur'an and *hadith*. They often earn instant popularity because of reference to the "sources", but, since their interpretations do not form a continuity with tradition, their impact is often partial and ephemeral. The new intellectuals are therefore continually compelled to search for dramatic, and often extremist, solutions.

Notes

1 Allama Ihsan Ilahi Zaheer (1940–87), born at Sialkot in a religious family, pursued traditional religious studies at Gujranwala and graduated from Jami'a Salafiyya in Faisalabad in 1960. After completing his studies at Medina University, he returned to Pakistan where he obtained MA degrees in Urdu, Persian, History, and Philosophy from Punjab University and an LL B from Karachi University. From 1966 he was *khatib* of Jami'a Masjid Ahl al-Hadith in Lahore. He edited various religious journals, published his own monthly magazine, *Tarjuman Ahl al-Hadith*, and wrote about fifteen books, most of them in Arabic. Towards the end of his life he became active in politics. He was the Nazim-i-A'la of Jam'iyyat Ahl al-Hadith whose public meeting he was addressing on 23 March 1987, when a bomb exploded and seriously wounded him. He died on 30 March at the Saudi Military Hospital in Riyadh (*Islamic Studies* 1987: 230).
2 The news story does not specify the Qur'anic verse. It only states that the young men referred to the verse in *sura* 4 that bade Prophet Muhammad to migrate. They might be referring to verse 97, which is mentioned in my main discussion.
3 Reforms such as the registration of marriages and restrictions on polygamy were introduced by the Muslim Family Laws Ordinance of 1962, despite severe protests by the *'ulama'*.
4 Dates in this chapter have been adopted from Hodgson (1974).
5 Numbers of the verses of the Qur'an as well as the English translation are from Pickthall (1953).
6 Khawarij: The earliest sect in Islam which rebelled against 'Ali (AD 656–61) because of his compromise with the Umayyids after the Battle of Siffin (AD 657). They revolted and fought against both the Umayyids and the 'Abbasids.

7 A group of Khawarij named after Nafi' b. al-Azraq (d. AD 685).

8 A group of Khawarij named after Zyad b. Asfar whom they followed. They opposed the Azariqa and Ibadiyya and held more moderate views.

9 A group of Khawarij who followed 'Abdullah b. Ibad. They rebelled against Marwan b. Muhammad (d. AD 744), the Umayyad caliph.

10 A group of Khawarij who, according to al-Shahristani, held that when the Imam committed an act of disbelief, his subjects also became disbelievers.

11 It appears that Donner has developed the argument restrospectively and explains the situation in early Islam in the perspective of 'Abd al-'Aziz ibn Sa'ud's (AD 1880–1953) policy to encourage bedouin to effect *hijra* from the nomadic to sedentary life in order to create the *ikhwan*, a para-military force which he used agains the Sharifians of Hijaz. Each settlement was called a *hijra*.

12 This author, 'Abd al-'Aziz b. Muhammad b. al-Siddiq, belongs to a family of scholars in Tangier. I have not been able to find much information on him. An autobiography of his elder brother (b. 1909), 'Abdullah b. al-Siddiq, makes occasional references to him as "my brother, the 'Allama, the Muhaddith" (e.g. 'Abdullah al-Siddiq 1985: 3). 'Abd al-'Aziz is also mentioned as one of his students ('Abdullah al-Siddiq 1985: 8).

References

'Abd al-'Aziz, Shah (1904) *Fatawa 'Aziziyya*, Delhi.

Abu Da'ud (1933) *Sunan*, vol. II, Matba'a 'Ilmiyya, Aleppo.

Abu Zahra (n.d.) *Al-'Ilaqat al-Duwaliyya fi'l-Islam*, Dar al-Fikr al-'Arabi, Cairo.

'Alamgiri (1932) *Fatawa 'Alamgiri* [Urdu translation by Sayyid Amir Ali], Nawilkashore, Lucknow.

Allama Ihsan Ilahi Zaheer [1940–87]: 'Obituary note' (1987) *Islamic Studies*, 26, no. 2, p. 230.

al-Ash'ari, Abu'l Hasan 'Ali b. Ismai'il (1950) *Maqalat al-Islamiyyin*, vol. II, Al-Nahda, Cairo.

'Awda, 'Abd al-Qadir (1959) *Al-Tashri' al-jina'i al-Islami, muqarinan bi'l-qanun al-Wad'i*, Dar al-'Aruba, Cairo.

Azad, Abu'l Kalam (n.d.) *Mas'alam-i-Khilafat*, Khayaban-i-Irfan, Lahore.

al-Baydawi, 'Abdullah b. 'Umar (1955) *Anwar al-Tanzil wa-Asrar al-Ta'wil*, Cairo.

al-Bukhari, Muhammad (1971) *Sahih*, vol. V, Majlis al-A'la li'l-Shu'un al-Islamiyya, Cairo.

al-Bursawi, Isma'il Haqqi (AH 1330) *Ruhal-Bayan*, Matbu'at Usmaniyya, Istanbul.

Clarke, Peter B. (1982) *West Africa and Islam*, Edward Arnold, London.

Donner, Fred McGraw (1981) *The Early Islamic Conquests*, Princeton University Press, Princeton.

Hodgson, Marshall G. (1974) *The Venture of Islam; Conscience and*

History in a World Civilization, University of Chicago Press, Chicago, 3 vols.

Hunter, W.W. (1964 [orig. 1871]) *The Indian Musulmans*, Lahore.

Ibn al-'Arabi (1972) *Ahkam al-Qur'an*, vol. I, Dar al-Ma'rifa, Beirut.

Ibn Hajar, Abul-Fadl Ahmad b. 'Ali [al-'Asqalani] (1959) *Fath al-Bari*, vol. VI, Mustafa al-Babi, Cairo.

Ibn Hanbal, Ahmad (n.d.) *Musnad*, vol. IV, Beirut.

Ibn Hisham (1963) in M. 'Abd al-Hamid (ed.) *Sirat al-Nabi*, vol. II, Muhammad 'Ali Sabih, Cairo.

Ibn Khaldun (1958) *Muqaddima*, vol. I, Routledge, London.

Isma'il (1985) *Jami' al-Fusulayn* [see al-Qannuji, 1985].

Jassas, Abu Bakr Ahmad b. 'Ali al-Razi (1916) *Ahkam al-Qur'an*, vol. II, Istanbul.

Kepel, Gilles (1985) *The Prophet and Pharaoh: Muslim Extremism in Egypt*, Al-Saqi Books, London.

Khalil, Sidi (1916) *Maliki Law* (translation of *Mukhtasar* of Sidi Khalil), F.M. Ruxton, London.

Mahmud, Raja Rashid (1986) *Tahrik-i-Hijrat 1920*, Maktaba 'Aliya, Lahore.

al-Maliki, Abu'l Hasan (n.d.) *Kifayat al-Talib al-Rabbani*, Mashhad al-Husayni, Cairo.

Martin, B.G. (1976) *Muslim Brotherhoods in Nineteenth Century Africa*, Cambridge University Press, Cambridge.

Masud, M.K. (1986) 'Shehu Usuman dan Fodio's Restatement of the Doctrine of Hijrah', *Islamic Studies*, 25, no. 1, pp. 56–77.

Maybudi, Abu'l Fadl Rashid al-Din (AH 1338) *Kashf al-Asrar wa-'Uddat al-Abrar*, Tehran University Press, Tehran.

Mushir, Mushir al-Haqq (1974) *Madhhab awr Jadid Zihn*, Jami'a, Delhi.

Muslim (1954) *Sahih*, vol. I, Dar Ihya al-Turath al-'Arabi, Beirut.

Najmi, 'Arif (1987) 'Lahore men bam ka dhamaka', *Jang* [Rawalpindi], 4 April, p. alif.

Pickthall, M.M. (1953) *The Meaning of the Glorious Koran: An Explanatory Translation*, New American Library, New York.

al-Qannuji, Siddiq Hasan (1985) *al-'Ibrat mima ja'a fi'l-Ghazw wa'l-shahada*, Islamiyya, Beirut.

Qureshi, M. Naeem (1979) 'The Ulama of British India and the Hijrat of 1920', *Modern Asian Studies*, 13, no. 1, pp. 41–59.

al-Qurtubi, Abu 'Abdullah (1967) *al-Jami'li Ahkam al-Qur'an*, vol. V.

al-Qushayri, Abu'l-Qasim (n.d.) *Lata'if al-Isharat*, vol. I, Dar al-Kutub al-'Arabi, Cairo.

Savi, Shaykh (1971) *al-Sharh al-saghir 'ala aqrab al-masalik ila madhhab Imam Malik*, vol. II, Cairo.

Schacht, Joseph (1966) *An Introduction to Islamic Law*, Oxford University Press, Oxford.

al-Shafi'i, Abul-Idris Muhammad (1903) *Kitab al-Umm*, vol. IV, Amiriyya, Cairo.

al-Shahristani, Muhammad (1899) *al-Milal wa'l-Nihal*, vol. I, Matba'a Adabiyya, Cairo.

al-Siddiq, Sayyid 'Abd al-'Aziz b. Muhammad (1985) *Hukm al-iqama bi-bilad al-kufr wa-bayan wujubiha fi-ba'd al-Ahwal*, Bughaz, Tangier.

al-Siddiq, 'Abdullah (1985) *Sabil al-tawfiq fi-tarjumat 'Abdullah b. al-Siddiq*, Dar al-Bayan, Cairo.

al-Tabari, Abu Ja'far Muhammad b. Jarir (1958) *Jami' al-bayan 'an ta'wil ayah al-Qur'an*, vol. XXIV, Dar al-Ma'arif, Cairo.

Van Dijk, C. (1981) *Rebellion under the Banner of Islam: The Darul Islam in Indonesia*, Martinus Nijhoff, The Hague.

Voll, John O. (1987) 'The mahdi's concept and use of "hijrah"', *Islamic Studies*, 26, no. 1, pp. 31–42.

al-Wansharisi, 'Abd al-Wahid Ahmad b. Yahya (1981) *al-Mi'yar al-Mu'rab wa'l-jami'-l-muqhrab 'an fatawa 'ulama' Ifriqiyya wa'l-Andalus wa'l-Maghrib*, vol. II, Dar al-Gharb, Beirut.

Watt, Montgomery (1971) *'Hidjra', The Encyclopaedia of Islam*, 2nd edn, Brill, Leiden, vol. III, pp. 366–7.

Willis, John Ralph (1979) *Studies in West African Islamic History*, vol. I, Frank Cass, London.

al-Zamakhshari, Mahmud b. 'Umar (1934) *al-Kashshaf 'an haqa'iq ghawamid al-tanzil*, vol. II, Cairo.

al-Zuhayli, Wahba (1962)[?] *Athar al-harb fi'l-fiqh al-Islami*, Damascus.

Chapter three

The search for knowledge in medieval Muslim societies: a comparative approach

Sam I. Gellens

> Anas b. Malik reported that the Prophet said: Those who go out in search of knowledge will be in the path of God until they return.
>
> (al-Tirmidhi, *Sunan*, 39: 2)

This chapter suggests how three medieval Islamic societies might be studied within a comparative historical framework. To do so, we have selected a prominent feature of everyday life, the *rihla* or *talab al-'ilm* (travel for the sake of acquiring religious knowledge), which was common to medieval Muslims throughout *dar al-Islam*. *Talab al-'ilm*, given its deep roots in the Islamic tradition, its popularity, and its ability to facilitate movement and exchange among Islamic societies, demonstrates the virtues of the comparative method in studying Islamic history. Its study reveals both universally shared sentiments and the strength of local ties as possibly no other societal trait could.

In an essay on the comparative history of European societies, Marc Bloch (1967 [orig. 1928]: 47) wrote that one use of the comparative method is:

> to make a parallel study of societies that are at once neighbour-ing and contemporary, exercising a constant mutual influence, exposed throughout their development to the action of the same broad causes just because they are close and contemporaneous, and owing their existence to a common origin.

Though Bloch restricted his analysis to Europe, his formulation makes eminent sense for several reasons when applied to medieval Islam.[1]

First, there is the vast physical expanse of *dar al-Islam*, a broad complex of peoples, geographies, and political structures that owes its existence and inspiration, in a fundamental sense, to a specific time and place: seventh-century Arabia. The Prophet Muhammad, the Qur'anic revelation, the Arabic language, and the cities of Mecca and Medina acted then as now as historical referents which bestowed a kinship on all Muslims regardless of birthplace or domicile. No matter how distant from Arabia, all medieval Islamic societies could claim a share in this common origin, this common Muslim heritage focused on the natal centre of Islam.

The dispersal of the Arabs and Arabic into the former Byzantine and Sasanid territories and beyond, the acceleration of the pace of conversion in the late third/ninth century, and the multiple influences and contributions of such newly Islamised peoples as the Iranians, Turks, and Berbers created a world civilisation extending from the Atlantic to the Oxus. Out of this vortex developed a multiplicity of local centres for traditional Muslim learning that did not, however, rob the Islamic world of its essential unity. Indeed, one of the most compelling aspects of Islamic history is the continuing dialogue among Muslims over the relative merits of local attachments versus perceived universal sentiments and obligations.

This civilisation – really a network of variegated societies united by their commitment to the *shari'a* – was one which in the fullest sense owed its vibrancy to constant movement. Travel in all its myriad forms – pilgrimage, trade, scholarship, adventure – expanded the mental and physical limits of the Muslim world, and preserved and nourished the various contacts that Muslims perennially maintained with one another. As Ross Dunn (1986: 5–6) has noted in his recent study of the renowned Muslim traveller, Ibn Battuta, Marco Polo visited China as a stranger and alien, whereas his Muslim counterpart compiled a *rihla* on the basis of distant journeys to lands either wholly or to some degree Muslim. Ibn Battuta may not have known the local languages of the places he visited, but he did know the *cultural* language of Muslims and hence felt at home.

Travel in its broadest definition ensured the unity of the Muslim community, but likewise encouraged appreciation of one's home. Spain, Egypt, and Iran were medieval Islamic societies each with a distinct character. Yet each region was part of a larger civilisational whole. These societies, to paraphrase Bloch's formulation, were neighbouring and contemporary, reciprocally influential, and subject to developments in religious learning, politics, trade, and warfare that were generally common to *dar al-Islam*. Travel bound them together and simultaneously stimulated the appearance of their local and regional identities. It is within the confines of this dialectic that we find the utility of the travel concept for the comparative study of medieval Muslim societies.

Travel as a meritorious activity is endowed with an ancient

Figure 3.1   Majnun at the Ka'ba with his father and other pilgrims. This miniature, taken from the *Khamseh* of Nizami, is later Herat/Timurid work of 898/1492–3. (British Library Ms. ADD.25900F. 114B. Used with permission.)

pedigree in the Muslim tradition. A rich vocabulary of words related in one way or another to travel is found in the Qur'an and the *hadith*. Sura Quraysh, 106: 2, refers to the *rihla* (the sole mention of the term in the Qur'an) in connection with the special accomplishments of the tribe of Quraysh and how much they owe their succes to God's providence. The Qur'an intends us to understand here that the Quraysh above all, with their talents for "journeys south and north" (presumably meaning to Yemen and Syria), should accept God's commands. Thus, embedded deep in Muslim consciousness is an identification of travel with pious activity, an appreciation that achievement in such endeavour is a sign of divine approval and munificence.

As an organising principle for comparative analysis, only travel for the sake of religious scholarship specifically concerns us here. Initially, we must consider the problem of terminology. In the period under consideration in this chapter (four–fifth AH/tenth–eleventh AD centuries), the expressions *rihla* (travel) and *talab al-'ilm* (seeking knowledge) could almost be used interchangeably. Throughout the Spanish *tabaqat* literature,[2] the two are often linked together, and when they are not they bear the same general meaning (travelling to seek religious knowledge). There are references to the *rihla* as *hajj*, but it is the former usage that is dominant. It is not until the late sixth AH/twelfth AD century that the two terms diverge. *Rihla* becomes identified primarily with the experience of the *hajj* – the examples of Ibn Jubayr and Ibn Battuta come immediately to mind – while *talab al-'ilm* retains its original meaning.[3] This change may reflect the institutionalisation of the *madrasa* system in place of the formerly more individualised, orally-oriented relationships which prevailed between students and teachers in the early medieval centuries of Islamic history. Thus, Ibn Battuta usually looks for buildings – i.e. colleges of Islamic law and Sufi convents – rather than the solitary but renowned scholar here and there on his itinerary. The bulk of the references in the *hadith* literature are to *talab al-'ilm* and not *rihla*. It is evident then that *talab al-'ilm*, as a concept describing a specific aspect of movement and exchange among Muslims, is the more precise and accurate of the two terms.

The *hadith* literature reminds the believer that the search for knowledge is intimately tied to the physical act of travel. In this regard, several themes recur in the principal *hadith* collections: teachers and the learned as the only valuable human beings; the high merit of seeking and spreading knowledge; travelling in order to gather it; and the possession of knowledge as a sign of grace which reduces distinctions of birth and rank among Muslims.

Provided it was done for the right reasons, travel in the classical Muslim conception, to use Paul Fussell's (1980: 39) words, "was conceived to be like study and its fruits were considered to be the adornment of the mind and the formation of the traveller".

The best-known *hadith* on the subject – i.e. "The seeking of knowledge is a *fard* incumbent upon every Muslim" – is coupled in the collection of Ibn Majah (*Sunan*, I, no. 224) with the admonition that "He who places knowledge with those with whom it does not belong is like he who gives jewellery, pearls, and gold to pigs". This report elevates *talab al-'ilm* to the status of a ritual obligation and stresses the care one must take in disseminating knowledge.[4] In his *Muwatta* (1951, II: 1002), Malik b. Anas transmits a *hadith* from the pre-Islamic hero, Luqman, who advises his son: "Oh my boy, sit with the learned (*'ulama'*) and mingle with them on your knees. For just as God gives life to people's hearts with the light of wisdom, so he enlivens the dead earth with the downpour of the heavens". The ideal company for a Muslim is the learned, for they represent a life-giving (and sustaining) force within the community. If indeed they are the best company, we could assume from this *hadith* that the believer should seek the presence of the *'ulama'* wherever they are; hence the importance of travel for the sake of attaining knowledge.

Recognised as a Companion by some, Abu al-Darda' was a younger contemporary of the Prophet and an authority on the Qur'an who served as a *qadi* in Damascus and died there in AH 32/ AD 652–3 (Jeffery 1960: 113–14). On one occasion, a class he was giving in the mosque of Damascus was interrupted by a man from Medina who had come to ascertain the validity of a Prophetic *hadith* which Abu al-Darda' had transmitted. The latter asked the man whether he had brought merchandise or anything else with him. When the man gave a negative reply, Abu al-Darda' responded with the following:

He who follows a road seeking knowledge, God will make the path to heaven easy for him. And the angels will place their wings so as to aid the seeker of knowledge. And all in heaven and on earth, even the snake in the water, will seek forgiveness from such a person. The merit of the learned man over the worshipper is like the merit of the moon over the rest of the stars. The *'ulama'* are the heritage of the prophets. The latter did not bequeath *dinars* and *dirhams*. Rather they left behind knowledge. He who takes it should do so with an abundance of good fortune.

(Ibn Majah, 1972: I, *hadith* no. 223)

The message here is obvious: God views with great favour those who pursue *talab al-'ilm* to the point that such activity facilitates entry into heaven. Worship (meaning prayer) undoubtedly brings the believer closer to God, but it is the learned one who enjoys an even more special relationship with Allah. It is the man from Medina who travelled to Damascus seeking to verify a *hadith* who is unstintingly praised, and we may assume that this adulation would apply to all Muslims who would travel for the same or similar reasons.

Given the intense interest in travel for the sake of scholarship in the *hadith* literature, it is no wonder that it became a normative feature of medieval Muslim education, at least until the sixth AH/ twelfth AD century. Though local and regional traditions were always influential in shaping religious and intellectual life, medieval Muslims really knew no boundaries in their desire to master the subjects which comprised the canonical syllabus of learning: among others, they included the Qur'an, *hadith*, *tafsir* (commentary on the Qur'an), and *qira'a* (correct recitation of the Qur'an). Scholarly peregrinations were frequent and often long, in terms of both time and distance.

A man could study in twenty different cities with as many different teachers in each and return home yearning for yet another trip. A representative example is the Cordoban *shaykh* who went east in AH 330/AD 941–2 at the age of fourteen (Ibn al-Faradi 1966: biography no. 1360). During his trip, he followed an extensive itinerary that included Mecca, Medina, Jidda, Yemen (Sana'a, Zabid, Aden), Fustat, Jerusalem, Gaza, Ashkelon, Tiberias, Damascus, Tripoli, Beirut, Caesaria, Ramla, Farama, Alexandria, and Qulzum. This tidal flow of scholars and scholarship across the Islamic lands eventually established the primacy of certain cities and regions as learning centres.

A shifting hierarchy of learning centres emerged. Depending on political and economic conditions, different cities in different periods could vie for pre-eminence in this regard. Whereas, for example, Baghdad set the standard in the third–early fourth AH/ ninth–early tenth AD centuries, it was Cairo under the Fatimids and Nishapur in the succeeding two centuries which attracted Muslim scholars. This hierarchy could also depend to a lesser degree merely upon opportunity – for instance, a scholar might opt for one city as opposed to another because it was closer to his place of origin or had a sufficient number of well-known divines residing in it. But it is evident from our sources that travelling scholars were exceedingly well-informed. They knew where the leading scholars lived and acted accordingly. A scholarly traveller of the type discussed eagerly contacted local *'ulama'* wherever he went, but he always knew where he would be most rewarded.

Although more research needs to be done on its exact nature, *rihla/talab al-'ilm* deserves its status as a unifying theme of medieval Islamic history. For Muslims who undertook it, it was an experience to be relished in a variety of contexts. Yet *rihla/talab al-'ilm* also contributed, as already noted, to regionalism and localism. Why is this so? First, the powerful forces that were generated – perhaps as early as the second century after the conquests – blended the ancient traditions of the Near East, transmitted by converts to Islam, with those of the Arab settlers. This blending produced new Muslim communities, each proud of its distinctive heritage, both old and new. The special qualities or merits (*fada'il*) assigned to Mecca and Medina in the Qur'an and the *hadith* literature established a precedent and a paradigm for newly-constituted Muslim communities. Mecca, of course, possessed both a privileged pre-Islamic status and a central place in Muslim tradition. This duality of distinction was copied and reproduced – initially perhaps in Egypt – by other Muslim societies, and gave birth to a literary genre called *fada'il*, which bred cultural competition among cities in particular.

Second, there was the psychology of the traveller himself. For example, a scholar who left Cordoba or Seville to perform the *hajj* and study with the learned men of North Africa and Egypt did not do so as a peripheral malcontent. He was usually at least a man of solid middle-class background and some local intellectual renown, and one fully imbued with the values of his native land. He marvelled at the sights that he saw in Mecca, cherished the memory of classes that he attended in Fez or Damascus, yet returned home still convinced that the homesickness he experienced was genuine and that no other land surpassed the merits of al-Andalus.

Perhaps all of this conforms to the three stages of Joseph Campbell's myth of the hero (quoted in Fussell 1980: 208): the setting out and separation from the familiar; the trials of initiation and adventure; and the return and re-integration into society. As our hypothetical Spanish scholar passed through these stages, he was reminded of both his citizenship in an international community of Muslims and his ties to his region and city in Spain. Unlike Fussell's British travellers of the modern inter-war period, most Muslim travellers returned home thankful to be there, and their re-integration was often a measure of how successfully the travel-for-study experience reinforced local identity and pride.

Spain, Egypt, and Khurasan are three examples of intellectual centres with strong local identities. Each contributed to and participated in the *rihla/talab al-'ilm* network. A Muslim in search of religious knowledge could find a warm reception in each region which would cement his ties to the international Muslim community of which he was a member. But he would also encounter that strength of local sentiment which we have described, as the following examples suggest.

Al-Subki (d. AH 771/AD 1369–70), the compiler of the most important biographical collection on the Shafi'i law school, tells us of a *shaykh* (d. AH 463/AD 1070–1) from a town near Baghdad who, wavering between a trip to Cairo or Nishapur, received the following advice:

> If you go to Cairo, you will go to only one man [Ibn al-Nahhas]. If he escapes you, your trip will be ruined. But if you go to Nishapur, there you will find a group of scholars. If one should elude you, you may obtain the help of one from among the rest.
> (al Subki 1964 IV, 30)

Needless to say, the man opted for Nishapur.

Egypt also had its adherents. In the late fourth AH/tenth AD century, the geographer, al-Muqaddasi (1906: 197), extolled the virtues of Fatimid Cairo. He declared it vastly superior to Baghdad, Damascus, and Nishapur in many respects, his most important comment for our purposes being that it was the habitat or breeding ground (*ma'dan*) of the *'ulama'*. Naturally we find echoes of this rivalry between cities and regions in the *fada'il* literature. Drawing in part on legends surrounding Egypt's pre-Islamic history, 'Umar b. Muhammad al-Kindi (1971: 45), the son of the famous Egyptian historian (Abu 'Umar Muhammad, d. AH 350/AD 961–2), could claim:

> Wise people agree that the people of the world strive to travel to Egypt and seek to make a living there. But the people of Egypt do not seek to make a living in any other country, and do not travel anywhere – even if there were a wall separating Egypt and the countries of the world, so much is available in Egypt that its people would have no need of them.

Suffice it to say that on the Egyptian side of that wall was a sufficient and vibrant network of scholars.

Muslim rulers were also drawn into the competition spawned by the *rihla*. The fourth AH/tenth AD century was the height of Spanish Umayyid power and visits by Spanish Maliki scholars to Egypt. In his invaluable guidebook to Cairo's tombs and cemeteries, Ibn al-Zayyat (d. AH 814/AD 1411–12) reports that the Caliph 'Abd al-

Rahman III al-Nasir regularly sent 10,000 dinars for the maintenance of Maliki *fuqaha'* in Fustat. Not to be outdone, the Egyptian ruler Abu al-Misk Kafur ordered that 20,000 dinars be distributed among the Shafi'is (1907: 190–1).

In sum, these examples should remind us of the close links between *rihla/talab al-'ilm* and *fada'il* as key ingredients in medieval Muslim self-definition. As noted, travel for the sake of study was a process which could emphasise universal traits common to all Muslims. For the scholar, it meant the exchange of ideas, books, and even addresses of teachers in distant cities; for the merchant, goods, services, and an awareness of new business methods and perhaps even technological innovations in manufacturing and agriculture; and for everyone, the experience of seeing other lands. If we accept Dunn's assertion that the *rihla* was above all "an account of a journey (or journeys) to Mecca", then the *hajj* was of course the most supremely universal trait of all (Dunn 1986: 310).

The frequency with which medieval Muslims pursued *talab al-'ilm* is an excellent indicator of their self-image and how much the *rihla* concept owed to the exigencies of time and place. Looking at Egypt first, we find that the term *rihla* itself rarely appears in biographies of Egyptian *'ulama'*. Primary sources for Egypt in our period (fourth–fifth AH/tenth–eleventh AD centuries) are limited to the abbreviated biographical work of Ibn al-Tahhan (d. AH 416/AD 1025–6) and the obituary list of Ibn al-Habbal (d. AH 482/AD 1089–90). But even from these materials we have the distinct impression that Egyptians felt that they were self-sufficient with regard to learning. Egypt's most celebrated early historian and first known compiler of a biographical dictionary devoted exclusively to Egyptians, Ibn Yunus al-Sadafi (d. AH 347/AD 957–8), never left Egypt. Yet his reputation as an *'alim* was unquestioned and we find his unfortunately lost biographical work frequently quoted by Muslim authors.

As al-Kindi's observation reminds us, the Pharaonic view of Egypt as the centre of the universe became part of the cultural heritage of Islam in Egypt. As a centre for Islamic studies, Egypt did not match the initial rate of development that Iraq enjoyed. But, by the fourth AH/tenth AD century, it was a much-respected regional entrepôt of learning. Its capital, Fustat (now Cairo), was a magnet for Muslims from all over the Mediterranean. Egyptians themselves saw little reason to seek knowledge elsewhere. The scarcity of Egyptians in the lists of *ghuraba'* (foreign scholars) in Spanish, Iraqi, and Persian biographical works underlines this attitude. Fustat was a teeming, sophisticated way-station, reception centre, and seat of learning for those making *rihlas*. But the *rihla* as a self-defining concept in Egyptian Muslim life seems to have played a minor role.

Turning to Spain, we find the exact opposite of Egypt. The *rihla* was the central feature of Spanish Muslim intellectual life. We are blessed with a rich biographical literature for Spain (Ibn al-Faradi, Ibn Bashkuwal, al-Dabbi, and Ibn al-Abbar) which is both local and primary in nature. The several thousand biographies in these collections trenchantly document the significance of *rihla/talab al-'ilm* for Spanish Muslims.

Initially, we should note the role of geography. Located at the western limit of the medieval Islamic world, it is very natural that travel for the sake of study would achieve its most impressive development in Spain. With the possible exception of their co-religionists in Sicily, Spanish Muslims had more contact with Christians and Christendom than any other region of *dar al-Islam*. Muslims, although constituting the dominant culture, ruled a large Christian subject population and, whatever the state of religious and political antagonisms, maintained economic relations with the Christian lands of northern Spain.

Far more crucial is the fact that from the late fifth AH/eleventh AD century, Muslim Spain was increasingly threatened by a militant crusading movement, fervently Spanish Catholic in orientation. Spanish Muslims had every reason to seek spiritual refreshment in areas where Islam was the majority culture. Egyptians could really afford, so to speak, to remain at home, whereas for Spaniards, *rihla/talab al-'ilm* truly meant the survival of Islam as a coherent, *shari'a*-based way of life. What began as "refreshment" conferring social benefit in the third AH/ninth AD century gradually became an unavoidable necessity by the sixth AH/twelfth AD, given the changing political and military conditions in medieval Spain and the increasing emigration of the corps of Maliki *'ulama'* to North Africa and Egypt. Embattled both physically and mentally, Spanish Muslims looked to other communities, the Maghrib in particular, for intellectual succour.

Our sources do not explicitly indicate that Spanish Muslims clearly perceived themselves as peripheral or marginal. However, given their distance from the early centres of Muslim scholarship, it is reasonable to assume that during the second–early fourth AH/eighth–early tenth AD centuries they would look eastward for appropriate models of learning in *hadith*. We may find a parallel in the early medieval Jewish communities of Spain, North Africa, Egypt, and the Franco–German region. These communities were initially dependent to one degree or another upon famous *yeshivot* (academies) of Iraq. So too were the Muslims of Spain, Tunisia, and Egypt upon their counterpart centres of learning in Iraq. Whereas the study of *fiqh* developed locally in Spain (inspired no doubt by the development of Maliki *fiqh* in North Africa) from an early date, *hadith* did not, hence the relatively substantial percentage of biographies of Muslims who went east to immerse themselves in that field. If a sense of intellectual periphery (Spain) and of centre(s) (Iraq and increasingly Egypt and Tunisia) did exist, it certainly was not something about which Spanish Muslims wrote. However, the biographies provide evidence of a perception of periphery that cannot be denied – at least as far as *hadith* study is concerned. On the other hand, this attitude was exaggerated and intensified by the political turmoil which prevailed among Spanish Muslims and by the accelerating advance of the Reconquista in the early sixth AH/twelfth AD century.

None the less, we should not assume that *talab al-'ilm* achieved acceptance as a *fard* in al-Andalus, despite the gravity of the situation. We referred earlier to the Prophetic *hadith* on the subject of *talab al-'ilm* as a *fard*. This *hadith* was hotly debated throughout the medieval Muslim world. For evidence of this, we need look no further than the Spaniard Ibn 'Abd al-Barr's (d. AH 464/AD 1071–2) *Jami' bayan al-'ilm wa-fadluhu* (*The Exposition and Excellence of Knowledge*). The author was the most famous *hadith* specialist of his time in Spain and North Africa and achieved his reputation without every having studied outside of Cordoba!

Ibn 'Abd al-Barr devotes the first nine pages of his work to the question of whether or not *talab al-'ilm* is a *fard*. As we read his presentation of the opinions of various early scholars, we realise that there was no consensus on the legal status of travel for the sake of study. For example, when asked about the problem, Malik b. Anas says: "How admirable is *talab al-'ilm*! As to its being a *fard*, no". And in a different transmission, he answers: "No. But it means seeking from a person that which one can put to good use in his religious faith" (Ibn 'Abd al-Barr 1975: 5). There is no doubt about the crucial importance of *talab al-'ilm*, but every doubt concerning its status as a ritual obligation. At best, the authorities quoted by Ibn 'Abd al-Barr are ambivalent, their commentary occasionally cryptic.

Talab al-'ilm may have come to represent a *fard* in a *de facto* sense, a way of dealing with an increasingly insecure and disturbing political, social, and intellectual reality for Spanish Muslims. It is likely that it reinforced both communal feeling *within* Spain and the bonds which Spanish Muslims maintained with their co-religionists in other regions. As such, *talab al-'ilm* was the Andalusian method of expressing how their peripheral Islamic society related to the more central heartlands of the *umma*, especially after the fall of Toledo (AH 478/AD 1085–6) and the steady progress of the Reconquista.

However, what one brought back, rather than the original motivation for going, could have been a decisive factor here. The physical search for religious knowledge was both an adventure and a religious duty. The *'ulama'* were, of course, not the only Muslims who undertook journeys, but the overwhelming testimony of the biographical literature shows that they were by far the most likely to do so, given their needs and vocations. The search for religious knowledge also conferred distinction. Those who completed the journey returned home not only with an expanded religious knowledge, but also – and perhaps more importantly – with the experience of other lands and other Muslims, which heightened their appreciation of their native land. The sections specifically set aside for foreign-born scholars in the biographical collections show a "diaspora" of Spanish and other Muslims who never returned home. The majority did return, however, to the merit of both themselves and the cities and regions which they had left. Undoubtedly, their perceptions of centre and periphery changed in the course of their travels; that is to say, the cultural enrichment and expansion of the periphery blurred the distinctions which had of necessity existed formerly between it and the centre.

The Spanish biographies yield a variety of characteristics that enable us to profile *rihla/talab al-'ilm* as it was understood in al-Andalus. First, it was the most important aspect of Spanish learning. The concept permeates the language of the Spanish biographical dictionaries. The experience was a multi-faceted intellectual endeavour, with neither *hadith* nor *fiqh* always enjoying primacy. It occupied a very special position in Spain in that those who travelled (*ahl al-rihla*) represented a distinct category of individuals. These men were heavily urbanised, ethnically heterogeneous, and solidly middle class in vocation and social outlook. They were drawn from the corps of Maliki *fuqaha'*, or jurists, which socially and politically stood between *khassa* (upper class or elite) and *'amma* (the "masses" or lower classes) in Muslim Spain (Benaboud 1980–1: 5–45). They were objects of praise but also had advantages of a practical nature in the sense that public offices such as the post of *qadi* were reserved for them by the ruler and his high officials. A famous teacher's reputation increased when he made a trip and, in addition, returned with a new or rare text previously unknown in Spain.

People of all ages engaged in *rihla/talab al-'ilm*, although those

between the ages of 20 and 50 appear most often in the *tabaqat*.
Trips were often family-oriented. Learning began at home and
one's renown was based on the intellectual foundation initially
passed on within the extended family unit. Sons (and occasionally
daughters) accompanied fathers and often then made a trip of their
own, usually in the company of a brother, cousin, or close friend.
We should add here that these customs were not peculiarly Spanish.
Muslims the world over pursued study for the same reasons and in
the same manner, whether they lived in Cordoba, Cairo, or
Nishapur.

In Muslim Spain, many travelled for the sake of study. In Egypt,
by contrast, it would appear that a minority among the corps of
'ulama' did so. Khurasan, through the example of its great city of
Nishapur, occupies a unique intermediate position between al-
Andalus and Egypt. In the fourth AH /tenth−eleventh AD centuries,
Nishapur was a wealthy and powerful urban entity under the suc-
cessive rule of the Samanids, Ghaznavids, and Saljuqs. A strategic
nexus on the trade routes to China and India, Nishapur was home
to an affluent and influential network of *'ulama'* families who,
during our period, controlled political activity within their city.
They are known to us through the *Ta'rikh Nisabur* by al-Hakim al-
Nisaburi (d. AH 405/AD 1015−16) and its continuation by 'Abd al-
Ghafir al-Farisi (d. AH 529/AD 1135−6). The several thousand
Arabic biographies in these works provide us with a very different
perspective on medieval *rihla/talab al-'ilm*.

Unlike the Egyptians, people from Nishapur did not stay home.
But the nature of their travels seems to have been different from
that of their Spanish peers. Spanish Muslims travelled all over al-
Andalus. Likewise, Nishapuris journeyed the length and breadth of
Khurasan and Iraq and Central Asia too. What is striking is the
contrast in linguistic usage between the Spanish and Nishapur biographical notices. Very rare is the phrase *lahu rihlatun* or the verb
rahala itself. Instead, we see the verbs *kharaja* and *qadama*
frequently. *Talab al-'ilm*, of course, is a major concern but not in
an explicit manner. For example, there is the following except from
the biography of Nasr b. al-Hasan b. al-Qasim al-Shashi (d. AH
487/AD 1094−5):

> He went to Nishapur as a young man on business . . . he went to
> lands west of Nishapur (*bilad al-gharb*) . . . and God blessed him
> with his acquisitions and commercial activities to the point that
> he had an abundance of wealth . . . then he returned to Nishapur
> and made his home there.

> (Frye 1965: 127)

Obviously, there is plenty of movement and exchange here and we should add that this example is not untypical of the Nishapur biographies. We find important information as well in this biography on the man's training in *hadith* study. Travel for the purpose of study is present but it somehow does not convey the intensity present in the Spanish sources.

Though subject to periodic political upheaval and economic dislocation, Nishapur and its Perso-Islamic culture area were never even remotely threatened by the likes of a Christian Reconquista (although the initially pagan Mongols devastated Khurasan in a manner that Christian knights never did in Spain). In our period, however, it was almost wholly Muslim – confident, prosperous, and self-assured. Nishapur scholars sought knowledge, particularly in the realm of *hadith*, as readily as their Spanish counterparts, but perhaps without that urgent sense of "mission", which may account for the Spanish preoccupation with *rihla/talab al-'ilm*. Travel for the sake of knowledge was possibly routine for the *'ulama'* of Nishapur. It was taken for granted in a way that it was not in Spain, hence its elevation to such a lofty status among Spanish Muslims.

Spain, Egypt, and Khurasan all embraced the ideology, which was the basis of travel for the sake of study. But, for a variety of reasons, they experienced it differently. In Spain, it was a primary aspect of one's identity as an *'alim* and reflected the country's peculiar status on the periphery of the Islamic world. For the Egyptians, it was just the opposite. They too respected the concept but felt little obliged to pursue it. With Nishapur and, in general, the Iranian/Central Asian culture region that looked towards not the Mediterranean but China and India, we encounter a corps of scholars who rarely used the "key term" itself but did engage in the process to which it was applied. They circulated within a "local" network and, to a greater degree than their Spanish and Egyptian peers, used the status conferred by their education effectively to influence and sometimes to dictate the political affairs of their cities.

In using this particular comparative approach, we have returned not to an "essentialist" or "reified" view of Islam or being Muslim. Instead, we have utilised *rihla/talab al-'ilm* as a means of comprehending how one activity fundamental to early medieval Islamic education was understood in three distinct Islamic societies so distant in time and place from our own.

Notes

1 The periodisation of medieval Islamic history remains a subject of debate. For the purposes of this paper, the approximate chronological boundaries are AH 236–545/AD 850–1150. It was during these centuries that the distinct characteristics of the fluid network of religious learning studied here developed and flourished.

2 *Tabaqat* literally means "classes" or "generations". It is a label for one of the most characteristic genres of historical writing in Arabic, Persian, and Turkish – the biographical dictionary. Usually arranged alphabetically, the *tabaqat* collections deal with all manner of individuals (such as caliphs, poets, and saints), but here we refer exclusively to those collections devoted to religious scholars (*'ulama'*).

3 It is interesting to note that in Morocco after the tenth/sixteenth century, the *rihla* shifts from association with the *hajj* to travel only within Morocco.

4 Though the question of *talab al-'ilm* as a *fard* (ritual obligation) is discussed on p. 60, it is worth noting at this point that an *'alim*'s status did not depend on the journeys that he pursued in order to acquire learning. The problems of which characteristics defined an *'alim* has generated substantial debate in recent years. Knowledge of *hadith* above all was a quality which certainly distinguished an *'alim*. But loyalty, status, reputation, and responsibility figured prominently as well. Making a *rihla* did of course enhance one's status and reputation but sanction for it was a local/regional matter. The need for and value of it depended upon time and place. Thus it is difficult to be precise about the criteria for an *'alim*'s status. As Richard Bulliet (1972) and Roy Mottahedeh (1980) have shown, access to religious learning was largely unrestricted and open to talent. There was an egalitarian sense to the process, yet this did not preclude the influence of inherited distinction and wealth. In the case of Nishapur, what mattered was not who learned but who taught. Moreover, there were identities and affiliations – membership in urban socio-political factions and Sufi brotherhoods, or ethnic bonds – which could co-exist with or even supersede one's being an *'alim*. These identities varied considerably over time and place. Bulliet's "patricians of Nishapur" had no counterpa in Egypt, although the Egyptian *'ulama'* possessed a cohesion which was encouraged by the country's geographic, economic, and intellectual significance in the fourth–fifth/tenth–eleventh centuries.

References

Benaboud, M'hammad (1980–1) ' *'Asabiyya* and social relations in al-Andalus during the period of the Taifa states', *Hespéris-Tamuda*, vol. 19, 5–45.

Bloch, Marc (1967) 'A contribution towards the comparative history of European societies', trans. J.E. Anderson, *Land and Work in Medieval*

Europe: Selected Papers by Marc Bloch, University of California Press, Berkeley and Los Angeles, pp. 44–82.

Bulliet, Richard W. (1972) *The Patricians of Nishapur: A Study in Medieval Islamic Social History*, Harvard University Press, Cambridge.

Dunn, Ross (1986) *The Adventures of Ibn Battuta, a Muslim Traveller of the Fourteenth Century*, Croom Helm, London.

Frye, Richard N. (ed.) (1965) *The Histories of Nishapur*, Harvard University Press, Cambridge.

Fussell, Paul (1980) *Abroad: British Literary Travelling Between the World Wars*, Oxford University Press, London.

Ibn 'Abd al-Barr (1975) *Jami' bayan al-'ilm wa fadluhu*, Dar al-Kutub al-Haditha, Cairo.

Ibn al-Faradi (1966) *Ta'rikh 'ulama' al-Andalus*, al Dar al-Misriyya li-Ta'lif wa'l-Tarjama, Cairo.

Ibn Majah (1972) *Sunan*, edited by Muhammad Fu'ad 'Abd al-Baqi, 2 vols, 'Isa al-Babi al-Halabi, Cairo.

Ibn al-Zayyat (1907) *al-Kawakib al-sayyara fi tartib al-ziyara*, al-Matba'a al-Amiriyya, Cairo.

Jeffery, Arthur (1960) *Abu al-Darda'*, *Encyclopaedia of Islam*, 2nd edition, Brill, Leiden and London, vol. I, pp. 113–14.

al-Kindi, 'Umar b. Muhammad (1971) *Fada'il Misr*, edited by 'Ali Muhammad 'Umar, Maktaba Wahba, Cairo.

Malik b. Anas (1951) *al-Muwatta*, edited by Muhammad Fu'ad 'Abd al-Baqi, 2 vols, 'Isa al-Babi al-Halabi, Cairo.

Mottahedeh, Roy P. (1980) *Loyalty and Leadership in an Early Islamic Society*, Princeton University Press, Princeton.

al-Muqaddasi (1906) *Ahsan al-taqasim fi ma'rifat al-aqalim*, edited by M.J. de Goeje, E.J. Brill, Leiden.

al-Subki (1964–8) *Tabaqat al-Shafi'iyya al-kubra*, edited by 'Abd al-Fattah Muhammad al-Hilu and Mahmud Muhammad al-Tanahi, 10 vols, 'Isa al-Babi al-Halabi, Cairo.

Part two
Travel accounts

Chapter four

The ambivalence of *rihla*: community integration and self-definition in Moroccan travel accounts, 1300–1800

Abderrahmane El Moudden

Travel (*rihla*) in Muslim culture is often valued for its integrating effects: the pilgrimage (*hajj*) leads the pilgrim to Mecca and Medina, and the search for knowledge (*talab al'ilm*) leads the student to one of the esteemed places of Islamic teaching, such as Medina, Cairo, or Fez. In all these cases, travel brings individuals and groups to centres and unites them with the wider community of the faithful (*umma*). This chapter considers the consequences of such travel for developing a sense of locality. Did *rihla* serve only to unite the faithful or did it also give to travellers a sense of local consciousness? I suggest that *rihla* is ambivalent: through it the traveller becomes more closely linked to the idea of the Muslim community as a whole, but at the same time learns what is specific to his own people and culture.

Rihla

Rihla, in the form of actual travel and travel accounts, was one of the main features of Muslim culture in the western part of *dar al-Islam* (realm of Islam). Since the early Islamic centuries, learned people ventured to the eastern lands of Islam, specifically to the Hijaz, seeking advanced learning in religious matters and spiritual fulfilment.[1] *Rihla* was particularly linked with the pilgrimage to Mecca and Medina, the fifth pillar of Islam. The travel was so long and risky that it was worthwhile for the literate to make written records of it which serve as useful guides for future pilgrims.

   Rihla literature flourished in North Africa, especially in Morocco (Turki 1979) from the sixteenth century onwards. Muhammad al-Manuni (1983: 186–92), a leading Moroccan archivist, divides *rihla* accounts for the sixteenth through eighteenth centuries into three types:

69

1 *Rihla* within Morocco, in which the traveller did not go beyond one region or, at the very most, the whole area of what is currently Morocco.
2 *Rihla hijaziyya*, travel to the Hijaz. This form of *rihla* resulted in oral or written comprehensive reports on the travel and on the various aspects of the pilgrimage.
3 *Rihla sifariyya*, including embassies and missions, in which the writer reported on his travels in foreign lands. From the seventeenth century onward, Morocco sent missions to Christian European governments, including France, Spain, and Britain, as well as to Muslim rulers. The most significant embassy travel accounts are those written by ambassadors to the Porte, the Ottoman central government, at Istanbul. These envoys, on their way to accomplish their diplomatic mission or on returning, often performed the *hajj* – thus explaining why many *sifariyya rihlas* are also *hijaziyya* ones. An example is al-Zayyani (d. AH 1249/AD 1834) in the late eighteenth century (al-Zayyani 1967).

Travels to the Hijaz were certainly the most important type of Moroccan movement abroad prior to modern times (Lewis 1971: 37–8). Not only were they the most frequent, but they were also the most comprehensive: the *hijaziyya* type could include the two other kinds of movement. Many pilgrims needed to travel within Morocco before starting the "real" travel towards the east. They needed to do so in order to join the pilgrimage caravan, which used to gather in specific cities before proceeding to the Hijaz, or in order to visit some of the more famous saints' shrines for the sake of safety *en route* in this world and greater rewards in the next (Brunel 1955: 77, 112). The path of pilgrims was rarely direct; it needed to be circuitous to enable them to visit most of the sacred spots on their way (Raphael 1973: 14). Moreover, journeys to the Hijaz were important because they often brought back new ideas or even initiated broad changes in the Maghrib. Examples include the Almoravid and Almohad revolutions in the eleventh and twelfth centuries AD and the introduction of Wahhabi ideas in the early nineteenth century AD (al-Iraqi 1984: 125–54).

Rihla in both its aspects, *hijaziyya* and *sifariyya*, had two elements. By accomplishing *rihla*, Moroccan travellers shared experiences with various components of the *umma*. At the same time, they were able to understand their difference through experiencing numerous comparisons. To show this characteristic of *rihla*, I will rely mostly on *hijaziyya* accounts because this kind of travel was a more comprehensive undertaking. However, the *sifariyya* accounts are also relevant to developing a conscious sense of difference. In some cases, the diplomatic and somewhat secular goal of the travel was clearly perceived and expressed, and the sensitivity to differences, especially political ones, may have even been stronger and clearer in these texts than in the *hijaziyya* ones. However, this distinction should not be overdrawn.

Rihla, *umma*, and consciousness of identity

Taking part in *rihla* altered consciousness of the *umma*. There was frequent travel for military, commercial, intellectual, and religious reasons since the early centuries of Islam (see Gellens, Chapter 3 of this volume). Travellers, scholars, and merchants participated in extending the sense of frontiers of the *umma* through their activities. *Rihla* accounts illustrated for local readers and listeners the extent of the Islamic community, and thus created "an integrated, ʒrowing, self-replenishing network of cultural communication" (Dunn 1986: 10). This network of cultural communication operated, however, in politically fragmented and socially localised contexts. The case of Morocco is significant in this respect.

Three dimensions characterise Moroccan society prior to the colonial era. On the socio-economic level, most Moroccans lived in small- or medium-sized tribal and village communities. Interaction within these local communities was intense and movement outside of them primarily involved a few seasonal workers or itinerant shepherds (Montagne 1930; Berque 1955).

Politically, the rural areas were more or less linked to the central government, the *makhzan*, which was basically well established in the cities and in the plains surrounding them. In order to function adequately, the central government had to be a travelling institution: the sultans used to settle part of the year in Fez, in the north, and the rest of it in Marrakesh, in the south (Nordman 1980−1: 123−52). Members of the local elites were often ordered to join the sultan in one of these capitals and, in this way, experienced some of the variety of Morocco's lands and people. Rarely, however, did their experiences range beyond the areas of the ruler's peregrinations (El Moudden 1983: 141−5). This administrative and military movement is noticeable in traditional sources at least since the eleventh century in the time of the Almoravid dynasty. Although the geographical extent of the Almoravid and Almohad states encompassed all North Africa and Muslim Spain, it was not until the sixteenth century, with the rise of the Sa'adi dynasty, that Morocco emerged as a distinct political unit more or less possessing its current political boundaries.

Finally, in intellectual and religious matters, religious intellectuals (*faqihs*) constituted a network cross-cutting Morocco's social and economic fragmentation. This elite of religious intellectuals also constituted an important link between Morocco and the rest of the Muslim world. Since they were among those who were likely to have travelled outside their local areas or regions, in their own localities they were the ones possessing a concrete idea of what the *umma* was like and able to convey this idea to others. A Moroccan from the south-western region of the Sus, Ahmad bin Ali al-Jazuli (d. AH 1197/AD 1782–3), epitomises the different directions of such a network. Al-Jabarti, the late eighteenth century Egyptian historian, wrote in his biography of al-Jazuli:

> He studied with us under the direction of my father, with the participation of Sidi Muhammad and Sidi Abu Bakr, the two sons of Shaykh al-Tawdi bin Suda [a leading scholar of eighteenth-century Fez], when they accompanied their father, that year, on the *hajj*; and with the participation of Shaykh Salim al-Qayrawani [probably from Qayrawan, Tunisia]
> (al-Jabarti n.d.: ɪ, 571–2)

This example shows that whether sitting at some corner of al-Azhar in Egypt or al-Qarawiyyin in Morocco, taking part in religious learning still provided an important opportunity for Moroccans from different regions in the late eighteenth century to unite. In this case, al-Jazuli, who was from the Sus in the south of Morocco, encountered at al-Azhar students from Fez (the sons of Bin Suda), others from Tunisia (al-Qayrawani) and still others from Egypt (al-Jabarti). Such encounters occurred frequently and symbolised the network of cultural communication linking men of learning throughout the *umma*. Although al-Jazuli never made it back home, a majority of travellers must have returned to their point of origin with their knowledge and experience, and shared these with their fellow tribesmen or townsmen. As a consequence, awareness of the areas outside the realm of Islam was often due to them (Dunn 1986).

These three spheres of practice and perception in Moroccan society – the socio-economic, political and intellectual, and religious – are clear in traditional sources at least from the sixteenth century onward (al-Nasiri 1954–6: ᴠɪ, 100). How were these three spheres interconnected?

Imagine al-Tamgruti, the Moroccan ambassador to Istanbul in the late sixteenth century, first in his local environment of Tamgrut, a famous *zawiya* (a religious brotherhood or lodge), located south of the High Atlas mountains on the northern fringe of the Sahara. In terms of society and local economy, he might have been taking care of his palm groves between prayer times, negotiating and sharing the costs of repairing a *saguia* (irrigation canal), or leading a delegation of members of his village to argue with the members of a village downstream about water rights and shares. Politically, on specific occasions, such as major religious feasts, he might have been ordered to come to wherever the sultan's capital was at that moment. At the intellectual level, he would certainly have met at the capital *faqihs* from other cities and regions of Morocco. He would undoubtedly have talked with recent *hajjs* (customary Moroccan form for *hajjis*, or pilgrims) about their adventures and encounters in the east and about the news from other Muslim lands.

Such an imbrication of the three levels in one personal experience was usual, particularly in the case of learned people, even though the majority of the rest of Moroccans experienced only their immediate environs. In such a socio-cultural environment, travel in its various forms constituted an important means of social, political, and religious integration.

Rihla to the Hijaz was especially important. More than an opportunity for Moroccans to accomplish a long and enriching, though risky, voyage,[2] it also provided a lasting personal experience. This is probably one of the reasons for the flourishing of the *hijaziyya* accounts in comparison to the other types of *rihla* accounts.[3]

For many centuries, the pilgrimage caravan was the most important, if not the only means of travel to the Holy Lands. On their way, Moroccan pilgrims were forced to cross the majority of Arab Muslim lands. This fact alone gives the Moroccan travels a complexity that is reflected in the texts and colours the perception of sacred space and time. Religiously significant dates punctuate the days and months of the journey, as do shrines and important holy centres along the way; they frame the whole narration. The *rihla* of al-'Ayyashi substantiates such an observation: at every stage of his two-year-long travel, he visited shrines and met learned people (al-'Ayyashi AH 1316: I–II; Kopf 1960: 785).

Two very important annual caravans left Morocco for the Hijaz cities – one from Fez, and the other from Sijilmassa, located in the south-east. *Rihla* texts indicate that travellers could quit the caravan in northern or south-eastern Morocco and rejoin it at one of its important stops during the journey – Tripoli, Alexandria, Cairo, Mecca, or Medina. Between each of these stages, the travellers recorded the name and condition of numerous stops of lesser importance.

For each of these stopping points, the *rihla* texts give more or less detailed descriptions of ecology, wells, sweet or salt water, hot or cold weather, and the ease and safety of the route. The descriptions also focus on some of the economic possibilities of each region and record the kind of trade that the pilgrims may have transacted there. Much attention is paid to the inhabitants' customs as well as to the religious and educational situation. Of course, throughout his text, the traveller kept close records on the most important men, scholars, and saints whom he met in each region, and on various scholarly or *belles-lettres* activities in which he happened to participate. It is for this reason that the *rihla* texts are usually encyclopaedic in character. Among other fields, they cover the religious sciences, history, biographies, and literature. Moreover, for modern scholars, they are a kind of documentary treasure, full of material of geographical, ethnographic, and even technological interest.

The medieval traveller was not, however, an aloof observer, detached from the matter of his depictions. He was often involved in the situation described and the *rihla* text must also be seen as an autobiography.[4] Yet it is not always constituted only by first-hand experience. When the traveller felt a shortage of interesting records about some point of his journey, he drew upon texts to fill the gap (Dunn 1986: 313; Morsy 1983).[5]

Through these various aspects, *rihla* texts testify that the journey to the Hijaz was an important means of integration of Moroccan pilgrims with the wider Muslim community. Moroccan travellers never felt completely foreign towards the inhabitants of the various pilgrimage itineraries. There was no great linguistic handicap for them, at least among the Muslim communities of the southern Mediterranean.[6] Indeed, on their way to the *hajj*, Moroccans sometimes felt so much at home that they considered it quite legitimate to try to impose their views of what they thought to be the right religious behaviour. Al-Jabarti recorded an incident of the sort for the year AH 1110/AD 1696, under the significant heading of "the Maghribi event":

> The Maghribi people of Tunis and Fez, who were accompanying the cloth cover that was to be brought to the *Ka'ba*, in a procession through the central area of Cairo, tried to prevent whoever was smoking, along their way, from doing so . . . This led to a conflict between them and the people of the bazaar of Cairo. The pasha arrested most of them, and consequently they missed the pilgrimage. Some of them died in prison, the others were released later.
>
> (al-Jabarti n.d.: I, 51)

This incident shows that an exaggerated feeling of being at home was not always without complication. It is nevertheless interesting to note that the pilgrims, and specifically the learned people among them, moved easily throughout large areas of the Muslim world.

The example of Ibn Battuta (d. AH 1368) illustrates this basic point. Departing from his native Tangier in northern Morocco, he covered no less than 73,000 miles during his almost thirty-year career. While of course not constantly on the move – he settled long enough in one locale to marry and have a family (Damascus), or to reach positions of authority in the local ruling establishment (India and China) – he was far from isolated. Rather, in India, for example, he was able to meet old acquaintances from Damascus and even Granada. As Dunn says:

> the scholarly class of the Islamic world was an extraordinarily mobile group. In the Maghrib of the later Middle Period the learned, like modern conference hopping academics, circulated incessantly from one city and country to another, studying with renowned professors, leading diplomatic missions, taking up posts in mosques and royal chanceries.
>
> (Dunn 1986: 3, 68; quotation at 24)

As a major factor of individual mobility in pre-modern Muslim societies, the pilgrimage in itself was a complex phenomenon that enabled its participants to share most of everyday life with co-religionists. This journey was not only a religious enterprise, but, because of its length (15–18 months in normal travel, but quite possibly longer as in the cases of al-'Ayyashi and Ibn Battuta), the pilgrims also observed and experienced common practices. For instance, in most of the important stages of the journey, Moroccan pilgrims converted their merchandise or slaves into cash, and purchased the different commodities that they needed for the journey, ˜uch as food and animals for transportation. For this reason, many *rihla* texts are in the form of market guides, advising future pilgrims about the best way to carry on advantageous trade on the way to the Hijaz (Zemmama 1984: 114–24). These guides, incidentally, show how business and pilgimage were so intimately connected that it is hard to detemine which one inspired the other.

At the main stages of the journey – Tripoli, Cairo, Mecca, and Medina – the pilgrims stopped for longer periods than they did at secondary places. There they were able to go to libraries, buy books, attend classes at al-Azhar in Cairo, or give lectures at the Prophet's mosque and shrine in Medina. They could also participate, as al-'Ayyashi did (Zemmama 1983: 156–68), in the great religious debates of the time.

75

Some Moroccan travellers or pilgrims preferred to settle permanently at one point of their journey. Al-Jabarti noted in his chronicles many cases of learned Moroccans who, after their return from the Hijaz, decided to stay in Cairo (n.d.: I, 327, 383, 572). One of them deserves particular attention because he could be seen as an example of how Moroccan travellers considered themselves as members of the larger Muslim community, even in the late eighteenth century – by which time Morocco had been an autonomous political unit for at least 200 years. Ahmad bin 'Ali al-Jazuli al-Susi, previously mentioned, first sought religious learning in his country. In AH 1182/AD 1768 he went on the pilgrimage and, on his way back, stayed in Cairo where, for a period, he studied at al-Azhar. Then he resumed his travels, going this time to the Rum, the central part of the Ottoman Empire. He participated there in a *jihad* (holy war), learned Turkish and was offered a high position in the capital. But, as was expected of a genuine *faqih*, he declined the invitation and returned to Egypt where he married and settled until he died in AH 1197/AD 1782–3 (al-Jabarti n.d.: I, 571–2). Through this example one can see how, in general, the *hajj* and the *rihla* were major ways for Moroccan travellers to realise their connections with other parts of the Muslim world.

One may wonder what impact the *rihla* accounts had on the rest of the people, who either did not go on the pilgrimage or, if they did, were unable to write a record of it. In fact, the pilgrims found a ready audience among those who could read. Among the illiterate, many listened to their long and frequently repeated oral reports. In effect, these travel accounts gave people who had never had the opportunity of leaving their native locality a chance to imagine a wider horizon. At the same time, however, they may have imparted something of the sense of difference from fellow Muslims that the travellers themselves experienced.

Al-'Ayyashi and his travels to the Hijaz: of differences and similarities

Abu Salim 'Abdullah al-'Ayyashi (AH 1037/AD 1628 to AH 1090/AD 1679) was a well-known seventeenth-century Moroccan traveller and scholar. Born in a small village in the eastern High Atlas mountains, his father was the head of the local *zawiya*. Al-'Ayyashi travelled to Fez to acquire the orthodox religious sciences, then went to Tamgrut to be initiated into one of the most active Sufi orders in Morocco at that time, the Nasiriyya (Hammoudi 1980: 615–41). Like many other Moroccan scholars, he soon felt the need to deepen his knowledge in eastern lands. He travelled three times to the Hijaz – in 1649, 1653, and 1661 – and stayed for long periods in Mecca and Medina, as well as Jerusalem and Cairo. Everywhere, he participated actively in theological debates, both learning and teaching. His feelings and observations are incorporated into his two-volume *rihla* text, *Ma' al-Mawa'id* [*Tables Water*].[7]

The title of this text signifies that the author intended it to be useful for the *'ulama'* in Morocco and elsewhere as well. Although he focused heavily on theological subjects, he was also a keen observer of contemporary life. His text is full of precise comments on many aspects of the social, economic, and political mores of the peoples he met along the way to the Hijaz. Autobiographical information is also scattered throughout the text. Indeed, during his three travel periods, al-'Ayyashi accumulated experiences and knowledge that helped him to constitute a more relative image of himself and his country. As a consequence, his judgements were neither absolutely negative nor completely positive towards such people of the eastern Muslim world as the Egyptians. While criticising some aspects of their lives, he did not omit, of course, to praise some of the positive sides. What remained constant was his sensitivity to differences.

Many of these differences he found insignificant, and treated them much as a tourist would in viewing an exotic scene. Some of them were of great significance, because he understood through them how his customs and even religious rituals differed from those that he was witnessing. While he felt neutral towards, or was even pleased, by the former, he was sometimes frankly embarrassed by the latter.

In Egypt, for example, al-'Ayyashi was struck by the enormous population of Cairo as well as the Nile Valley in general. Its crowded markets and people hurrying in the streets contrasted with what he was accustomed to in the High Atlas region (AH 1316/AD 1898–9: I, 121–2). This was more or less the impression of many previous Moroccan travellers, such as al-'Abdari and Ibn Battuta. Al-'Ayyashi also noticed differences in food habits: for example, drinking coffee was a general and useful habit in Egypt, and it sufficed to make a guest content, but the same was not true for Morocco, where guests expected large meals (1898–9: I, 132–3). He also noted the great attention shown to mosques in Egypt in comparison to the relative neglect accorded to those of Morocco. In general, through his acquaintance with Egypt, he revealed an acute consciousness of the anarchy of Morocco in the 1660s and 1670s due to rivalries between local principalities (1898–9: I, 152).

However, al-'Ayyashi could not help commenting on the negative characteristics of fellow Muslims. The Egyptians, suffering from lack of pride, endured arbitrary government from the Mamluks without reaction or rebellion (1898–9: I, 121–1). He also disapproved of how Islam had been bureaucratised and corruption was tolerated in Ottoman Medina. He generalised:

> All judiciary offices in eastern lands, whether in Egypt, Syria or the Hijaz, are acquired in return for money. Governors sell the offices of *imam* (prayer leader), *khatib* (sermoniser), *muezzin* (caller to prayer), *qadi* (judge) . . . to whoever offers best, without considering whether he has or not any competence for the office. This results in enormous dangers for Muslims and Islam. Concerning the office of judge, we have not heard, in all eastern lands, of a *qadi* whose judgements rely on the *shari'a* (sacred law). Their judgements depend on bribery, and a verdict may change many times during the same day in relation to the more or less great amount of the bribe.
>
> (1898–9: I, 128)

Al-'Ayyashi related the case of such a *qadi* who wanted to apply the *shari'a* to the affairs of prominent men in Medina, but ended by being assassinated. He concluded: "One can only complain to God" (1898–9: I, 289).

Different ways of organising everyday life were especially disconcerting:

> The teachers' custom in Medina is to vacation on Tuesdays and Fridays and classes meet on the other days, contrary to our custom of vacationing on Thursdays and Fridays in Morocco. When I was teaching in the Haram [Medina], they forced me to teach on Thursdays. It was hard for me because it was different from what we were accustomed to . . . I asked them and insisted upon replacing Thursdays with Tuesdays, but they obstinately refused. I was forced to follow their custom.
>
> (1898–9: I, 289)

Al-'Ayyashi could only console himself by reciting a verse of poetry: "If you come to a land in which all people are blind/Close your eye, even if you have only one eye!"

The differences noted by al-'Ayyashi include prayer ritual. In the Maliki school of law, Muslims let their arms down while standing in prayer, whereas, in the other schools, worshippers fold their arms on their chests. But this latter custom soon spread to eastern lands including those where the Maliki school had influence. It widely came to be assumed that only heretical people (*rafidi*) let their arms down. Al-'Ayyashi noted the ironic case of a western

Maliki accused, in a Syrian village, of being heretical for precisely that reason, even though his accusers were Maliki themselves (1989–9: I, 292).

Often comparisons are realised through a theological challenge. It was customary for western Maliki *faqihs* to become involved in debates about the *hadith* (Prophet's traditions), and many of them like to report that they found their antagonists' knowledge weak. True to this tradition, al-'Ayyashi reported how in Jerusalem he outwitted an Egyptian Hanafi scholar, who was believed to be very learned (1898–9: II, 321–2).

In some paragraphs, al-'Ayyashi generalised his comparisons:

> Nomads of Darb, Hijaz, Tihama and Najd are the most ignorant and tough people among Arabs. Only few of them care about prayers or Ramadan. Common people, Arabs and Berbers, in our Morocco, are *faqihs* in comparison to them. In Morocco, no one, however ignorant he might be, and even if illiterate, would be ignorant about how to do his prayers.
>
> (al-'Ayyashi 1898–9: I, 313)

Here we meet the subjective aspect of comparison. When al-'Ayyashi decided to stay in Mecca for a long period, he justified it by saying that Mecca was the homeland for all the faithful. But, in the last pages of his *rihla* account, he showed just how deeply he was longing to return home: his thirty-month stay abroad seemed as if it had been a whole century (1898–9: II, 418). Within the *umma*, therefore, al-'Ayyashi felt closer identification to his own country and people, for the things that differentiated him from eastern peoples were exactly those that linked him to his compatriots in Morocco.

Al-Tamgruti and his *rihla* to Istanbul: competition over the *umma*

If we look at another Moroccan, but of the sixteenth century, we will find similar sentiments. I have avoided choosing the text of another eighteenth-century traveller for two reasons: first, the chronological development of the themes in *rihla* literature is not my principal concern here; second, by the eighteenth century, Morocco and the Ottoman Empire had reached a kind of *modus vivendi* and *rihla* texts were less interested in expressing difference and competition.

The text of Abu'l-Hasan 'Ali al-Tamgruti is one of the earliest accounts of Moroccan–Ottoman relations in the late sixteenth century, when competition over legitimacy within the *umma* was still intense. Reading through *Kitab al-Nafha al-Miskiyya fi'l-Sifara al-Turkiyya* [*The Book of the Musky Breeze of the Embassy to Turkey*] serves to indicate his reactions to the numerous aspects and events of his travel to Istanbul in 1589–90. He travelled there as the ambassador of the Sa'di Sultan Ahmad al-Mansur (ruled 1578–1603) to the Ottoman Sultan Murad III (ruled 1574–95).

H. de Castries stated in his introduction to the French translation of the *Nafha* that little is known about al-Tamgruti outside of what we can infer from his own *rihla* account (al-Tamgruti/de Castries 1929: iv). Born about 1560 in Tamgrut, he died in 1594 or 1595 in Marrakesh. He belonged to the region in which the Sa'di dynasty originated and might thus have been expected to be unconditionally faithful to Sultan al-Mansur.

Al-Tamgruti provided us with an interesting insight into the relations between his family and the Sa'di dynasty when he wrote (1929: 45) that his late brother, Sidi Muhammad, had been sent as ambassador to the Ottoman lands before him. We can infer from this detail that al-Tamgruti's family was in charge of an inherited office that involved diplomacy between Morocco and Istanbul. At any rate, we can safely assume that al-Tamgruti was acquainted with Ottoman affairs well before his mission, especially through his brother's accounts (1929: 45). The knowledge of the Ottoman provinces, Istanbul, and Ottoman society and state that is contained in his travel account did not therefore depend on first-hand experience alone, but was representative of what was known of the Ottomans among prominent families of the Sa'di regime.

Al-Tamgruti said nothing of the real purpose of his official mission. Were the contents of the mission top secret? Or were oral reports on such matters more common? We simply do not know why al-Tamgruti's account is silent here, but on other matters, such as itineraries and cities that he visited, he was prolix. He said of Istanbul: "In this city, there are so many people, craftsmen, properties, commodities, stores, and books that the traveller is struck by their number, which only God could count and know" (al-Tamgruti n.d.: 94; al-Tamgruti/de Castries 1929: 54). The size of the city and the variety of its activities were so unlike what he had known and so fascinated him that his colourful descriptions remind us of modern *cartes postales* of Istanbul.

The author's general reaction to the Ottomans alternated between fascination and rejection. Al-Tamgruti was fascinated by the strength and power of the empire; after all, the Ottoman sultan was the most important Muslim ruler, able to oppose and fight the Christians. The same fascination could be noticed in his sensitivity to the language spoken by the Turks: in many places, he made specific comments on the rules of Turkish grammar (al-Tamgruti 1929: 85, 99, 103).

At the same time, al-Tamgruti clearly recognised his difference from the Ottomans, particularly in matters of law. Yet, surprisingly for a *faqih*, he did not record the name of any scholar during his six-month stay in Istanbul. He only wrote: "we attended the seminars of scholars who were in Istanbul and we learned many things from them" (al-Tamgruti/de Castries 1929: 68). It is possible that, as a Maliki, he was reluctant to detail the Hanafi school and its scholars, as he had done for the Maliki scholars of Tunis. Speaking of the *fiqh* (jurisprudence) taught in Istanbul, he merely concluded: "they teach their law" (*fiqhuhum*).

On the political level, he expressed his rejection of the style of Ottoman rule much more clearly. When he was still on his way to Istanbul, he witnessed a rebellion among the Arab tribes in the countryside of Tripoli (al-Tamgruti/de Castries 1929: 31–4; Hess 1978: 113–14), which afforded him the opportunity to record Ottoman practices:

As a matter of fact, the Turks had oppressed the inhabitants of Tripolitania very much. They had devastated the country with cruelty, depriving people of part of their lands and houses and ransacking their wealth. They had been so unrespectful to Muslim women that, if they liked a girl, be she the daughter of a notable or of a prominent man, no one could have prevented them from [marrying] her. It was impossible to marry her to someone else.
(al-Tamgruti/de Castries 1929: 32–3)

As a consequence, many of the North African Arabs, from Egypt to Ifriqia (Tunisia), were turning their eyes towards the ruling dynasty in Morocco:

We have noticed among them an extraordinary willingness to being ruled by the *sharifs*, our lords. They want to share peace, equity, mercy and benefits that the Maghribis [Moroccans] enjoy thanks to [the *sharifs*].
(al-Tamgruti/de Castries 1929: 33)

We should not forget that it was a member of the Sa'di regime who was speaking; a laudatory style would not have been unexpected. Nevertheless, these paragraphs go further and make a substantial claim for the Moroccan dynasty: because the *sharifs* were, or proclaimed themselves to be, descendants of the Prophet, they were the true caliphs. This is clearly shown in the text when al-Tamgruti contrived to speak of the Ottoman sultan and the Sa'di sultan in the same sentence:

> The [Ottoman] sultan gave us his response to the credentials of the caliph, our lord sultan, *sharif* Ahmad al-Hasani. And in order to thank him, he gave us magnificent presents for him.
>
> (al-Tamgruti/de Castries 1929: 68)

Over many Islamic centuries, travellers, pilgrims, scholars, and ambassadors felt themselves linked to the wider community of Muslims. While this trend continued of course, at the western edge of the *umma* from the sixteenth century onward, historical trends favoured the more conscious expression of a distinct identity for Morocco: Moroccans became more aware of being at an extreme frontier of the Islamic world and of the need to resist the Iberian offensives. They also became increasingly aware of being the only area outside of Ottoman rule in the south Mediterranean Muslim world. Travellers and travel accounts refer, from then on with greater frequency, to a more precise and self-conscious geographical, socio-cultural, and political homeland. While noting that they shared many characteristics with fellow Muslims throughout the broad community, therefore, writers such as al-'Ayyashi and al-Tamgruti discovered other characteristics that they did not share and that distanced themselves from the *umma*. *Rihla* as text and as actual travel contributed to making both similarities and differences manifest, and left a sense of ambivalence that complicated what might have been assumed to be a natural identification with the *umma*.

Acknowledgements

I would like to thank S. Khalaf, D. Eickelman, and J. Piscatori for their comments and F.Z. Salah and V. Winder for their assistance with the English of this chapter. Remaining imperfections are mine.

Notes

1 There is, often, a chapter on the *rihla li-talab al-'ilm* (travel in search of knowledge) in Prophetic traditions. See, for example, Abu Dawud, *Sunan*, III, 317, tradition no. 3641.
2 Risks ranged from the danger of being assaulted by bandits, to exposure to plague, desert, and sea.
3 Al-Manuni gives twenty-two titles of texts concerning the period 1660–1790: two of them are *sifariyya* texts, three cover travel within the country, and seventeen are *hijaziyya* texts.
4 Very often most of the biographical evidence available about the traveller is contained in his *rihla* account. This was the case of Ibn Battuta and al-Tamgruti.

5 This vice, however, seems to be common to travel accounts in other cultures. See Morsy (1983).
6 It is worth noticing that such a feeling is still at work today. In a recent interview, Faqih al-Basri, one of the most radical leaders of the opposition to the Moroccan monarchy during the last twenty-five years, answered a question in these words:

> *Question*: "Le pays a dû vous manquer . . . ?"
> *Réponse*: "Bien sûr le Maroc me manque . . . J'étais loin de mon village, de mes racines, mais j'évoluais dans une partie plus vaste que j'ai appris à découvrir et à aimer . . . le croyant est partout chez lui en terre d'Islam."

(See *Jeune Afrique*, 15 July 1987, no. 1384, p. 24)

7 Al-'Ayyashi's *rihla* is only partially translated into French: Berbrugger 1846 and Motylinksi 1900.

References

al-'Ayyashi, A.S. (AH 1316/AD 1898−9) *Ma' al-Mawa'id*, Fez, I and II.

Berbrugger, L.A. (1846) 'Voyages dans le sud de l'Algérie', in *Exploration scientifique de l'Algérie*, vol. ix.

Berque. J. (1955) *Les structures sociales du Haut Atlas*, Presses Universitaires de France, Paris.

Brunel, R. (1955) *Le Monachisme errant dans l'Islam, Sidi Heddi et les Heddawa*, Libraire Larousse, Paris.

Abu Dawud (n.d.) *Sunan*, III.

De Castries, H. (1929) *Relation d'une ambassade marocaine en Turquie, 1589−1591*, Guethner, Paris.

Dunn, R.E. (1986) *The Adventures of Ibn Battuta, a Muslim Traveler of the Fourteenth Century*, University of California Press, Berkeley and Los Angeles.

Hammoudi, A. (1980) 'Sainteté, pouvoir et société, Tamgrout aux XVII−XVIII siècles', *Annales; Economies, Sociétés, Civilisations*, 35, nos. 3−4, pp. 615−41.

Hess, A. (1978) *The Forgotten Frontier, a History of the Sixteenth-Century Ibero-African Frontier*, The University of Chicago Press, Chicago.

al-Iraqi, A. (1984) 'Al radd al-Maghribi', *Al-Manahil* [Rabat], 30, pp. 125−54.

al-Jabarti, A. (n.d. [1970?]) *Tar'ikh Aja'ib al-Athar fi'l-Tarajim wa'l-Akhbar*, Dar al-Faris, Beirut, 3 vols.

Kopf, L. (1975) 'Al-'Ayyashi', *Encyclopaedia of Islam*, Brill, Leiden, vol. I.

Lewis, B. (1971) 'Hadjdj', *Encyclopaedia of Islam*, vol. III, 31−8.

al-Manuni, M. (1983) *Al-Masadir al-'Arabiyya li-Tar'ikh al-Maghrib*, Mohammad V University, Rabat.

Montagne, R. (1930) *Les Berbères et le Makhzen dans le sud du Maroc*, Alcan, Paris.

Morsy, M. (1983) *La relation de Thomas Pellow, une lecture du Maroc au 18ième Siecle*, Edition Recherche sur les civilisations, Paris.

El Moudden, A. (1983) 'Etat et société rurale à travers la *harka* au Maroc du XIX Siècle', *Maghreb Review*, 8, pp. 141–5.

Motylinksi (1900) *Itinéraires entre Tripoli et l'Egypte*, Algiers.

al-Nasiri, A. (1954–6) *al-Istiqsa*, vol. 6, Casablanca.

Nordman, D. (1980–1) 'Les expéditions de Moulay el Hassan, essai statistique', *Hespéris-Tamuda*, 19, pp. 123–52.

Raphael, F. (ed.) (1973) *Les pèlerinages de l'antiquité biblique et classique à l'Occident médiéval*, Geuthner, Paris.

al-Tamgruti, A.H. (1929) *Kitab al-Nafha al-Miskiyya fi'l-Sifara al-Turkiyya*, Lith.

al-Zayyani, A.Q. (1967) *al-Turjumana al-Kubra*, Wizarat al-Anba', Rabat.

Zemmama, A.Q. (1983) 'Ma'a Abi Salim al-'Ayyashi fi Rihlatihi ila'l-Mashriq', *al-Manahil* [Rabat], 27, pp. 156–68.

—— (1984) 'Ma'a Abi Salim al-'Ayyashi fi Rihlatihi ila'l-Mashriq' [continuation of 1983 article], *al-Manahil*, 30, pp. 114–24.

Chapter five

The pilgrimage remembered: South Asian accounts of the *hajj*

Barbara D. Metcalf

The pilgrimage to Mecca is unquestionably one of the great phenomena in the history of Muslim peoples. It has largely been studied from the perspectives of medieval travel and learning, of modern administrative issues and of topics in the religious study of rituals.[1] These studies provide a context for yet another approach, that of eliciting meaning in the pilgrimage, examining not only uniformities in the experience of Muslims but differences over time. The accounts written by pilgrims themselves invite an analysis of individual experience against the background of the social and political world in which they were produced. They are accounts of journeys that are at once inner and outer; and they are guides for us, both to changing patterns of religious sensibilities and to a world in technological, social, and political transition.

The South Asian accounts[2] take shape initially in the period of British rule, a period of complex and extensive re-definition of Islam and of community life; they continue, since 1947, in an Islamic republic and in a secular state where Muslims live as a minority. Nowadays, they are written in a world where Islamic values and Muslim identity seem increasingly significant. The *hajj* accounts produced in all these contexts show us important dimensions of Islam as a modern religion, of modes of self-presentation, and of Muslim social and corporate life as recounted in distinctive individual lives.

The scope of the accounts

The accounts of the *hajj* written by South Asians take many forms: travelogues, journals, letters, and guides.[3] They describe to different degrees and in different ways experiences of travel, judgements of other people and cultures, the meanings of the *hajj* and other central symbols of Muslim religious life, and – in so doing – offer self-representations of the pilgrim authors themselves. The

85

authors include some well known figures: major religious thinkers like Maulana Siddiq Hassan Khan Bhopali (1872), the poet Shefta (1841), the Begum of Bhopal (1870), and the Nawwab of Rampur (1872), and, in this century, literary figures from 'Abdu'l-Majid Daryabadi (1929) to Shorish Kashmiri (1967) as well as statesmen like Muhammad Zafrullah Khan (1967). A very substantial number of writers are from families touched by the institutions that emerged under British rule: they are well-born, literate in Urdu, of families with some mix of connections to government service, professions, and land.[4] But some are not from this type of background. Khwaja Hasan Nizami, himself scion of an illustrious Sufi family and a public figure in the first decades of this century, introduced, for example, the memoir of a craftsman, one Mistri Chiraghu'd-din Pasruri (1926), insisting on its usefulness and telling the reader that it was pointless to object to its Urdu – on the grounds that the author was, after all, from the Punjab! A handful of accounts have been written by women, from the wife of an army captain in Madras (Saba Mustafa 1979) to a former school principal from Lahore (Zainab Kakakhail 1976). Recently the well-known writer Imdad Sabiri has published the first of what promises to be a multi-volume series of collections of *hajj* accounts preserved in the records of his family. The accounts thus offer a very concrete and specific subject presented by a relatively wide range of observers over a considerable period of time.

Perhaps surprisingly, however, the accounts are concentrated in the years of British rule and after. Despite the splendid travelogues written in Arabic in the centuries after the 'Abbasids, there does not seem to be a continuous genre of travel writing in Muslim societies generally. In the Indian sub-continent, even travellers to the holy places of Mecca and Medina did not write about their travels before the late eighteenth century, except in so far as they recorded visions or wrote treatises while there.[5] In 1787, one Maulana Rafi'u'd-din Muradabadi (1961 edn), a disciple of the great *hadith* scholar and reformer of Delhi, Shah Wali'u'llah, performed the *hajj* and later set down a record of his trip; his is generally taken by later Indian writers as the first such account to have been written from the Indian sub-continent. Only a few pilgrims were to do likewise for the next hundred years. Between 1870 and 1950, however, the pace quickens when several dozen published their accounts. Since then, ever more people have written accounts, probably as many in the last four decades as in the eight decades before.[6] Many more, of course, wrote unpublished letters and accounts, known only to family and friends. Written accounts of the *hajj* thus seem a modern phenomenon. They share the impulse and context of other writing that emerges in this period, including travel accounts that range as far as Europe.[7]

The *hajj* accounts as a modern genre

The impulse to write is clearly related to the changes engendered by British domination and western technology, including the printing press, which permitted easy dissemination of writings, and new modes of transport, which permitted easier travel. Writers were discovering new worlds as they were discovering, or creating, new ways of thinking about themselves. The first two Indian Muslims to leave accounts of their trips to Europe, for example, were each from areas of intensive contact with the British in the late eighteenth century, Bengal and Oudh respectively. The traveller from Oudh, Mirza Abu Talib Khan, was a revenue official for the East India Company and wrote – at least in part – with a European audience in mind.[8] The *hajj* accounts share important characteristics with other new forms of modern literature which are, for example, increasingly conceived as occasions for constituting a persona, a representation of a self that focuses on individual experiences, perceptions, and feelings, much like the autobiographies that began at the same time. Authors began to present themselves not only as observers but as active participants in what they describe: the *hajji* and not the *hajj* takes centre stage.

Many accounts take on characteristics, if not the shape, of novels, including dramatic vignettes of episodes with directly quoted conversations. Some abandon what one might call the built-in pattern of a pilgrimage account – beginning with the departure, climaxing in arrival at the destined goal, and, on occasion, describing the journey home – in order to structure their story by some other principle.[9] In recent decades many of the most popular accounts have been written by literary figures. Thus the novelist Mumtaz Mufti in his opening apologia makes clear that he is writing neither an entertainment nor a religious treatise, but simply the life story (*ap biti*) of an "unknown, ignorant, but sincere pilgrim" (not a *hajji* but a *za'ir*); he opens with a series of compelling vignettes that show what propelled him, as a sometime secular leftist, to undertake the journey (Mumtaz Mufti 1975: 10).

Studies of Persian and South-east Asian travel literature, including *hajj* literature, suggest, broadly speaking, a similar pattern. Fragner (1979) finds the earliest Persian memoirs for the nineteenth century to be in fact travel accounts; only in the twentieth century does he find autobiography and what he calls attention to one's "development and fate" (*Werdegang und*

Schicksal) as characteristic of either travelogues or memoirs. Matheson and Milner (1984) analysing five Malay texts, identify as one theme an increased emphasis on personal experience in the most recent texts.

The *hajj* accounts turn out not to be an isolated genre, a continuation of a static medieval form, but rather a genre that develops in ways broadly similar to the modern novel and autobiography. The accounts should be read, moreover, in the context of modern biographies, particularly the biographies of the Prophet Muhammad, a subject that has seen a virtual explosion from the late nineteenth century on. The representation of the central personal symbol of the faith has been increasingly emphasized as Muslim cultures have focused more on issues of individuality and personhood. This emphasis is evident not only in biography and poetry, but in a reformist emphasis on the *hadith* of the Prophet, and in increased celebration of devotional practices related to the Prophet's birthday *(mawlud)*. Since the *hajj* to Mecca often included pilgrimage to the Prophet's grave in Medina, the accounts themselves may include reflections on the Prophet as well.[10] The accounts should be read as part of an enduring yet shifting constellation of three poles: changes in society generally, changes in concepts of individuality, and changes in the interpretation of central religious symbols, of which two, the *hajj* and the Prophet, are relevant here.[11]

The *hajj* does not decline in modern times. In contrast to European Christian pilgrimage, it is rarely called into question. It is a canonical duty, an unalloyed good; it is always better to go. Christian pilgrimage to Jerusalem or saints' shrines is always problematic, even in centuries when such practices flourished. Similarly suspect can be Muslim pilgrimage to saints' tombs whose devotees, from Morocco to Senegal to Baluchistan, may even identify a visit to a shrine as equivalent to the *hajj*.[12] What questioning there has been of the *hajj* has not been associated with modern change but with some streams of Sufi mysticism that deplore external duties with no focus on inner purification.[13]

There is, not surprisingly, lively cynicism about a practice so revered. The *hajj* can be seen as a cover for worldly greed – contacts for smuggling – or honour. But far from diminution, modern decades have seen the *hajj* grow, not only from South Asia but from all Muslim societies, until today the annual pilgrimage numbers up to two million. As McDonnell (this volume) shows, modern currents of reform have in fact encouraged the *hajj* and modern transportation has facilitated it. Far from being seen as an alternative to ethical duties or piety, Islamic rituals like the *hajj* have been seen in periods of reform as essential to both.[14]

By the nineteenth century in Europe, however, travel accounts had little to do with pilgrimage. The image remained as metaphor, for pilgrimage had in fact often given way to exploration and quest.[15] The romantic quest, our most persistent mode of literary travel, made of pilgrimage a new image of a journey into the self, with the antagonist neither the exterior temptation of the Middle Ages nor the external nature of writers like Defoe; it was, instead, identity and selfhood that gave the challenge (Howard 1980: 8). We now take for granted that travel, removing a person from local identities and ties, familiar languages and people, and placing him amid different ways of living and thinking will force at least the sensitive and thoughtful to reassess exactly who they are. As S. Naipaul puts it: "All travel is a form of gradual self-extinction" (1984: 65).[16]

The *hajj*, however, even if it partakes of adventure, practical account, or inner exploration, remains a pilgrimage in the specific sense of the visitation of the Ka'ba at Mecca under prescribed circumstances as an essential duty of an able Muslim. *"Hajj"* is not a metaphor as "pilgrimage" is in English; even if used as a vehicle for a personal quest, the *hajj* in fact remains and is the structure for whatever experience the *hajji* creates. That experience, filtered by distance and literary conventions, becomes the remembered *hajj* of the written account and, for its readers, part of a shared understanding of religious symbols, self-expression, and interpretation of peoples and places.

Perspectives on the *hajj*

Travel accounts in general are richly revealing because they at once purport to describe an objective reality yet in fact reveal the cultural world through which the traveller filters what he sees. Sometimes it is possible to identify some central implicit set of issues that shapes an entire account.[17] Perhaps surprisingly in writings on a core religious ritual, many travellers in late nineteenth-century British India, for example, wrote with a range of imperial issues close to the surface of their perceptions. Thus Mirza 'Irfan 'Ali Beg (1895–6) explicitly wrote to provide useful information and describe interesting events for the Anjuman-i Islamiyya, a voluntary association of Muslims – presumably well-born and educated urban professionals, landlords, government servants, and traders – with whom he was associated. Like many *hajjis*, he wanted, presumably in all sincerity, to pass on the blessings of a journey like his and to make such a journey easier for those who would follow. At the same time, however, as a deputy collector in the eastern United Provinces, as high a civil servant as any Indian in the imperial bureaucracy, he was clearly a person who had internalised British concerns for governance and had an identity as a British subject and functionary. He knew English, his tastes were English (from cricket to tea) – and he knew how a government ought to behave.

For him, the significant group in his journey was "Indian Muslim", a category of increasing salience in the social and political context of his day, and one that takes on new meaning for him in the course of his travels. He looks for Indian Muslims and in a foreign context takes pride in what is special about them. He rejoices in their piety, describing, for example, their unceasing circumambulations and barefoot journeys to Medina. He remarks on their generosity in endowing hospices, gardens, and mosques. In the Haramayn and *en route*, he readily takes on the role of civic leader – whether acting as examiner at the Indian-founded Madrasa-yi Saulatiyya in Mecca or meeting the pilgrim protectors in Bombay and Jidda to ascertain their role. At every point he reflects on the way in which government should act to provide order, protection, comfort, and cleanliness. He speaks to the imperial government of their responsibilities and addresses himself as well, in the Hijaz, to the Turks. The plight of the poor Indian Muslim – vulnerable, abused, and cheated – is his overwhelming concern. Two years after publishing his Urdu account, 'Irfan 'Ali personally translated and revised his journal in English, adding a table of each occasion when he found the situation amiss – his main goal being to influence the government of India to act responsibly to project their Muslim subjects on *hajj*.

There is more in his account than this. There are also his deep bonds with his friends, his kindness to his servant, his ready response to a holy and learned man he comes to know in Mecca, his cosmopolitan interest in touring, and his congenial relationships with non-Muslims as well as Muslims. However, his particular political perspective is central, and it is enhanced and made public by the very act of writing. Other writers in this period have a somewhat similar experience in the *hajj* and its recording, notably the Begum of Bhopal who so internalised the British ideals of an "improving" ruler – committed to cultivating good character and installing drains – that she urged the Turks to withdraw and leave the running of the holy places to her (Sikander Begum 1870: 140–1)!

Some of the accounts are shaped by a specific religious orientation. Muhammad Ma'shuq 'Ali (1909), for example, described his experience as a disciple of the great Sufi, Maulana Ashraf 'Ali Thanawi. His *hajj* followed residence at the hospice of this saint and was part of the training in ritual fidelity and personal formation that was set for him. Other accounts (for example Abu'l-nur Muhammad 1960) argue a sectarian perspective and use the *hajj* as a platform for asserting its validity. Yet others are essentially scientific – written like government gazetteers to review history, local customs, the educational system, and the organization of the government (for example, Hasanu'd-din 1935). In each case, to present the *hajj* is to present a certain kind of self.

Many of the accounts in recent decades are explorations of the self in a more specific sense, looking to the great communal ritual as an occasion to test a person's place in relation to nothing less than Islam itself and to the Muslim *umma*. Somewhat like the quest for meaning, for authenticity, outside of one's own culture – such as we know in some forms of modern European or American travel – self-described secularists embark on the *hajj* to test themselves, to experience faith vicariously, perhaps in some sense to participate in that faith themselves (Cohen 1979). Thus 'Abdu'llah Malik (late 1970s) explicitly calls himself a *tahzibi Muslim* – a cultural Muslim – who goes on *hajj* reluctantly: and sets out looking over his own shoulder as he learns, he says, a new vocabulary. He struggles to find an intellectual equivalence for his Communism and Islam. He finds himself ever more emotionally involved, but thanks to the structure of the travel narrative, in contrast to a more sustained kind of essay writing, he can savour a thought or emotion ("My eyes were moist and I wept – quite apart from what my beliefs were and what they weren't"), then just move on. Indeed, the formal structure of the travel account, it has been argued, makes it particularly appealing to a certain kind of modern personality which prefers not to resolve but to sample and explore (Bridgeman 1986). Malik calls his account *Hadis-i dil*, the testimony of the heart and not of the canonical scripture. One characteristic of the self-conscious intellectual, playing off connection and lack of connection, is to find ways to assert his difference from those around him. One sometime secular leftist, for example, whose story I heard orally in 1985, made a point that in contrast to most *hajjis* who – as they are told over and over is normal – feel fear in Mecca but love in Medina, his experience was the reverse.

Whether as part of a re-identification with Islamic symbols or not, recent accounts tend to take as their central theme what one writer (Zainab Kakakhail 1976: 6–7), explaining her list of favourite accounts, calls "matters of the heart" and "inner experiences". The freshness of *hajj* accounts, she explains, rests not only in their documenting actual changes to benefit the reader, but in their showing "the singular and unique experiences", the individual heart and gaze, that refract the beauty of the Ka'ba – in every case in a distinctive way. For her, given her emphasis on feeling, it is not surprising that she draws her vocabulary for central religious symbols – God, Unity, the Ka'ba – from Sufism, distinguishing the *hajj* from other duties which are ethical in purpose and seeing the pilgrimage "alone as a matter of the heart", "easing the pain of separation", its customs those of the world of passionate longing (*'ishq*).

Zainab Kakakhail's account is not alone in using such language. In the past however, the Sufi tradition was expressed by the insertion of couplets into the ongoing prose account. Indeed, to be able to quote aptly the Persian or Persianate Urdu couplets of the Sufi tradition has long been the mark of a refined and educated person in this culture. The recent accounts seem to demonstrate a convergence of what had been two levels of discourse: a prose discourse focused on external events; and a poetic discourse of passion, longing, and separation offered without comment and not claimed as one's own speech. Now the poetic language is appropriated as one's own.[18] As the content changes, the rhetoric and forms of the accounts change as well. If we take the accounts from the late eighteenth century on, they clearly become a continuing genre, building on each other, shaping each other. Do they develop in certain directions as possibilities of the form are simply played out?

Howard (1980), in his study of the pre-Chaucerian accounts of the pilgrimage to Jerusalem, shows how certain "built-in" possibilities of the pilgrimage genre – in that case, irony above all – do develop over time. Do the accounts shape their own landscape, so that the traveller sees through lenses honed through literature? Fussell (1980), in the case of British travellers to the continent, has particularly shown how reading creates the experience of travel; Kabbani (1985) has argued the significance of the European discourse of Orientalism, including travel accounts, in precluding a traveller like V.S. Naipaul from even seeing the Muslim countries which he purports to describe. Writers also learn from those who have gone before, at least in part, the form they must give their account, a form that changes over time – for example, from the conventional self-deprecation in Zardar's account described on p. 93, to the now obligatory trope of denying that one ever intended to write at all.

Much that is in the accounts is, of course, implicit. Some aspects of the world of writers can be elicited by focusing on the audience, explicit or implied, in the accounts. The writers, while telling their stories, pursue conversations whether consciously or not, of which their written words form largely one side. Sometimes they present, in effect, a response to questions they know would be asked, sometimes they assert the kind of person they want to be known to be – in contrast to some alternative kind of person – sometimes they declare by their assessments and emphases a position in ongoing controversies of a religious or political nature. Sometimes they may not even be conscious that they are writing to a range of concerns, expressed in their societies and internalised in their psyches, shaping the experience which they create as they write.

Visual representations in the texts

One way to elicit these themes is to look not only at the words but also at the physical presentation of the texts.[19] One need go no further than the title pages, for example, to see the increased tendency to make the author's experience central and to present each account as distinctive. Figure 5.1 juxtaposes two title pages, on the left that of Zardar Khan (1873) published by the great Hindu Kayasth of Lucknow, Nawwal Kishur. Zardar shared with Nawwal Kishur the Persianate culture of the well-born, often, as in Zardar's case, typical of people employed by the government or a prince. Zardar's book was conventionally entitled *Safarnama-yi haramain* [*A Travelogue to the Two Sanctuaries*]. Its lack of colour, its floral border, the medallion for the title, and the inscribed panels top and bottom present the immediately familiar cover of innumerable publications of the day. The top panel replicates in words the balance and symmetry of the page, setting out in the elegant calligraphic style, *nastaliq*, a two-part rhyming invocation, in Persian, that sets the tone of humility common to publications of the day: "With the help of the Maker of the man [*makin*] and the place [*makan*] and the aid of the Shaper of the land [*zamin*] and the age [*zaman*]". The author's name does not even appear on the cover, but only in the midst of the formulaic phrases of self-described abjection set out on the opening page.

The jacket on the right appeared some hundred years later (Mumtaz Mufti 1975), a three-colour design, with the one-word title, *Labaik* ("I am here", the call of the *hajji* in Arabic as he enters Mecca). The background, yellow-green, significantly deepens to dark green, the Islamic colour *par excellence*, as field for the black Ka'ba centered at the top. The title is written in a swinging free form so that the first letter, *lam*, points to the shrine and the elongated final *kaf* encircles it: the calligraphy thus recalls drawings of the plan of the Ka'ba like those in Figure 5.3. The author's name,

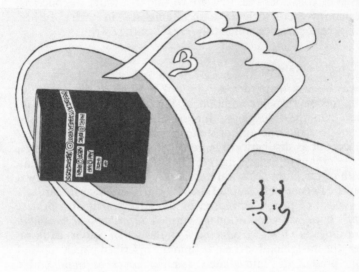

Figure 5.1 Book covers. (Left) Muhammad Zardar Khan (1873) *Safarnama-yi Haramain*; (right) Mumtaz Mufti (1975) *Labaik*.

Mumtaz Mufti, is boldly written in the loop formed by the downward stroke of the same letter; the name is written at an upright angle that identifies it not with Persian but with the Arabic of the Qur'an and the larger Muslim world. The jacket makes the book look like a novel, and indeed the friend who first mentioned this account to me thought that it was just that – a logical assumption given the poetic title and the reputation of the author as a literary figure.

Like a novel, the goal of this account, and many recent ones, is to convey an immediacy of experience. Over and over, the successful accounts written in recent decades are praised for their making the *hajj* vivid and present before the reader's eye; the reader identifies with the writer and vicariously lives his experience. Readers' letters prefaced to the publication of Muhammad Riza Ansari's account (1965) for example, praise it for being a veritable cinema and avow that the reader feels he has made the *hajj* himself. The text itself serves as the *hajj*. Here *Labaik*, the title, says, "I am present" and its calligraphy circumambulates the Ka'ba just as the author's words will effect the *hajj* for the person about to read.

Drawings of monuments similarly suggest significant transitions. Early drawings published in the accounts show balance and patterning (reminiscent of Zardar's title page) and may incorporate miraculous elements presumed visible once or expected to appear in a time to come. Figures 5.2 and 5.3 show drawings published in Zardar's 1873 account. Figure 5.2, left, shows his drawing of the site of the miracle of the splitting of the moon, with the split moon also visible; Figure 5.3 shows the Aqra mosque in Jerusalem as well as the pool of Kausar, the bridge, the balance, and the throne of God, all associated with the Day of Judgement, which is expected to begin in that place. He thus includes both visible and invisible reality. Figure 5.3, left, is a drawing of the Sacred Mosque (1880) depicted in a characteristic medieval style, seen from above with the side walls flattened out (Wazir Husain Khan 1880–1). Drawings like this are very schematic and patterned, almost mandala-like in their focus on the centre. The drawing on the right eschews formality for realism, drawing an accurate ground plan of the mosque without attention to walls, domes, and doors, and distinguishing by slashed lines what did not seem of interest before: the distinction between the old building and new additions (Sultan Da'ud 1963). The early author shows himself as part of a long historic and aesthetic tradition; the modern author gives us accuracy and new information.

The charming drawing in Figure 5.4 records the climactic event of the *hajj*, "the standing" at 'Arafat ('Abdu'r-rahim 1915). The

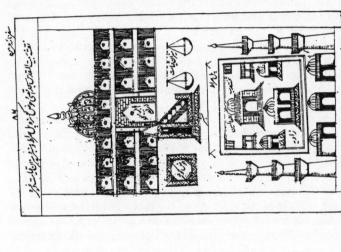

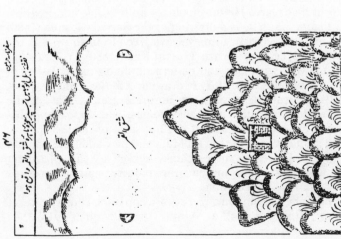

Figure 5.2 Drawings of sacred places and symbols. (Muhammad Zardar Khan (1873) *Safarnama-yi Haramain*.)

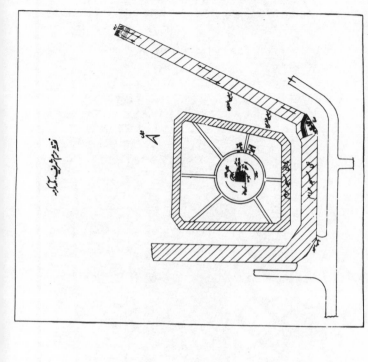

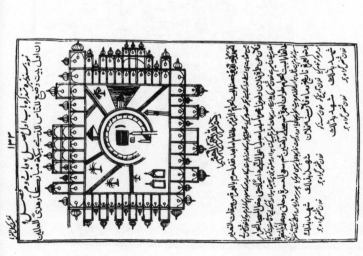

Figure 5.3 Floor plans of the Ka'ba. (Left) Wazir Husain Khan (1880) *Wakilu'l-ghuraba*; (right) Sultan Da'ud (1963) *Safarnama-yi hijaz*.

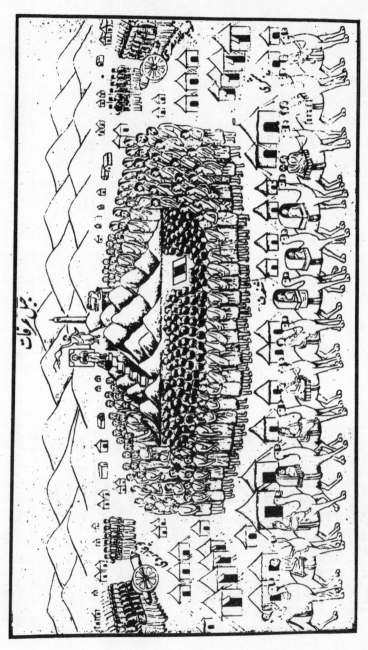

Figure 5.4 Mount ʿArafat. (ʿAbduʾr-rahim (1915) *Safarnama-yi rahimi*.)

Figure 5.5 Photographs of authors. (Left) Ghulamu'l-Husnain (1935) *Safarnama*; (right) Saba Mustafa (1979) *Paharon ke daman men.*

simple line drawing and design recall the block prints of northern Indian textiles, as do the sketches of the ladies, who all wear saris. The repetitive camels, tents, and mounted pilgrims form a strong line across the bottom, the Turkish artillery in their modern military uniforms balance the two sides, and the hills provide the top frame for the central focus – the gathering, preaching, and prayer on the sacred hill. An account written in more recent decades would probably include an aerial photograph, rather than a balanced and patterned drawing of this sort.

Finally, Figure 5.5 offers two photographs of authors. Not many authors provide photographs, perhaps fearing to offend the sensibilities of those who find photographs suspect or who might think the author vain. But even from the limited number of photographs available, the contrasts are again suggestive of the increasing tendency to focus on what is individualistic. The photograph on the left shows a venerable figure dressed in *ihram* (Ghu'lamu'l-husnain 1935); the second, a wonder-struck woman, wife of a Madrasi army officer (Saba Mustafa 1979). Her photograph is meant to communicate the personal emotional quality of the *hajj* – the theme that her text as a whole is meant to demonstrate. The earlier photograph, in contrast, is as much a generic representation of a *hajji* as a photograph can possibly be.

Conclusion

Travel to Mecca is travel of a very particular kind. To go to Mecca is to go home, to return to one's *ruhani watn*.[20] To go to Mecca is to perform an act of unquestioned value. Not only is the goal clear, but the place, in contrast to the destinations of some kinds of travel, is thoroughly known by vast resources of the culture in story and devotional song – now reinforced by techniques of reproduction and communication that make the Holy Places ever present.[21] Moreover, the journey moves on the invisible lines which believers create by every prayer, posture at sleep, and burial in the grave; on the day the *hajjis* perform the ritual sacrifice, fellow Muslims everywhere perform their sacrifice and all are linked world-wide in celebration of the feast. By undertaking the *hajj*, the pilgrim in principle affirms his individual responsibility for obedience to God and claims his place among the community of faithful people. However much the pilgrim seeks in his experience and in his writing to explore a unique and self-conscious self – the theme, as suggested, of many of the recent accounts – his undertaking must be in some tension to the normative programme of the *hajj*, and of all of mainstream Islam, to hone himself to the prophetic model, the person of the Prophet Muhammad, in whose footsteps on this occasion he can literally walk.

Such a context suggests that we have more than a simple mirroring of European individualism explored in alien settings as we trace changing patterns of self-representation in the *hajj* accounts. If a person is "finding himself" he is doing so in a crowd, following a ritual programme of dress and behaviour meant precisely to obliterate the markers that make a believer distinct by class, race, or region. The accounts, even if imitative of European travel writing and made salient by the socio-political change engendered by European technology and domination, are written in the context of interaction with the core tradition of Islam.

All this would be true of any Muslim account. Those from South Asia share their own characteristics – characteristics rooted in the peculiarly plural character of Indian cultures and in the long experience of colonial rule. That rule provided a range of alternative values, so that indigenous cultures became self-conscious and, in Geertz's (1968) phrase, oppositional. At the same time, the very idiom of British rule encouraged religious identities in a plural society. These experiences shape all forms of self-statement by South Asian Muslims, but accounts focused on such central symbols as those represented by the *hajj* present themes particularly suggestive of the specific issue of how being Muslim has been experienced and conceived. A Muslim identity has not been the only one significant to those we label South Asian Muslims, but it has, assuredly, been an important one. In the accounts we see something of the shifting content of that identity as well as its relation to competing and complementary strands – of occupation, moral formation, spiritual quest, gender, and territoriality. The texts let us hear people speak, telling us, in a wide variety of ways, what kind of people they are and how they think of Islam, the places they go to, and the people they meet.

Acknowledgements

I am grateful to the John Simon Guggenheim Foundation for support during 1983–4 as well as to the American Institute of Pakistan Studies and the American Philosophical Society for grants to support travel, all of which enabled me to collect materials and undertake preliminary work on this project. I returned to the project in Autumn 1987, thanks to the Davis Humanities Institute which provided released time from teaching and the company of excellent colleagues.

Notes

1 For an excellent introduction to these topics, see Lewis (1971). On administrative issues, see Long (1979) and Roff (1975, 1982). On the *hajj* as ritual see Roff (1985); von Grunebaum (1951); and Partin (1967).

2 As will be clear in the discussion that follows, by South Asian I limit myself primarily to those written mostly in Urdu, a few in Persian, a handful written in or translated into English.

3 I currently have in hand, or have made use of, almost 150 accounts. I have found these accounts in London (British Library, India Office Library), Lahore (Dayal Singh Trust Library, Oriental College Library, Punjab Public Library, and Punjab University Library), Islamabad (Islamic Research Institute [IRI]), and the libraries of the University of California. I am grateful to the staffs of all these libraries and to Dr Muhammad Khalid Masud of the IRI for their generous help. I have also acquired books in shops in Lahore and Delhi as well as an excellent collection of accounts from old book shops in Hyderabad, India, thanks to the skilled help of Dr Gail Minault. Dr Michael Fisher kindly provided an account by a Keralite; Dr Francis Robinson, one by a Farangi Mahali. I have not yet had an opportunity to consult libraries in India where many more accounts are presumably to be found.

4 This "sharif culture" is evoked for the late nineteenth century in Lelyveld (1979), Chapter 2.

5 See Pearson (1986, 1987a, 1987b). Pearson suggests that as many as 10,000 pilgrims a year may have undertaken the *hajj* during the period of Mughal rule. The best-known example of early writing about experiences in the Hijaz is that of Shah Wali'u'llah (1730), the *Fuyuz al-haramain*, a collection of his visions.

6 This assumes that those I have identified are in proportion to the total written.

7 I am grateful to Dr J.P.S. Uberoi for reminding me of this and for presiding over a lively session on my work at the Sociological Research Colloquium, University of Delhi, on 11 December 1987.

8 The writers are Sheikh I'tisam al-Din from Bengal and Mirza Abu Talib Khan from Lucknow as noted in Lewis (1982).

9 Howard (1980), analysing the pilgrimage literature of pre-Chaucerian unknown pilgrims to Jerusalem, argues that the inclusion of the return journey – exemplified by a monk's account that touchingly ends with his welcome by the monastery dog – specifically points to an account that focuses on personal experience more than on the externals of the journey.

10 For excellent material on the whole range of expressions related to the Prophet in the modern period, see Schimmel (1985).

11 See Brown (1975) for a discussion of eleventh- and twelfth-century AD changes in social structure, as communities became less coherent and intense; in relationships; and in conceptions of the supernatural "as an upward extension of the individual". Colin Morris (1972) delineates a

new focus on inwardness in the twelfth century AD as shown in sermons describing personal experience, lyric poetry, ritual injunctions to confession with a focus on intention, and more personal portraits. New social roles and a new focus on personal relationships were the context for new interpretations of religious symbols, including a focus on the sufferings of Christ and devotion to him and a new conception of the Virgin. See also Bynum (1982). Other periods have, of course, seen this complex interplay in changes in society, religious symbols, and self, but this period is one that has been particularly well studied.

12 This is the case for the visit to Touba on the part of the Mourides of Senegal as it is for Demah on the part of Javanese. It is apparently the case also for the shrine of the Merinid sultan Abu Yusuf (AD 1258–86) in Rabat where tradition holds that seven circuits of the passageway around the *mihrab* gives merit equivalent to the trip to Mecca (Ellingham and McVeigh 1985). The contemporary Zikri sect of the Baluch, studied by Dr Akbar S. Ahmed, identify a local pilgrimage shrine in Makran with similar merit.

13 Thus the eighteenth-century Punjabi poet Bulhe Shah, celebrating the love of Hir for Ranjha, the type of the soul's love for God, sang:

> The *hajji* go to Mecca, world by world,
> My Ranjhu is Mecca for me. . . .
> The *hajji* is within
> The *ghazi* is within. . . .
> I have become a fool.
> The *hajji* go to Mecca.
> We must go to Takht-i mir [the birthplace of Ranjha].
> *This* is the road to Mecca.

(Provided by Dr Denys Matringe, Ecole des Hautes Etudes en Sciences Sociales, Paris, June 1986)

In his poem, Bulhe Shah recalls themes that go back at least to Junaid (d. AH 298/AD 919) in insisting on an inner component to the external trip.

14 For the "reformational" quality of Islamic ritual, see Graham (1983).

15 This was true whether for well-known figures like Byron or a traveller like Mrs Fanny Parks (1850) who travelled in India in the 1820s and 1830s. When Mrs Parks returned to London she concluded her two volumes by hanging up, she wrote, her long staff and stripping the scallop shell from her hat – the medieval emblems of the pilgrim to the shrine of Santiago in Compostella (2: 496).

16 Naipaul begins his published account of a trip by recalling these opening words of his notebook: "All journeys begin in the same way. All travel is a form of gradual self-extinction."

17 In studying European travelogues to Latin America, Roberto Gonzalez-Echevarria (1987) is able to identify what he calls a shifting "hegemonic discourse", so that travellers in one era, for example, will speak to legalistic concerns and use a legalistic vocabulary, travellers of another period will shape their account by science.

18 For an analysis of the interplay of these two levels of diction in another context, see Abu-Lughod (1986).

19 I am grateful to Dr Catherine Asher for pointing this out to me and for ably helping me with her art historian's eye, to reflect on the visual materials presented here.

20 This is the phrase used by Gilani Kamran (1978). His is one of the few scholarly works that surveys the Urdu *hajj* accounts, and I have benefited from it as from the personal helpfulness of Professor Kamran.

21 Today the climax of the *hajj* is transmitted by television satellite and watched live throughout the world. Calendars and art of all kinds make the image of the holy shrine the most familiar distant building of many Muslims. Pakistan television, like the television of many countries, transmits special programmes during the *hajj* season, including a six-part mini-series, which I viewed in 1985, to prepare intending pilgrims for their trip.

Accounts cited

'Abdu'llah Malik (late 1970s) *Hadis-i dil: ek komunist roznamcha-yi hajj* [*Testimony of the Heart: A Communist's Hajj Diary*], Lahore, Kausar.

'Abdu'l-majid Daryabadi (1929) *Safar-i hijaz* [*A Journey to the Hijaz*], Calcutta, Idara-yi Insha-yi Majidi, 4th edn, 1980.

'Abdu'l-nur Muhammad Bashir (1960) *Labaik ya saiyidi: Musafir-i Madina Bashir ki da'iri* [*Here I am Lord: The Diary of Bashir, The Traveller to Madina*], Kotli Loharan, Siyalkot, Kutbkhana-yi Mah-i taiyiba.

'Abdu' r-rahim, Munshi (1915) *Safarnama-yi rahimi ma'ruf ba Rafiqu'l-hajj* [*The Book of Rahim's Travels, or, A Companion to the hajj*], Calcutta, Matba'i-ghausiya.

Chiraghu'd-din Pasruri, Mistri (1926) *Roznamcha-yi safar-i hijaz* [*Diary of a Journey to the Hijaz*], Delhi, Matbu'a-yi mahbub'l mataba'.

Ghulamu'l-Husnain Sahib Fazil Panipati, al-Hajj Maulana Khwaja (1934–5) *Safarnama-yi hajj ma'ruf ba Saman-i akhirat* [*A Travel Account of the Hajj, named, Provisions for the Afterlife*], Delhi, Mani'a Pres.

Hasanu'd-din, Khamosh (1935) *Muraqa'-i hijaz* [*A Scrapbook of the Hijaz*], Agra, 'Azizi Pres.

'Irfan 'Ali Beg, Mirza (1895) *Safarnama-yi hijaz* [*A Travel Account of the Hijaz*], Lucknow, Nawwal Kishur.

——— (1896) *Pilgrimage to Mecca*, Benares, The Chandraprabha Press.

Muhammad Imdad Sabiri (1986) *Allah ke ghar men bar bar haziri: 1953 se le kar 1983 tak ke hajj ke safarname* [*Again and Again at God's House: Hajj Travelogues from 1953 to 1983*], Delhi, Jamal Press.

Muhammad Kalb 'Ali Khan (1872) *Qindil-i haram* [*A Candle of the Sanctuary*], Rampur, Matba' Husaini.

Muhammad Ma'shuq 'Ali (1909) *Safarnama-yi hajj-i bait allah sharif* [*A Travel Account of the Hajj to the Noble House of God*], Lucknow.

Muhammad Mustafa Khan Shefta, Nawwab (1841) *Siraj-i munir* [*The Illustrious Sun*], trans. (from Persian to Urdu), Agra, Matba'-i Akhbar-i Agra, 1910 edn.
Muhammad Riza Ansari (1965) *Hajj ka safar* [*A Journey for hajj*], Lucknow, Farangi Mahal Kitab Ghar.
Muhammad Zafrullah Khan (1967) *Pilgrimage to the House of Allah*, London, The London Mosque.
Muhammad Zardar Khan (1873) *Safarnama-yi haramain* [*A Travel Account of the Two Holy Places*], Lucknow, Nawwal Kishur.
Mumtaz Mufti (1975) *Labaik* [*I am Present*], Lahore, al Tahrir.
Rafi'u'ddin Faruqi Muradabadi (1786) *Safarnama-yi hijaz* [*A Travel Account of the Hijaz*], trans. (from Persian to Urdu) Maulana Nazim Ahmad Faridi Amrohawi, Lucknow, Tanwir Pres, 1961 edn.
Saba Mustafa (1979) *Paharon ke daman men: Safarnama-yi arz-i muqaddas* [*At the Skirt of the Mountains: A Travel Account of the Hallowed Land*], Bangalore, Alaktrik Qaumi Pres.
Shorish Kashmiri (1967) *Shab ja'e ki man budam: hijaz men chauda din* [*'The place where I was at night': Fourteen Days in the Hijaz*], Lahore, Matbu'at Chirtan.
Siddiq Hasan Khan Bhopali (1872) *Rihlat as-siddiq ila'l bait al-'atiq* [*The Journey of Siddiq to the Excellent House*], trans. (from Persian to Arabic), Bombay, Sharfu'd-din & Sons, 1961 edn.
Sikander Begum of Bhopal, Nawab (1870) *A Pilgrimage to Mecca*, trans. Mrs Willoughby-Osborne, with Afterword by Lt. Col. Willoughby Osborne and Appendix, trans. the Reverend William Wilkinson, London, Wm. H. Allen & Co.
Sultan Da'ud (1963) *Safarnama-yi hijaz* [*A Travel Account of the Hijaz*], Lahore, Nur Kampani.
Wazir Husain Khan Sahib Bahadur, Saiyid (1880–1) *Wakilu'l-ghuraba* [*Advocate of the Poor*], Lucknow, Nawwal Kishur.
Zainab Khatun Kakakhail, Profesar (1976) *Jalwah gah-i tauhid ke rubaru: Safar-i hajj aur astana-yi nabuwwat par haziri ki rudad* [*Facing Unity's Site of Effulgence: An Eye-witness Account of a Journey for Hajj and the Prophet's Abode*], Lahore, Himayatu'l-Islam Pres.

Secondary references

Abu-Lughod, Lila (1986) *Veiled Sentiments: Honor and Poetry in a Bedouin Society*, University of California Press, Berkeley.
Bridgeman, Richard (1986) *Traveling in Mark Twain*, University of California Press, Berkeley.
Brown, Peter (1975) 'Society and the supernatural: a medieval change', *Daedalus*, 104, pp. 1–2 and pp. 133–151.
Bynum, Caroline Walker (1982) *Jesus as Mother: Studies in the Spirituality of the High Middle Ages*, University of California Press, Berkeley.
Cohen, Erik (1979) 'A phenomenology of tourist experiences', *Sociology*, 13: 179–201.

Ellingham, Mark and Shaun McVeigh (1985) *The Rough Guide to Morocco*, Routledge & Kegan Paul, London.

Fragner, Bert G. (1979) *Persische Memoirenliteratur als Quelle zur neureren Geschichte Irans*, Franz Steiner Verlag, Wiesbaden.

Fussell, Paul (1980) *Abroad: British Literary Travelling between the Wars*, Oxford University Press, New York.

Geertz, Clifford (1968) *Islam Observed*, University of Chicago Press, Chicago.

Gilani Kamaran (1979) '*Hajj* ke safarnamon ki riwayat', in *1978 ke bahtarin maqalat*, ed. Sajad Taqwi, Maktaba Urdu Zaban, Sargodha, pp. 51–67.

Gonzalez-Echevarria, Roberto (1987) 'A lost world re-discovered: Sarmiento's Facundo', a paper presented at the conference 'Difference, Authority, Power' (University of California, Davis, 26 February 1987).

Graham, William A. (1983) 'Islam in the mirror of ritual', in *Islam's Understanding of Itself*, ed. Richard G. Hovannisian and Speros Vryonis, Jr., Undena Publications, Malibu, pp. 53–71.

Hajj Studies, Volume 1 (1979), The Hajj Research Center, Jeddah.

Hardy, Peter (1972) *The Muslims of British India*, Cambridge University Press, Cambridge.

Howard, Donald R. (1980) *Writers and Pilgrims: Medieval Pilgrimage Narratives and their Posterity*, University of California Press, Berkeley.

Kabbani, Rana (1985) *Europe's Myth of Orient*, University of Indiana Press, Bloomington.

Lelyveld, David S. (1979) *Aligarh's First Generation: Muslim Solidarity in British India*, Princeton University Press, Princeton, N.J.

Lewis, Bernard (1971) 'Hadjdj', *The Encyclopaedia of Islam*, 2nd edn, Brill, Leiden and London, vol. III, pp. 31–8.

—— (1982) *The Muslim Discovery of Europe*, W.W. Norton, New York.

Long, David (1979) *The Hajj Today: A Survey of the Contemporary Pilgrimage to Makkah*, State University of New York Press, Albany.

Matheson, Virginia and Anthony C. Milner (1984) 'Perceptions of the *Haj*: Five Malay Texts', Institute of Southeast Asian Studies, Research Notes and Discussion Paper no. 46, Singapore.

Morris, Colin (1972) *The Discovery of the Individual 1050–1200*, Harper & Row, New York.

Naipaul, Shiva (1984) *An Unfinished Journey*, Viking Press, New York.

Parks, Fanny (1975 [orig. 1850]) *Wanderings of a Pilgrim in Search of the Picturesque*, Oxford University Press, Karachi.

Partin, Harry B. (1967) 'The Muslim pilgrimage: journey to the center', unpublished PhD dissertation, University of Chicago.

Pearson, Michael N. (1986) 'The *hajj* (pilgrimage) from Mughal India: some preliminary observations', *Indica*, 23, pp. 143–88.

—— (1987a) 'Pious passengers: Muslim pilgrimages from India in the early modern period', a paper presented to the conference 'Sailing Ships and Sailing People', University of Western Australia, Perth.

—— (1987b) 'Portuguese records and Indian history: the case of the "*hajj* market"' (transcript).

Roff, William R. (1975) 'The conduct of the haj from Malaya and the first Malay Pilgrimage Officer', National University of Malaysia, Institute of Malay Language, Literature, and Culture, Occasional Papers no. 1, Kuala Lumpur, pp. 81–111.

—— (1982) 'Sanitation and security: the imperial powers and the nineteenth century *hajj*', *Arabian Studies*, 6, pp. 143–60.

—— (1985) 'Pilgrimage and the history of religions: theoretical approaches to the *hajj*', in Richard A. Martin (ed.) *Approaches to Islam in Religious Studies*, University of Arizona Press, Tucson, pp. 78–86.

Schimmel, Annemarie (1985) *And Muhammad is His Messenger: The Veneration of the Prophet in Islamic Piety*, The University of North Carolina Press, Chapel Hill.

von Grunebaum, G.E. (1951) *Muhammadan Festivals*, Henry Schuman, New York.

Part three

Pilgrims and migrants

Chapter six

Patterns of Muslim pilgrimage from Malaysia, 1885–1985

Mary Byrne McDonnell

Scale

Over the past hundred years, dramatic change in the scale, conduct, and composition of the Malay *hajj* has occurred. Over time, these transformations have modified how Malay pilgrims have experienced the *hajj*. In the 1880s, an average of 2,500 Muslims from the Malay States performed the *hajj* annually. This number doubled by the 1920s, and, since the mid-1960s, it has risen to 9,130 – an increase of approximately 400 per cent. The most dramatic increase has been since 1970. In 1982, approximately 25,000 pilgrims from Malaysia participated in the *hajj*. Significant dips in this general trend can be attributed to major world events, while minor fluctuations have normally been related to internal economic factors.[1]

The growth in the numbers of pilgrims cannot simply be due to population growth. Although it is impossible to determine the percentage of pilgrims within the Malay Muslim population at any given point, the average numbers of pilgrims in relation to the total Muslim population would appear to indicate that the increase in pilgrimage numbers is due to population growth. However, if we examine Malay pilgrims as a percentage of the Muslim population of *hajj* age (35 + years), it becomes clear that the percentage performing the *hajj* is increasing at a faster rate than the *hajj*-age segment of the Muslim population.

With respect to world-wide pilgrimage attendance, trends in Malaysia appear to be representative. In the early 1900s, 80–90,000 pilgrims annually performed the *hajj*, with more than 800,000 performing the *hajj* today. *Hajj* attendance has steadily increased since the 1950s, when it averaged 100,000, and has made major strides following the 1973 oil embargo, which heightened Saudi Arabian prestige. Indeed, an augmented position in the world of nations has enhanced the Saudi position in the eyes of Muslims. It can be argued that this heightened prestige has enabled Muslims to

111

feel safer and more secure in the Saudi ability to manage the *hajj*, and has enhanced the perception that there is a single centre. Funds from oil have also allowed pilgrimage to be better managed at the Saudi end, lending reality to the pilgrims' sense that a more powerful country can afford better protection and facilities.

The number of overseas pilgrims has also increased.[2] It rarely reached 100,000 before the Second World War. Today, more than 300,000 overseas pilgrims perform the *hajj* yearly. Malaysian pilgrims have formed 7.4 per cent of the total of overseas pilgrims. Indonesians have formed 15.2 per cent, and Indians 20 per cent before the creation of Pakistan, and 10 per cent since 1947. Although real numbers of pilgrims from Indonesia and India and their percentages of the overseas pilgrims are greater than Malaysia's, we know that their Muslim populations are also substantially greater. If we examine the above percentages of overseas pilgrims in relation to the respective Muslim populations of Malaysia, Indonesia, and India, we discover that Malaysia has sent twelve times as many pilgrims from its Muslim population as Indonesia, and ten times as many pilgrims as India before 1947. Since then, Malaysia has sent fourteen times as many pilgrims as has India.

Conduct

Since the 1880s, the conduct of the *hajj* from Malaysia has been completely altered. From initial control by British colonial officials with only a peripheral interest in it, the *hajj* from Malaysia has come to be the sole concern of large numbers of highly-trained Muslim managers in Saudi Arabia and Malaysia. Because *hajj* management was previously tied up with the stability of the British Malayan colonial government, its main concerns were with the health of pilgrims and the possibility of their acquiring ideas subversive to the empire while in the Hijaz. Today pilgrimage is managed as a tool of national economic development and nation-building within Malaysia. From an initially haphazard group of directives, pilgrimage management progressed in the colonial period to a system attached to merchant shipping and police intelligence,[3] a system with little impact once British ships docked in Jidda. Today, however, the regulatory system encompasses every aspect – from the decision to perform the *hajj*, through the entire journey, to return to the point of origin. The Malaysian government agency, Lembaga Urusan dan Tabong Haji (LUTH) [The Pilgrimage Management and Savings Corporation], regulates when Malaysians go, how they may go, and how much money they may

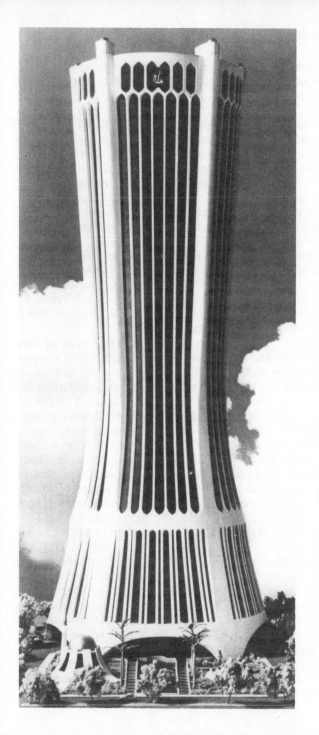

Figure 6.1 The architects intended the design of the headquarters building for LUTH (the Pilgrims' Management and Savings Corporation), Kuala Lumpur, to suggest that saving for the pilgrimage can also serve to channel funds into local enterprises "lawful of Islam". (Photography courtesy of LUTH, Kuala Lumpur.)

take. It organises such practical matters as registration, visas, passports, transportation, and medical and welfare care (LUTH Annual Reports 1971–82).

Thus, in recent years, the pilgrim's experience in practical terms has been substantially altered. Until the early 1930s, the *hajj* was a physically unsafe, insecure, unsanitary journey of long duration, in cramped and squalid conditions. By the end of the decade conditions had been upgraded substantially, and the journey was more organised, safer, and easier – especially in those areas amenable to Malayan governmental control such as shipping. However, little could be done to improve medical and sanitation conditions within Saudi Arabia or to mitigate extortions by *mutawwifs* (*shaykhs* who act as agents for pilgrims).

Transportation, welfare, and medical facilities have now been vastly improved, and the time and scope of the journey have been greatly reduced. Problems remain but these are relatively minor. The modern pilgrim travels in comfort by air, is supervised by Malay officials throughout the journey, and returned home promptly one month after departure.

In statistical terms, these improvements are mirrored by vast reductions in death and destitution figures. Destitution was never particularly high for Malays, who were long considered an affluent element of the *hajj* population. In the 1880s, the destitution rate for pilgrims was about 0.85 per cent. Since the Second World War, destitution is claimed to have been completely eradicated through increasingly severe government measures to restrict pilgrimage to those who are financially able to make the journey without jeopardising their own, or their families', financial security. Death rates have also declined dramatically since statistics first became available in the 1920s. At that time, rates fluctuated widely, peaking at roughly 13 per cent. By the 1950s, highs reached only 8.8 per cent. In the past fifteen years, the highest rate has been 3.7 per cent, and rates more often range between 1.5 per cent and 2 per cent.

Founded in 1969 as a division of the Ministry of National and Rural Development, LUTH has shown marked success in its welfare, financial, and developmental goals. It has particularly mobilised savings in the rural areas. Savings in kind, as opposed to cash, have greatly decreased, and selling land and other items to participate in the *hajj* has become a thing of the past. In addition, LUTH, through a policy of erecting large and prominent buildings in each district to underscore its solidity and prestige (and that of the *hajj*), has given visible proof that Muslim Malay needs are being addressed at the national political level. LUTH is thus playing a role in "Islamising" the peasantry and altering their perception of economic change.

Composition

An analysis of who participates in the pilgrimage is important for understanding the *hajj* as an agent of personal social mobility and change within Malay society.

In the past century, the social groups participating in the *hajj* have varied. In 1900, a typical pilgrim was a wealthy member of the traditional elite,[4] male, and elderly. By the 1920s, newly monied but not financially stable elderly peasants made up the bulk of pilgrims, with the increasing involvement of students and the emerging middle-class intelligentsia and elite. These trends were exaggerated in the next decades as the three groups – the traditional religious and secular elite; petty bureaucrats and their student sons; and elderly pensioners and peasants – became more clearly definable. In addition, women and younger students increasingly made the journey, as did pilgrims from urban centres. Within individual Malay states, rural areas experiencing rapid development appear to have sent the most pilgrims, whereas the poorest areas, least involved in economic and social change, continued to send the fewest pilgrims. There began to be evidence of urban pilgrims. The beginnings of a shift from the predominance of rural pilgrims to that of urban pilgrims reflected the general shift of the middle class from a rural to an urban setting – the son of a *penghulu* (lesser Malay chief or district level state bureaucrat) or a farmer, for example, who became a teacher or bureaucrat in the capital. In the process, rural middle-class expectations and symbols of legitimacy moved to the cities as well.

After the Second World War, these trends continued, and entire families began to be identified as middle class through the title *hajji*. As Malay power shifted to an urban setting, the *hajj* increasingly became urbanised. Indeed, as costs rose, the *hajj* became prohibitive for all but those whose participation in the cash economy was already substantial.

Since the 1960s, pilgrims have become equally rural and urban and predominantly middle class, middle aged, and relatively affluent. Most have ancestors who were involved in the *hajj*, and it is most popular among the new bureaucratic elite. It is a journey undertaken with spare funds and spare time, and, following its completion, there is no return to poverty as in previous years.

Half of the pilgrims today are women. Before the 1920s, there is no reference to women performing the *hajj*, but in the late 1930s, the numbers of women began to rise as it became more common for the peasant elite to take their entire families. A few wealthy women, having outlived their husbands, seemed to have performed the *hajj* on their own. By the mid-1940s, there are far more references to women performing the *hajj*. Some had undertaken the journey previously, while a number were widows whose husbands had previously gone to Mecca; most were the daughters of *hajjis*. These women tended to be younger than their male counterparts, and were largely from Kelantan. In the post-war period, as more families undertook the journey, the number of women increased, and it became popular for pregnant women to perform the *hajj* in the company of their husbands. In 1960, male and female participation drew even. Since then, female participation has markedly increased, exceeding male participation by 5 to 6 per cent. Only in Selangor are there still more male *bakal haji* (Malay term for an individual preparing to perform *hajj*).

Intellectual change

From the last decades of the nineteenth century until the second decade of the twentieth, the pilgrim spent long months in travel and often years in Arabia. He had a great deal of interaction with the *Jawah* (members of the Malayo-Polynesian language group resident in Mecca) community, and with teachers from among them and from a variety of Arab countries. He also had time for prayer, study, and induction into Sufism, generally choosing the Naqshbandi *tariqa* (order or brotherhood).

It is likely that he had been influenced by the Islamic revival then evident in Cairo and Mecca, through direct exposure, friends made on the journey, or literature disseminated from Singapore. Even had he remained for the minimum period in the Hijaz, he would have been exposed to the Islamic revival at work in Arabia – the revolutionary result of pan-Islamic and modernist trends – and to Wahhabi teachings. When combined with exposure to the hundreds of thousands of Muslims gathered together from all over the world and to anti-imperial propaganda, the Malay pilgrim may well have resolved to engage in further involvement in *tariqas*,[5] and co-operation with the vernacular-speaking, educated elite once he returned home. In turn, the enhanced status and influence of *hajjis* within the local community enabled these new ideas to gain wider validity and dissemination at the village level.

By the 1920s, the average stay was about six months and it was becoming more common for pilgrims to reside in Mecca permanently after retirement. Contact with the *Jawah* was strong, exposing the pilgrim to much of the political and intellectual turmoil that marked these years. Between 1919 and 1923, the troops of 'Abd al-'Aziz ibn Sa'ud, extending their hold throughout Arabia, left only Mecca and Jidda to their rivals. Yet even in these settings Wahhabi religious influence was gaining ascendance. A pilgrim would have been keenly aware of the new Wahhabi restrictions on his worship and actions in Medina, and to some extent in Mecca, and of the intensifying violence and extortion associated with venturing outside of Jidda.

From the Malay pilgrim's contacts with the *Jawah* community, his Malay-speaking *mutawwif*, and his mosque teachers, he would have learned of the growing anti-colonial and pan-Islamic movements in other Muslim countries and of Islamic modernist and reformist ideas. He may also have heard something of the increasing discontent of the Muslim peoples under western domination and of western ideas of democracy and self-determination (Roff 1974: 32–90).

In the period 1924 to 1945, both the number of *Jawah* and their contact with Malay pilgrims increased. Annual Pilgrimage Reports by Malayan colonial officers often noted the large number of pilgrims who yearly choose to remain several seasons or to retire permanently in Mecca. The stable *Jawah* population hovered between 500 and 600. Intellectual trends in the Hijaz, such as anti-colonialism and Wahhabism, were in general an intensification of those evident in earlier years, heightened by newly-won Saudi control of the Hijaz and by Wahhabi dominance.

Pilgrims had different levels of involvement with their surroundings during the *hajj*. The casual pilgrim would have had far less involvement in the issues of the day than an intellectual or a member of the traditional elite, interested in mixing with the leadership of Saudi society. Someone such as Hajji Abdul Karim,[6] the leader of Kampong Jawa, a village near Klang in the Malay State of Selangor, who remained to study in Mecca for several years, would have become far more involved with these intellectual trends than those remaining for only six months.

Since the end of the Second World War, the length of the *hajj* journey has shortened. Time and contact have been gradually reduced, so that the pilgrimage is now a controlled, four-week, packaged journey. The *Jawah* have decreased and cannot be augmented by new arrivals due to modern Saudi immigration restrictions. At the same time, there has been an expanded predisposition among Malay pilgrims to absorb the symbols, feelings, and ideas prevalent in Arabia. Pilgrims have been previously exposed to the beliefs held by the centre through the media and are

117

re-exposed through such vehicles as the annual pilgrimage address
given by the reigning Saudi king and through identification with the
larger Muslim community of which they are keenly aware, even if
involvement can be only superficial. In the pre-independence
period, Malay nationalism was especially important and had certain
affinities with Arab nationalism. Today, in Saudi Arabia, the
pilgrim is confronted by a powerful Muslim state – conservative,
moderate, modern, and opposed to radical tendencies within Islam.
Although the *bakal haji* does not study in Saudi Arabia, he studies
before the *hajj* and already understands a great deal about the centre
of the Muslim world through the media. What is transferred now is
a predisposition to be a good Muslim by emulating Saudi Arabian
orthopraxy and Saudi Arabian political moderation.

External change

Before the late 1930s, the length of the journey, the advanced age
of the pilgrims, and the extreme physical deprivations and hardships encountered allowed the returned pilgrim to bear little resem-
blance to the man who had departed. He was physically and
financially exhausted and often returned home to a life spent in
dependence on family and neighbours – if he returned home at all.
This pilgrim had saved all his life for this journey and often accomplished it by selling his land or his home. In expectation of death,
or at least of a lengthy absence followed by change significant
enough to preclude return to his former life, the pilgrim paid his
debts, settled old scores, and put his worldly affairs in order.
Pilgrimage was often undertaken at particular life junctures – after
finishing school, before marriage, upon retirement, or with the
approach of death. Before departure, he consulted a *bomoh* (traditional Malay medical practitioner or curer) to determine an
auspicious day and time for departure, gave a *khenduri* (communal
meal) to bid goodbye to his friends and to pray for a safe journey,
and, relatively confident that these would keep him from harm, did
not look back as he left his home. A large crowd accompanied him
to the wharf.

The returning pilgrim was severely changed. He was likely to be
dressed in new Arab garments, and his physical appearance altered
by the privations of his lengthy absence. He would have been
addressed with the prestigious and respectful title of *hajji* or even
shaykh (if he had purchased a license to recruit pilgrims). As the
new *hajjis* – who had formed powerful bonds through shared
experience under strained circumstances – made their farewells to
one another, they would have addressed each other by their new

Arab names, giving the waiting crowd of relatives further reason to wonder whether these were in fact the same people seen off a year earlier. Back in the village, the pilgrim would have been welcomed home by a *khenduri* and honours. If he had sold his land to finance the journey, he would now have to live on charity or become an itinerant religious wise man, communally supported by virtue of his new status.

In succeeding years, the Saudi Arabian and Malayan governments have worked to reduce the time spent on the *hajj*, to improve its conditions, to circumscribe movement within Saudi Arabia and contact with non-Malays, and to lessen the financial hardships associated with the journey. Today, the pilgrim leaves his old life only briefly and returns physically and financially unchanged. The physical changes engendered earlier as outward symbols of internal change no longer exist. He saves through LUTH and rarely sells anything to make the journey. He has also received no new concrete knowledge and has little chance to absorb alien experiences or enjoy prolonged contact with Muslims from different backgounds. He is isolated among Malays and significantly buffered from the alien environment.

None the less, his preparations today are more elaborate. He attends pre-*hajj* classes, and performs extra prayers and fasts. Registration procedures force him to begin thinking about and planning for the journey a year in advance. New and elaborate travel wardrobes are sewn. As departure nears, a *khenduri* is arranged at which friends and relatives often give monetary gifts, and weeks are spent visiting friends in neighbouring towns. While preparations are lengthy and elaborate, they no longer include putting one's worldly affairs in order in anticipation of death. Rituals associated with long and unsafe journeys are rarely performed and consultations with a *bomoh* are less usual for the average pilgrim. However, the mystical associations with Mecca is still evident, even among well-educated, modern, urban-dwellers.[7]

As in the past, a large crowd gathers to see the pilgrim off. On his return, a brief four weeks later, he wears Arab clothing, may have a beard, and often bears a new Arab name. *Hajji* is today an official form of address and is inevitably adopted as part of the individual's formal name. A woman's head is usually covered once she has become a *hajja*. Although returned pilgrims may later revert to Malay dress, a small beard for men and a head covering for women may be retained. These remain as external signs, although physical, financial, and intellectual changes have greatly lessened in recent times. In a society where it is increasingly important, politically and psychologically, to be identified as a good Muslim, these outward symbols of having been on the *hajj* and achieved religious status are increasingly desirable. The pilgrim is seen as the dispenser of *berkat* (blessings) and is fêted and visited for several weeks on return. Although many more persons in a locale have performed the *hajj* than was previously the case, *hajjis* still receive great respect, even though outward manifestations of this often depend on the individual pilgrim's socio-economic status.

Internal change

Perhaps the most elusive aspect of this transformation is inner, personal change, which was assumed by others to result from the journey and entailed more than the respect or admiration attributable to association with an elite activity. That it was assumed an individual became internally holy and religious and somehow a better person is clear from his elevation within society, not just as a more worldly person who had travelled beyond the village confines, but as a wise and holy person, sanctified by his experience, and therefore possessed of both the duty and the power to influence the thinking and deeds of other villagers.

Of the period before 1920 we have little indication of how the individual felt as a result of his experience, and no sense of his expectations. There were intimations that a person may have undertaken the *hajj* in thanksgiving, especially following an illness. *Hajj* was also associated with atonement, a linkage strong enough to have been transformed into legal precedent and accepted by British courts. To sentence a criminal to perform the *hajj* was seen to serve the same rehabilitary purposes as a prison term.[8] Moreover, we are told by observers such as Hurgronje (1931) that pilgrims are emotionally affected by such sights as the Masjid al-Haram. Written accounts of the *hajj* presented the experience in terms of an outward experience and of *kerajaan* (symbolic nationhood or kingdom), not in terms of personal, inner change. However, unanalysed emotionalism was recorded, as was association with magic and *berkat*.

By the mid-1920s, there began to be evidence of the internal transformations associated with the *hajj* that the individual had undergone – partly because this was the first period to produce detailed, first-hand accounts of the pilgrimage process. We learn that the *hajj* was associated with both real and symbolic death, and real and symbolic rebirth. Hj. Abdul Majid bin Zainuddin, the first Malay Pilgrimage Officer (MPO) who served from 1924 to 1939, attested to the auspiciousness of death in the Holy Land while in a state free from sin as a result of the pilgrimage rituals (see Abdul Majid 1926).

The pilgrim prepared himself as if he expected to die, and performed rituals marking important junctures in the Malay life cycle. His journey cleansed him of the sins of his old life and prepared him for a reformed life – accounting perhaps for his acceptance as wise and holy upon his return.

By the late 1930s, and increasingly following the Second World War, pilgrims seem to have become concerned with the prestige they would gain from the journey. Harun Aminurrashid, a prominent nationalist and teacher at the Sultan Idris College, in his *hajj* account (Matheson and Milner 1985: 25–6), is clearly concerned "for the status gained within Malay society by undertaking [the] *hajj*", and with the title "Hajji" or "al-Haj". *Hajj* is seen as a symbol of "Muslimness" and "Malayness", which were becoming increasingly inseparable, but he also describes it as an interior experience. Internal expectations of change appear to be associated with social mobility, cultural and political identity, prestige, and a sense of belonging.

The analysis of data from a survey, combined with in-depth interviews that I conducted between 1981 and 1984, has allowed internal expectations and transformations to be better apprehended for a wider range of pilgrims.[9] The *hajj* seems no longer to represent simply an external juncture in a pilgrim's life. It is not undertaken at any particular time relative to the human life cycle. However, it appears increasingly to be related to an internal spiritual juncture that occurs at a point when a variety of social, political, and personal pressures make the individual susceptible to government encouragement of a journey that would reaffirm cultural identity. Interviews indicate that people have very definite expectations with respect to internal and external changes in their lives as a result of undertaking the *hajj*. In general, they expect to be closer to Allah, to be more knowledgeable about Islam, to be a better person, and to be honoured within their community upon their return. They feel the journey will free them from vices and negative emotions (impatience, jealousy, hatred), help them to be less materialistic and pray better, and enable them to give a better example to the community. The status that will accrue to them is also important, as evidenced by the high interest that they show in the outward symbols of their inwardly-altered condition, such as: the title "Hajji"; Arab clothing; facial hair; and change of name. In essence, *hajjis* expect to be perceived by others as better Muslims, to behave as such, and, in fact, to be better Muslims.

Pilgrims also discuss an intense feeling of belonging to a community of Muslims. The communal bond developed during the journey is still strong, although perhaps it is now perceived more in relation to the Malay community. Because the *hajj* is performed within an almost wholly Malay context, shepherded and buffered by Malay officials, it is seen as a shared national experience as well as a religious one.

Personal change: motivation, mobility, and Muslim self-identity

The fact that, in some basic sense, individuals conceive of the notion to perform the *hajj* because they are enjoined to do so by Qur'anic prescription (22: 91) does not explain why some individuals choose to do so and some do not (see Eickelman and Piscatori, Chapter 1 of this volume). It does not explain why even those not enjoined to perform the *hajj* (individuals who are financially or physically unable to endure the journey) often feel compelled to embark, or why pilgrimage to Mecca is particularly popular among the groups described during certain historical periods. It offers few clues as to why individuals choose to perform the *hajj* at a particular time in their lives. Motivational patterns are involved with both "ability" and "desire", and increasingly with government manipulation of these factors.

In the decision to perform the *hajj*, ability must coincide with desire. In the nineteenth century, this desire was fostered by contact with Singapore – the archipelago's focal point for Islamic intellectual activity and information disseminated from the Middle East – by a growing cultural insecurity in response to increased alien immigration; by the general expansion of colonial domination over Malay life; and by the possibility of upward mobility upon return from the *hajj*. Desire, economic ability, and increased opportunity would generally have been present in a man who already enjoyed some status in the community and wished now to add religious status to his financial, educational, or political status in order to legitimise it. In effect, the *hajj* made those already respected and part of the power structure respected in a new way.

As vernacular education increased, Islamic modernism gained a wider audience, including a dissatisfied new elite, which, though having emerged from the upper levels of the peasantry, and newly monied, was unable to put its new skills to work in jobs commensurate with its new status. In these circumstances, the *hajj* acted as both a step in the search for increased social mobility and a form of rebellion in response to the cultural threat posed by foreign domination and alien immigration. Indeed, the importance of Islam and of the *hajj* as a symbol of "Muslimness" was growing as a sign of Malay power and Malay cultural identity.

For the traditional elite, the *hajj* continued to reaffirm traditional status in the early decades of the twentieth century. For the peasant who undertook the *hajj*, his status was increased in a rural setting. His short-term economic position may have suffered, however, as he generally sold his land before the journey and returned penniless. For the new intellectuals, whose desire to undertake the *hajj* and to increase their status was affected by expanded educational opportunities provided by the colonial government without matching opportunity, and by an increasing threat to an intensified Malay–Muslim identity, the *hajj* was coming to symbolise and affirm middle-class status.

By the mid-1920s, students returned to a new range of jobs as a result of skills acquired abroad and of their newfound aura of Muslim orthodoxy. Many who went to the Middle East for education joined, upon their return, Islamic reformist or modernist groups (Roff 1974: 56–90). They became part of Malaya's Middle-Eastern-educated intelligentsia, for whom the search for identity was involved with pressures associated with Malay nationalism. Those who, through education and jobs, were already part of the emerging middle class were legitimised by the *hajj* experience within an expanding setting as the scope of Malay power broadened. For the first time, elderly pensioners and peasants were able to perform the *hajj en masse*, the former owing partly to governmental subsidy. These grants were not numerous and were provided on a case-by-case basis to individuals deemed "deserving" via a screening process. Criteria changed over the life of the system, which began in 1921 and seems to have continued through the 1950s. It was initially a state, rather than a national, system and was generally confined to employees of the individual state and, later, of the national government. Beneficiaries of this system, and of the general economic prosperity of the period, returned to an enhanced status within village life, and participated in the formation of a Malay economic middle class.

The post-war, pre-independence years saw a wider scope for personal mobility after performance of the *hajj*. This was due to the wider involvement of Malays in government, growing nationalist aspirations, and the expansion of both the secular and religious bureaucracies in response to the need for Malays to widen their role within "the Contract" – the multi-party, multi-racial agreement that led to Malaysia's independence from Britain in 1957. Evolution towards independence increased the power and prestige associated with religion and the role of Islam in society, and of *hajjis* in particular, as Malay participation in government intensified. The association of wealth and the prestige connected with religion began to take on new importance as a way not only of becoming middle class, but as a means of validating that achievement. It became possible to achieve upper-class status through political and economic power rather than birthright, if that power was validated by its linkage with sources of traditional prestige – religion and the Islamic centre – and thus seemed moral. Pilgrimage legitimised wealth and, while they had been associated for centuries elsewhere (see El Moudden, Chapter 4 of this volume), religion, commerce, industry, and politics now seemed to go hand in hand in Malaysia as well.

Since the 1960s, the *hajj* has continued to provide traditional rural social mobility. In addition, it provides access to power for the bureaucratic middle-class elite, especially for those whose economic and educational prestige is already intact. While government workers are by no means the majority of *bakal haji*, pilgrims are well and increasingly represented in the top echelons of the civil service. In the 1980s, not only is it popular for top echelon bureaucrats in government and public corporations to perform the *hajj*, but it is increasingly popular for their immediate juniors – having seen the Director-General or Minister, on his return from Mecca, placing "Hajji" or "al-Haj" on his office-door nameplate – to perform the *hajj* themselves. The *hajj* performance by top government officials during political crises at home is also becoming increasingly common.

While it is difficult to tell whether individuals perform the *hajj* to achieve power or whether people rise to power who have gone on the *hajj*, or who are of the type to have the predisposition to go, it is evident that the *hajj* has become a part of the national power configuration. In recent years, the ruling Malay party, the United Malay Nationalist Organisation (UMNO) has accepted that the *hajj*, as a symbol of orthopraxy, must be encouraged if it, and the government, are to succeed within the Malay community. The *hajj* is particularly encouraged in order to stem *dakwah*-type fundamentalism, and in begrudging recognition of the powerful pressures and forces at work in modern Malaysian society that have allowed the *dakwah* movement to prosper (Nagata 1984). As the secular elite that inherited independence a quarter of a century ago is being transformed to meet these new political and personal challenges, seeming to be a better Muslim has become synonymous with being a better Malay and citizen. "Muslimness" and "Malayness" have become intimately connected now, whereas, in the 1880s, Islam was but one element in a traditional Malay prestige system.

Given that the *hajj* has become fashionable among the secular, urban, middle class – who are coming to see Islam, prestige, and upward mobility as going hand in hand – we see that an individual can view himself as a member of several groups at once. He can be Malay, Muslim, and a PhD. He can perhaps remain attached to certain concepts associated with his animist past while being a competent, well-educated lawyer or politician. These simultaneous identities may not exist in any hierarchy. Rather, ideas, decisions, and reactions may depend on which identity is predominantly operative in a given situation. The identities appear, moreover, to co-exist without being perceived by the individual as contradictory.

Social change: becoming "more" Muslim

In the late nineteenth century, growing numbers of more orthopraxic Muslims, exposed to modernist ideas, and the increasing influence of these prestigious persons over community life, planted the seeds of later political, economic, and religious changes. The vehicles for dissemination of these currents of intellectual change were: the intellectual life of Cairo initially (and of Mecca after 1882); the *Jawah* community; the pilgrims, students, teachers, and *tariqa shaykhs*; and the Islamic community of Singapore. The growing desire to perform the *hajj* led to economic change through the greater involvement of peasants in the colonial cash economy in order to acquire the ready cash for a journey bound up with prestige and upward social mobility.

By the early decades of the twentieth century, the transformation within the traditional elite from a secular to an increasingly Islamic orientation – which was just beginning in the pre-1910 period – continued to be evident. A certain politicisation of this newly orthopraxic elite emerged as secular power was usurped by the colonial government, and, in this context, the *hajj* became involved in the growth of Malay nationalism. In economic terms, the *hajj* was involved in the evolution – just discernible in this period – of both a Malay–Muslim middle class and its intellectual leadership. The former rose from the ranks of the newly cash-conscious peasantry, and the latter from among the newly educated young members of the traditional upper strata of peasant society.

Between the late 1920s and the Second World War, the *hajj* was involved with legitimising the traditional elite, creating a new economic middle class from among the peasantry, and legitimising the growing and discontented elite of this emerging Malay–Muslim middle class. The *hajj* also altered the fabric of Malay society by raising its orthopraxic component as increased proportions of the Muslim population performed it in the Wahhabi and reformist

125

atmosphere of this decade. In this climate, the *hajj* began to create a more uniform Islamic dimension to Malay identity.

As nationalism matured, roughly in the period between the 1920s and independence in 1957, there appeared to be a strong relationship between time spent at the Muslim centre and social and political discontent upon return. Currently, contact with the centre seems to lead, on return, to dissatisfaction with one's own personal, interior, spiritual life, but not with the larger social and political world. This may be because the Malaysian government encourages interaction with the centre and is perceived (largely through LUTH) as having concern for the well-being and needs of Muslims. Moreover, because the centre is non-revivalist, the centre and the periphery espouse a similar view of Islam at present. The *dakwah* revivalist movement is thus not viewed by the average Malay *hajji* as being representative of the view at the centre and deserving of emulation. The political and social discontent manifested in the *dakwah* movement clearly does not appear to be related to contact with the Hijaz.

The journey to the centre is creating increasing numbers of orthopraxic individuals who are concerned with being better Muslims within the context of a common interpretation of Islam currently acceptable to the guardians of the centre – i.e. the Saudi royal family – and the federal government of Malaysia. A "more" Muslim society is evolving, a society determined to perceive itself as increasingly Muslim and to behave in what is commonly identified as a "good" Muslim manner. In the process, however, this society has become more susceptible to manipulation and control through a commonly approved Islamic idiom.

Notes

1 This chapter is about patterns. The sources from which the patterns have been deduced vary over the hundred year period covered by the inquiry. Materials were collected and analysed over a three-year period using a variety of methodologies including archival research in London and Kuala Lumpur, in-depth interviews in two carefully chosen villages in the Malaysian states of Kelantan and Selangor and survey research. Written sources included both primary and secondary materials such as British and Malaysian government records and files, published memoirs and texts, and unpublished theses and papers.

For the earliest periods discussed, information about pilgrims and pilgrimage can be found primarily in published memoirs and eyewitness accounts, in the records of the British Foreign and Colonial Offices, especially CO273 (1869–1912), FO685 (1859–1887), FO368 (1909–1918), and in the reports of British Consuls stationed at Jidda.

By the late 1920s, indigenous Malayan sources become richer and much information can be found in the reports of the Malayan Pilgrimage Officer; the annual administrative reports for the Federated and Unfederated Malay States (FMS and UFMS); federal and state establishment lists; the ordinances and legal codes of the straits settlements, the FMS, the UFMS, and the individual Malay States; the federal and state census reports; and the state and district level records of Kelantan and Selangor. FO686 (1917–1925), FO905 (1934–1947), FO371 (1906–1950), and CO727 (1922–1923) remain helpful. Written sources for the past twenty years come mostly from the files and records of the Malaysian pilgrimage regulatory organisation, Lembaga Urusan dan Tabung Haji, from articles in the indigenous press and from the annual reports of officials involved with regulating pilgrimage. Personal interviews (1981–4) and a survey conducted in 1981 (see note 9) account for much of the descriptive material in the most recent period and provide the basis for analysis, particularly concerning questions of pilgrimage composition and of personal and social change.

2 The term "overseas pilgrims" is commonly used to define pilgrims not from the Islamic "heartlands". It may sometimes have meant pilgrims arriving at Jidda by sea. The term is used throughout the relevant historical literature. In 1981, the figure for overseas pilgrims was 322,621 according to LUTH statistics.

3 In the late nineteenth and early twentieth centuries, European interest in the conduct of the *hajj* centred on health concerns. In the decade between 1910 and 1923, some colonial officials viewed sanitation problems in the Hijaz and on shipboard as the main reason for regulating the Muslim pilgrimage. Others were concerned that anti-colonial, nationalist stirrings in the Middle East would be transmitted to the colonies. This tendency to equate pilgrims with anti-colonial subversion was less strong in Malaya than in Indonesia or India. Nevertheless, the first Malay Pilgrimage Officer, assigned in 1924, was under the direction of the Political Intelligence Bureau of the Criminal Investigation Division of the Police Department of the Federated Malay States. Ten duties were outlined for him – with intelligence gathering while in the Hijaz being far down on the list. His appointment called attention to the relationship between the *hajj*, Islamic orthodoxy, and political discontent.

4 The term "traditional elite" refers to those who governed Malay society prior to and (under supervision) during the colonial era. Sometimes, although not necessarily, members of this group were involved in the diverse federal bureaucratic structures. The term is still common today. It includes members of the various royal families, their staffs, and retainers, *kathis*, *penghulus*, and magistrates. It also includes individuals who have received various royal titles such as "Dato" and "Tan Sri".

5 There is strong evidence that *tariqa* induction was especially popular for pilgrims from the Malay archipelago. A nineteenth-century observer provides lengthy discussion of this and of the complex interconnections between *tariqa shaykhs* in Mecca, their representatives in the East Indies, *Jawah* members of the brotherhoods and pilgrims in both Mecca and

after their return home (see Hurgronje 1931: 215–92). The emotional bonds established during the pilgrimage journey fostered a feeling of oneness with Islam and of identification with the greater Muslim world. *Tariqa* induction and participation upon return home provided a means of continued communion with the Muslim centre. In addition it appealed to Malay Muslims whose personal Islam found roots in a syncretic past. There is also much evidence that *tariqas* played an important role in the development of the Kaum Muda Islamic reformist movement, which in turn played an important role in the early development of Malay nationalism (Roff 1974: 56–60).

6 Ketua Kampong (village headman), Hajji Abdul Karim bin Hajj M. Noor of Kampong Jawa, Selangor, performed *hajj* in 1927 and remained to study. While residing at Kampong Jawa, in the home of one of his daughters, I interviewed Hajji Karim on this topic on numerous occasions between August and December 1981.

7 Evidence of this is generally anecdotal. It is important to understand that modern, sophisticated, educated Malaysians continue to recognise a variety of spiritual and mystical occurrences. Illustrative examples are common in daily life. As noted in note 5, Islam in Malaysia is tied up with both indigenous and Sufi mysticism, the latter often carried directly from Mecca via the *hajj*. Despite LUTH efforts to eradicate the practice and to divorce the Malay interpretation of Islam from "pre-Islamic, animist" beliefs, both peasants and university lecturers occasionally consult *bomohs* before departure on the *hajj*. Previously, consultation with a *bomoh* was considered normal and acceptable. It is now officially frowned upon and occurs less frequently. Stories of individuals undergoing mystical transformations which produce tangible economic consequences following the *hajj* are not uncommon. In addition, there is a strong association between Mecca, the *hajj* as the reference point for entrance into the world of Mecca, and the importation into Malaysia of *toyols*, a type of spirit believed to come to Malaysia via the *hajj*. This spirit is thought to produce economic prosperity for its owner. Belief in this spirit is as strong among educated urban dwellers as among villagers.

8 By the second decade of the twentieth century, requests to proceed to Mecca, in lieu of serving a jail term, were so numerous that they began to be refused on the grounds that too many criminals were avoiding prison punishment, preferring the journey to Mecca to atone for their social transgressions: K473/14; BAK "M" 64/19. BAK refers to the files of the British Advisor to Kelantan which are available at the Arkib Negara, Kuala Lumpur. There are also numerous examples of this association in current daily life. Political figures released from prison will head for Mecca to become reborn in the eyes of their constituencies. The same is true of individuals who somehow fall from political grace. Some people may perform *hajj* or *'umra* following an accident or illness or other misfortune. For example, former Foreign Minister Tan Sri Ghazali Shafie undertook the journey following the January 1982 crash of his private plane in which he was the sole survivor. The crash took place amidst

rumours of improper behaviour which threatened to ruin the minister's political career. Public opinion considered his journey to Mecca as an appropriate element in his political rehabilitation and, despite the controversy surrounding the crash, he was renamed to his cabinet position following the April 1982 elections.

9 The survey was conducted at the Kelantan and Selangor airports as pilgrims departed for the 1981 *hajj*. My hope was to obtain information on pilgrims' socio-economic backgrounds, feelings, expectations, fears and desires with respect to the pilgrimage experience. The information was intended to supplement archival and in-depth interview data. Statistically appropriate quantities were chosen, given the numbers of 1981 pilgrims registered for the *hajj* from these states. The total sample contained approximately 1,400 pilgrims. Kelantan and Selangor were chosen as opposite ends of the rural–urban scale, and as extreme representations of divergent colonial experiences within British Malaya. In addition, Kelantan has historically sent large numbers of pilgrims and has been the centre of Partai Islam politics in Malaysia and of the *dakwah* Islamic revival in recent decades.

References

Abdul Karim ibn Hajj Muhammad Noor, Interviews, August–December 1981 at Kg. Jawa, Selangor, Malaysia.

Abdul Majid (1926) 'A Malay pilgrimage to Mecca', *Journal of the Malaysian Branch of the Royal Asiatic Society*, 4, part 2, pp. 269–87.

British Foreign Office (F0371) on Arabia, 1906–50, available at Public Record Office, London.

British Advisor to Kelantan (BAK files), available at Arkib Negara, Kuala Lumpur.

Hurgronje, C.S. (1931) *Mekka in the Latter Part of the 19th Century*, Brill, Leyden.

Kelantan Prime Minister's Department (K files), available at Arkib Negara, Kuala Lumpur.

LUTH Annual Reports, 1971–82, available at LUTH Headquarters, Kuala Lumpur.

Matheson, V. and Milner, A. (1985) *Perceptions of the Hajj: Five Malay Texts*, Institute for Southeast Asian Studies, Singapore.

McDonnell, M.B. (1986) 'The conduct of the hajj from Malaysia and its socio-economic impact on Malay society: a descriptive and analytical study, 1860–1981', unpublished PhD thesis, Columbia University. Please see this study for details of the interviews and archival materials on which this chapter is based.

Nagata, J. (1984) *The Reflowering of Malaysian Islam*, University of British Columbia Press, Vancouver.

Qur'an, trans. R. Bell (1939) T. & T. Clark, Edinburgh.

Roff, W.R. (1974) *Origins of Malay Nationalism*, Penerbit Universiti Malaya, Kuala Lumpur.

Survey conducted September 1981 at Kelantan Airport and Subang International Airport in Kuala Lumpur.

Chapter seven

The *hijra* from Russia and the Balkans: the process of self-definition in the late Ottoman state

Kemal H. Karpat

Introduction

This chapter deals with the identity change among those Muslims living in an area that corresponds more or less to the Ottoman territories in the Balkans, Caucasus, Anatolia, northern Iraq, and Syria. In these regions, the most significant change in social identity in the last decades of the Ottoman empire was defined by the migration, self-defined as *hijra*, which originated in European areas of the empire and had as its destination the Ottoman provinces of Asia. This migration may be regarded as a continuous process that extended over a period of roughly sixty-five years from approximately 1850 to 1914. Intensive mass movements of the European Muslim population occurred in the period 1862–5 and again in 1878 in the face of coercive measures by Russia and Bulgaria. Both before and after these periods of mass exodus, smaller groups moved steadily from Slavic lands towards Anatolia.

The "Muslim" identity of these populations consisted outwardly of certain objective symbols and acts such as names and rituals, through which an individual related himself to a group or community that called itself Muslim. The actual active practice of the faith did not appear to be necessary for one to consider himself Muslim, nor was it a precondition for his acceptance by his Muslim group. For the average Muslims in the groups I have studied, the *besmele* (Arabic, *bismallah*, ritual invocation of God's name) and *kelime-i shehadet* (Arabic, *shahada*, profession of the faith), if seemingly sincere and expressing serious commitment to the faith, were considered sufficient proof of one's identity as a Muslim. (Of course, fasting during Ramadan and the observance of other Muslim rites were additional proofs.)

It will be my contention, first, that at the place of origin the migrants tended to identify themselves with Islam in terms of social behaviour and ritual rather than in terms of a political system;

131

second, that the process of migration transformed this relatively passive communal Muslim identity into a more dynamic political consciousness by enlarging its geographic and ideological scope; and, third, that the process of migration not only changed the original communal Muslim identity of the migrants but also helped to politicise the identity of Muslims in the areas to which they went.

The historical migrations: a brief sketch

Migrations into the Ottoman state began at the time of Russia's annexation of Crimea in 1783. Muslims began to leave their ancestral homes largely because they desired to live under the authority of a Muslim ruler rather than under the Russian Orthodox Czar, but there were compelling economic reasons as well. As the Russian presence in Crimea increased, Muslim peasants became the tenants of new Russian landlords, who tried to maximise their income by bearing hard on the cultivators. The peasants and, eventually, the Muslim aristocrats, who had served in the Czar's administration until their places were taken by Russians, found salvation in emigration. Emigration intensified after the wars of 1806–12 and 1829, especially after the Crimean war of 1853–6, since the Muslims had supported the Ottoman and allied armies in the hope of regaining their old autonomy and independence. After 1812, the Russian authorities, caught in the political–religious fervour of orthodoxy, increasingly sought to rid themselves of the Muslim population by encouraging or forcing emigration (Karpat 1984–5). The last gasp of this policy came as late as 1944, when the entire Muslim population of Crimea, including Communists and partisans who fought the Germans in 1941–3, were forcibly uprooted and sent to central Asia.

A major wave of emigration from the Caucasus – which reached its peak after 1862 – began after the anti-Russian resistance of the Muridists led by Shaykh Shamil was finally crushed in 1859. This Caucasian migration, which continued well into the twentieth century, is sometimes referred to as the Cherkes, or Circassian, migration, but it actually involved a great variety of groups that were ethnically and linguistically unrelated to each other.

The last large wave of migrants came from the Balkans after the Turco-Russian war of 1877–8 and the Balkan war of 1912–13. The Muslim population of the Balkans, which was a majority in many areas, was parcelled among various new non-Muslim nation-states in the area as these were broken off from the empire, and in each case the Muslims were immediately encouraged or forced to emigrate. Serbia had begun expelling the Muslims after it acquired a degree of autonomy in 1815; Greece, Bulgaria, and Romania followed in 1878, 1892, and 1913 respectively. Albania declared its independence in 1912 in order to avoid being incorporated into Serbia, which had already seized most of Macedonia and its huge Muslim population, consisting of Albanians in Kosovo and Turks in Uskup (Skopje).

The total number of people immigrating into the Ottoman Empire between 1860 and 1914 was approximately five to seven million. The Ottoman statistics indicate that the total population of the country rose by about 40 per cent in the period 1860–78 and by about 10 per cent to almost the end of the century. As the Ottoman birth rate during this period was barely 1.2 per cent, the conclusion that the growth of population was due chiefly to immigration is inescapable (Karpat 1985).

Behind these migrations, in addition to the political–historical causes already cited, lay another reason: the practice of *hijra* itself. As Masud shows in Chapter 2 of this volume, the concept of *hijra* has exercised a profound influence on Muslim thought and practice over the centuries. It is thus not surprising that it became an intrinsic part of the Ottoman intellectual heritage. But the special position of the Ottoman sultan as the caliph of all the Muslims – the idea of a universal caliphate was politically revived in the nineteenth century – and the insertion of a clause in various treaties signed with Russia and the Hapsburgs, allowing Muslims in those territories to declare allegiance to the caliph in their Friday prayers, greatly enhanced the position of the Ottoman Empire as a centre and a haven open to all Muslims. This principle was given new meaning in the late 1880s, when the sultan was persuaded to declare the empire open to all Muslims who wanted to migrate and settle there. In sum, the Muslims living on the periphery of the empire, who were faced by threats to their cultural existence and material welfare, sought salvation by moving closer to the centre – whose attraction and importance had risen in proportion to the weakness of the periphery.

It should be noted, however, that more than one centre was envisaged. Although Muslims of Russia and the Balkans preferred Ottoman lands for historical, political, and religious reasons, the empire was not always the final destination for all Muslims. The religious elites – notably from central Asia, Afghanistan, and the Caucasus – brought the *hijra* to its natural conclusion by migrating to, and settling in, Mecca and Medina where many of their descendants, although "Arabised", survive as a distinct group today. It is essential to point out, however, that for the Muslims of central Asia the *hajj* was considered somewhat incomplete without a stop, sometimes for years, in Istanbul. The multi-sided cultural and political significance of this "second-tier *hajj*" deserves a full study.

The migrants

The migrants were extraordinarily diverse in social, ethno-linguistic, and historical background. The Crimeans spoke their own Turkic (Tatar) dialect, as did two or three of the groups from the Caucasus, and this dialect was divided into several sub-dialects. The Caucasian groups – the Cherkes, Chechen, Abkhazians, and Georgians, among others – who were not racially or linguistically related to Turks, spoke a variety of languages. The bulk of the immigrants from the Balkans were ethnic Turks and spoke the Rumilian dialect, but among the Balkan migrants there were also large groups of Slavic-speaking Bosnians, Herzegovinians, Montenegrins, and Pomaks. Many Cretan Muslims spoke Greek, and the Albanians their own tongue.

Most of them, however, shared two characteristics. The first was a tribal background. In their place of origin the Caucasian migrants had lived under the authority of tribal chiefs and feudal lords. Only in Daghestan had the fundamentalist, egalitarian, anti-Russian movement of Gazi Molla and Shaykh Shamil, known as Muridism, created a degree of unity and a sense of Muslim identity that superseded tribal loyalties and identities. This was possible because of the struggle against the common enemy, the Russians. The same sort of tribal affiliation prevailed also in most of the rural areas of Crimea, although here the Khanate had fostered a degree of political awareness and Islam had been accepted much earlier than in the Caucasus, so that the various groups felt a high degree of religious and, to a lesser extent, political identification. Moreover, the Crimeans included a highly developed merchant group linked to the old aristocracy and inhabiting the coastal areas; with them tribal affiliations were weak, while among the peasants in the interior, tribal loyalties were strong. The Slavic-speaking Bosnians in the rural areas were under the authority of their own feudal lords, who had bitterly fought the Ottoman centralisation policy in the 1840s in order to preserve their autonomy. Many of these feudal lords had, at the time the province was conquered in 1463, accepted Islam as the new faith; it supposedly was close to their native faith of Bogomilism, a mixture of Christianity, paganism, and Manicheism. In doing so, they hoped to preserve their land holdings and ethnic identity. The Albanians and Montenegrins had preserved their old tribal mores, although these were considerably weakened over the centuries under the joint impact of Islam and Ottoman political culture.

The groups that had developed a degree of political–ethnic consciousness prior to their conversion to Islam tended to maintain it after conversion. This was notably true in the case of the Muslim Slavs, especially the Bosnians, who had their own kingdom prior to its conquest by Mehmet II in 1463. The Albanians, the oldest people in the region, who had lived under various rulers and feudal lords, also maintained a degree of ethnic consciousness. The sense of ethnic identity of the non-Turkic groups in the Balkans was expressed, prior to migration, in a negative manner: they insisted that they were Muslims but not Osmanlis (Turks), but this sense of separateness appeared not to have had any political significance. It is essential to stress the fact that, except for the Crimeans, none of these groups identified itself with a Muslim political state of its own prior to migration. Among the Crimeans, the memory of independent statehood had become blurred during Ottoman rule, despite the fact that their aristocracy and the ruling dynasty preserved a sense of historical continuity. Thus, it may be stated that before their migration into the heartlands of the Ottoman state, most of these Muslims identified themselves with their tribe and ethnic groups, while Islam provided principally a norm for social behaviour and secondarily an identity source.

The situation in sections of the Caucasus was different, however. There, Islam was the most important source of identity change prior to migration – mainly due to particular socio-economic and political forces at work. Initially, the highly diversified tribal society of the north-east, known as Daghistan desired to preserve its traditional social organisation, which ranged from democratically self-governing communities to feudal lordships and slave trading. Muridism, which started late in the eighteenth century, was initially a conservative resistance force against Russian occupation but soon changed its ideological content. It became a Sunni fundamentalist Islamic movement for social justice that called for the liberation of the peasants from feudal servitude and the elimination of old, barbaric traditions. Transformed rapidly into a populist mass movement, it was joined later by the *beys* of Circassia and other feudal lords, who decided that the Muridists could better serve their interests than the Russian occupiers. The Muridists were instrumental in converting many animist tribes to Islam and in sharpening the Islamic consciousness of the adherents to a degree hardly known elsewhere in the Islamic world, notably under the leadership of Shaykh Shamil in the period 1834 to 1859.

In the Caucasus, therefore, Islam became a rallying point for political mobilisation and a militant movement that helped it become rooted as a religion. In this, it was immeasurably aided by the Naqshbandi *tarikat* (Arabic, *tariqa*, brotherhood or order), the dominant Sufi order in the Caucasus. Its worldly, politically militant attitude was to a great extent conditioned by the events in the Caucasus, for most of the Muridist leaders, including Shaykh Shamil, were Naqshbandis. Indeed, Caucasian migrants were in good measure responsible for strengthening the Naqshbandi movement in the Ottoman state and in Turkey.

For the overwhelming majority of Muslims in the Balkans, despite the fact that most of them were living on the border of the Islamic world facing a hostile European–Christian world, Islam remained apolitical until they were uprooted. Their passive cultural–religious consciousness was easily converted to a dynamic Muslim identity when the circumstances required; however, in general, until the migration occurred, the Islamic identity of these Muslims was reflected largely in non-political rites and social practices.

The second common characteristic shared by the migrants was the Ottoman political culture.[1] This culture was Islamic in origin, but in practice it aimed at creating a social and political order in accordance with the ethnic and religious realities of the entire population of the realm. It began to evolve as early as the fifteenth century when Sultans Mehmed II (AD 1451–81) and Suleyman the Lawgiver (AD 1520–66) laid the foundation for it through a variety of *kanunnames*, or edicts issued by the ruler and not forming part of the *shari'a* or revealed Islamic law, which in fact made up the Ottoman Constitution. Theoretically, the *kanunname* was bound to conform to Islam; in practice, deviations necessitated by practical consideration were possible. The *Şeyhülislam* (Arabic, *Shaykh al-Islam*, paramount religious official at court), who was appointed by the sultan, seldom refrained from issuing a *fetva* (Arabic *fatwa*, religious–legal opinion) approving the government's decisions; thus formal conformity to Islam in tradition was achieved. The Ottoman courts and legal system were both Islamic and "secular" – in the sense that they could adapt themselves to social, economic, and political changes outside the realm of religion but without appearing to do so. The Muslim courts were spread throughout the country and generally enforced the rules of the *shari'a*, which together with the *kanunnames* thus produced a degree of uniformity in family affairs, contracts, and other civic matters. This brought about a collective mode of social behaviour among Ottoman Muslims.

The central administrative system also contributed to the

development of the Ottoman political culture, with secular over-
tones as necessitated by local interests. The sultan's authority was
well represented by the officials appointed by and working at the
discretion of the central government in Istanbul. The field administrators, such as the *beylerbeys* and *sanjak beys*, were appointed by
the central authority and had at their disposal fairly large con-
tingents of Janissaries, whom they used to maintain the authority
and enforce the decisions of the central government. The appointment of natives to various local administrative positions and the
granting of a degree of *de facto* administrative autonomy (as was
the case in the Arab provinces) was commonplace. But all of these
local appointments were formally sanctioned by the central government, although they were often in reality an expression of local
interests and preferences.

Most of the migrants were from regions in which the Ottoman
central government had enforced a relatively uniform judicial and
administrative system and philosophy of state, society, rights, and
obligations.[2] The result was a political culture that was in essence a
secular political culture legitimised through Islam, but – for that
very reason – capable of adaptation to and evolution into new
patterns, including territorial statehood. Muslims – especially in
the Balkans, the Crimea, the coastal areas of the western Caucasus,
northern Iraq, and Syria – reflected this Ottoman political culture
in the similarities of their social behaviour patterns, and in the fact
that the elites of the migrant groups were predisposed to accept the
decisions of the central authority.

Conditions favouring a change of identity

The initial Ottoman policy towards immigation was devoid of ideological significance, as indicated by the statutes of the immigration
offices. The early Muslim *muhajir* (migrant) had been accepted as
part of a general sense of Islamic duty, but also because of the
traditional Ottoman practice of granting asylum to anyone,
Muslim or non-Muslim, requesting it.

By 1880, however, the government's policy towards immigration
had taken a definite ideological bias in favour of Muslims. The old
policy was officially changed in 1887 after the office of the *Şeyhülislam* wrote to the incumbent Sultan Abdülhamid II that the lives
of Muslims under foreign rule had become intolerable and that
every Muslim wishing to live in an Islamic country should be
allowed to immigrate. Implicit in this recommendation was the
suggestion that the Muslims wishing to enter the Ottoman realm be
given priority over non-Muslims (Karpat 1981). It is symbolic that

the office charged with overseeing immigration matters was renamed at this date the Muhacirin-i Islamiye Komisyonu Alisi (High Islamic Immigration Commission) and was placed directly under the sultan–caliph. One of the consequences of this change of policy was that by 1901 the mass settlement of non-Muslims in Palestine was prohibited. The Jews, in particular, while allowed to immigrate and settle in Ottoman lands, were expressly prohibited from settling *en masse* in Palestine as they wished to do.[3]

The reforms began chiefly with Sultan Mahmud II (1808–39), entered a new phase in the Tanzimat era (1839–76), and, finally, took an entirely different course after 1876 under Abdülhamid II.[4] Under Abdülhamid II (1876–1909), the reforms became self-consciously Islamic in character, due in good measure to the changes brought about by the migrations. Indeed, it was the migration of the Muslims from the periphery of the Muslim world that forced him to adopt his so-called "Islamic" policy, and to follow a political course different from that of his predecessors. This policy, promoted often as Ottomanism, actually represented a new concept of state, nationhood, territory, and Islamic identity, and had little in common with the classical Islamic ideas of state, government, and territory.[5] That Abdülhamid's policy of building a unitary Islamic national territorial state was backed by a large part of the *'ulama'* shows that even the most orthodox Muslim scholars would accept a change of political identity as long as it was carried out within the cultural perimeters of Islam and was enforced in accordance with its methods, especially when the survival of the Muslim society as an independent entity was at stake.

The migration process as a catalyst for identity change

The causes that triggered the migration were instrumental in preparing the migrants for a change of identity. Basically, all of the *émigrés* acted because of threats, implied or overt, to their lives and property.

The ill-armed Caucasian rebels resisting the Russian army were mercilessly massacred or uprooted. British consular statistics place the number of Caucasian deaths – many from starvation and disease – at over half a million (Pinson 1972: 71–85; *Voennyj Sbornik* 1884: 158–96).[6] The Caucasians remaining in their ancestral homes were given the opportunity to convert to Christianity and settle in the easily controllable plains of Kuban; later they were asked to serve in the Czarist army, raising the possibility that they might be forced to fight other Muslims. Many, as a consequence, migrated to Ottoman lands in the period 1862–5.

In 1878, about a million Muslims were forced out of the area which is now known as Bulgaria and Romania, by the Russian army and Bulgarian armed bands, which, according to British embassy reports, also killed some 300,000 Muslims. Russia wanted to establish a national Bulgarian client-state and sought by brutal force to turn the Orthodox Christians into a dominant majority. These migrants lost all their land, houses, and even personal belongings. Very few received any indemnity for these losses, although, in the case of the refugees from Bulgaria, some were allowed to go back and sell part of their property at derisory prices. Thus, the migrants who belonged to the upper classes found themselves as poor and destitute as the humblest citizen of the community.

This forceful action was given wide coverage throughout the Ottoman state by the newly emerging press. The reports in hand indicate that one of the most widely discussed topics among the pilgrims at Mecca after the 1860s was the fate of Muslims in the European Christian lands. Thus, the citizens in the heartland also were made increasingly aware of their own Muslim identity, and this in turn had an effect on the way they received the immigrants. Following the well-established Qur'anic obligation to provide shelter and help to the *muhajirs* (see Masud, Chapter 2 of this volume), the migrants were sheltered and fed for months, and even years, in private homes. In many areas the local Muslims helped build homes for the newcomers. Although there were unpleasant clashes, caused by the warlike attitude of the Cherkes tribes as much as by negative reaction towards the migrants, these were the exception. The manner in which they were welcomed by the Muslim population of their new home further solidified the migrants' Muslim consciousness and eventually facilitated their integration into the society.

In itself, the act of mass migration, which was experienced in common by both the lowest- and the highest-ranking Muslims of the communities, helped to increase the sense of Muslim communal solidarity and to bring down those social barriers that had separated the migrants in their original homes. Not only did attitudes of mind undergo transformation; concrete changes in their economic and social conditions resulted in greater equality as well. The leadership position of the traditional chiefs was eroded when migration deprived them of the economic and political power that had bolstered alignments in the old hierarchies. Occasionally, the attempt was made to re-establish the traditional social system in the new home, but, as will be explained later, the settlement policies of the Ottoman government made the re-establishment of the migrants' traditional power structure difficult, if not impossible. For individuals with latent leadership ability, the migration was to some extent a liberation from the constraints of the social and cultural mores and from the hierarchy of authority prevailing at the place of origin. For individuals with personality characteristics conducive to innovation and the easy acceptance of socio-political change, the migration provided an opportunity for self-affirmation. The overwhelming need to survive and adapt to new places and conditions of settlement called for vision and initiative, and the individuals with those personality characteristics rose to positions of leadership.

This argument is supported by data showing changes in social structure and leadership cadres among the Crimean migrants established in Dobruca following the Crimean war of 1853–6. At the bottom of the social scale among these Crimeans were the Nogay, who had maintained a tribal form of organisation and leadership and were involved in agriculture on the Crimean plateau. The upper class, which had lived in the cities along the Crimean coast and were better educated, continued after migration to regard the Nogay as inferior and attempted to monopolise the positions of power in Dobruca. However, the Nogay, who were no longer willing to remain a permanent under-class, protested vehemently (in protest a group of them even returned to Russia), forcing the Ottoman government to accord at least symbolic recognition of their equality by giving them medals and salaries as it did to other Crimean leaders (Karpat 1984–5). After Dobruca was ceded to Romania in 1878, the social differences among the Nogay, Yaliboy, Kerish, and other Crimean groups vanished as they all amalgamated into one single Muslim–Tartar group in an effort to preserve their Muslim identity. To this day Romania classifies its 60,000 Muslims as Turks and Tartars.

If a tribe or village emigrated *en masse* and then was resettled as such in a geographical, cultural, economic, and political environment very similar to the place of origin, it was possible that the old social structure, including the leadership, might survive to hinder identity change. However, the Ottoman government took steps to prevent this. It already had long experience with the settlement of tribes in the fifteenth through the eighteenth centuries, and had established a pattern designed to facilitate integration. The tribal confederations, notably the Caucasians, were divided into several groups and settled in different places. Many tribal and communal chiefs were given special incentives to encourage them not to continue to assert their leadership: some were enrolled in the army with officer ranking, while others, along with the religious heads, were encouraged to settle in cities. The leaders of the settled and well-established communities from the Caucasus and the Balkans preferred, in any case, to settle in the cities.

The effect of this policy was that the immigrant elites were rapidly incorporated into the body of the Ottoman elites and thus became part of the establishment, while their former constituents, free of the burden of loyalty and obedience to the old leaders, could adapt themselves to their new environments as they saw fit. The immigrant elites and their offspring played a major role not only in helping to define and shape the emerging Muslim–Ottoman identity but also in promoting successfully the acceptance of this new identity among those they formerly led. Furthermore, the new leadership cadres that arose in the settled communities also came to play a major part in this transformation, as they sought in a conscious fashion to identify themselves and their communities with the values and the political goals and aspirations of their new motherland.

Those of the old leadership who did not settle so easily into new roles as integrated members of the Ottoman establishment found that despite their best efforts they were, in the new conditions, unable to maintain themselves in their traditional positions of power *vis-à-vis* their fellow migrants. Many of those who, in former times, would have placed the interests of themselves and their own social group above those of the community as a whole, now became the advocates for the entire community. They hoped by identifying themselves more intimately with the larger group to maintain their leadership positions, and to gain influence in government circles by virtue of their position. However, as it seemed obvious that these former chiefs, now far away in the urban areas, were bent mainly on perpetuating the old order and their own ascriptive privileges, they were soon replaced by new leaders who were better able to articulate the needs and aspirations of a people seeking to cope with a changed geographic and social environment. The first generation of these new communal leaders maintained contact with the old chiefs, but the second and succeeding generations defined their position and role in accordance with the conditions prevailing in the community rather than in accordance with the advice of the elders. They soon began to define their identity in terms of the new Ottoman–Muslim constituency promoted by the sultan–caliph.

Pan-Islamism and identity change

Pan-Islamism, actually Islamism (*islamcilik*) in the Ottoman state can be considered as a grass-roots fundamentalist movement seeking socio-political accommodation in Islamic terms.[7] It was, to a rather large extent, a by-product of the mass nineteenth-century immigration, which brought with it into the Ottoman realm many of the different religious ideologies of Muslims on the fringes of the disintegrating empire. The movement played a vital role in the change of identity of both newcomers and old residents of the Asian provinces of the Ottoman state.

The press of the 1860s and, especially, of the 1870s expressed a deep dissatisfaction with the condition of economic and political affairs in the Ottoman state. Thousands of workers in the traditional textile industry had been left unemployed when cheap cloth from England and France flooded Ottoman markets after 1840: unemployment among craftsmen rose to approximately 70 per cent. Muslim merchants and small landowners in the countryside, dominated and exploited by the European economic interests via the local Christian commercial intermediaries, shared the discontent of the peasants and workers (Issawi 1966; Pamuk 1987). The government was accused of being unable to stop the country's territorial disintegration or uphold Muslim rights. These accusations became far more widespread and vehement – encompassing now the discontent of the upper classes and religious establishment – after the debacle of the 1877–8 war with Russia. The millions of destitute Muslim immigrants pouring in from the Balkans and the Caucasus (Istanbul alone received about 200,000 refugees in 1878) further increased the general apprehension. It was about this time, moreover, that various obscure princes and sultans from Asia and Africa, threatened with occupation by the European powers, wrote to Sultans Abdülaziz (AD 1861–76) and Abdülhamid II asking for protection and offering allegiance in exchange. These factors appeared to foreshadow the development of pan-Islamism as an international movement, but despite European fears, this kind of movement failed to materialise.

The Islamic current that did emerge manifested itself in the form of grassroots demands – from both low-level religious leaders and laymen – for Islamic unity and action to assure the survival of the state as a Muslim entity and to better the lives of the faithful. The existing administration was considered to be both incompetent and so corrupted by the European-style reforms of the Tanzimat that it was unwilling to follow a truly Islamic path. The refugees gave their full support to this movement, in the hope that a revitalised

Ottoman government would reconquer the European territories and they would be able to return to their homes. This hope was soon dashed, however, as Sultan Abdülhamid refused outright to enter on a policy of reconquest.

The central idea of the Islamic populist–fundamentalist movement was that the Ottoman Muslims were a *millet* – a nation – deserving of a land of their own where a Muslim way of life under Muslim rule would prevail (Lewis and Braude 1982). Whereas in the past the term *millet* was applied only to non-Muslim communities, now even the sultan began to refer to the Muslims as "my nation" (*benim milletim*). The fundamentalists regarded the remaining Ottoman territory as the land wherein the expectations of this Muslim nation could be fulfilled; territory therefore appeared as an indispensable condition for Muslim survival. The literati of the movement attempted to prove that Anatolia was the predestined homeland of the Muslim Turks by associating it with such mythical heroes as Ayub al-Ansari (who died at the Arab siege of Constantinople), Mehmet II (the conqueror of Istanbul), and the present sultan himself. Thus the idea of a multi-religious, multi-ethnic nation unified under the doctrine of "Ottomanism" (as enunciated by the Tanzimat reformers), was turned back on itself by the fundamentalists and became a concept of a homogeneous Muslim nation occupying its own territory – i.e. the "motherland". Although the Islamists, principally the high *'ulama'*, theoretically rejected this concept as undermining the unity of, and allegiance to, the *umma*, it was adopted as basic to the preservation of their Muslim culture and religion.

The fundamentalist movement included a large number of immigrants, among whom were the leaders and members of both Sunni and non-Sunni *tarikats*. These *tarikats* had strong popular bases, and many were instrumental in the perpetuation of egalitarian populist ideas: e.g. the Bedreddinis of Serres; the Qizilbash of Deliorman and Dobruca; and the Naqshbandis and Muridists of the north Caucasus. Traumatised by their experiences as refugees, they were anxious to know how such a fate could befall them, and they found the answer in the incompetence of their top leaders. What was needed was an uncorrupted, authentic Muslim leader who would dedicate himself to the fulfilment of Islamic ideals.

Some appear to have been willing to take violent action against the government. In 1878, for example, Ali Suavi, the publisher of the journal, *Ulum* (*Sciences*), together with about a hundred followers – mostly refugees from the Balkans – landed on the pier of the palace of Sultan Murat V at Ciragan with the intention of bringing him back to the throne, then occupied by Abdülhamid II.

143

Suavi was associated with many dervishes, or popular preachers. He had studied in Europe, was married to an Englishwoman, and, for a period, was the head of the Galatasray, the French school established in Istanbul in 1868. But he was also known to preach in the mosques against European imperialism and the deterioration of the Islamic way of life, and was thus an outstanding forerunner of contemporary Muslim fundamentalism. He apparently wanted to replace Abdülhamid because of his authoritarian policies, his failure to back the Muslim guerrillas fighting the Russians and Bulgarians in the Rodoppe mountains, and his readiness to cede Muslim lands to the infidel. Although Suavi was killed in the action, his followers arrested, and 178,000 refugees living in Istanbul exiled to Anatolia ostensibly to preclude further trouble, the event was extraordinary in that it marked the first time that a group of civilians, rather than a military cabal, had attempted to overthrow a ruling sultan.

The migrants generally accelerated social differentiation in the fundamentalist movement and gave it a class dimension. After the forced mass emigrations from the Caucasus and the Balkans, during which both rich and poor were uprooted from their homes, there still remained large Muslim groups: in the north-eastern section of what is now Bulgaria; in Dobruca; in Bosnia; in parts of the Caucasus; and in Crimea. After the Balkan war of 1912–13, these Muslims also began gradually to migrate in order to avoid the fate of their co-religionists, and were encouraged to do so by the national states of Bulgaria and Romania, which allowed them to sell their properties and carry part of the proceeds with them to Turkey. Consequently, a large number of *beys* and other notables, many of whom had owned large tracts of land, carried considerable capital with them to Istanbul. These relatively well-to-do immigrants bought properties, mostly in cities, and became part of the Ottoman urban elite. Many of them invested their capital in commercial and small industrial enterprises, and thus enlarged the emerging urban entrepreneurial class by adding to it a Muslim dimension.

Included among the new Muslim commercial class were aristocratic families and learned *'ulama'* – from the Balkans, the Caucasus, and Crimea – as well as military officers, some of whom had served in the Czarist armies. Some of these had received a European type of education in their original homes or had studied in European universities, but also joined the Islamist movement. Islam had become, in fact, the chief identity symbol and focus of political allegiance. Two examples illustrate this point. A Muslim member of the ruling dynasty of Montenegro, who enjoyed great popularity at the royal court and owned extensive tracts of land, abandoned all of these and came to live in Istanbul on a small pension provided by the government. The English consul, who reported the incident in great detail, but who of course must not be regarded as an unimpeachable source, observed that, to this Slav aristocrat, the upholding of his faith was dearer than all his riches and titles.[8] The second example is that of General Musa (Kondukov), a Chechen who had reached a very high position in the Czarist army. Eventually, under the pretext of joining a survey commission, he came into the Ottoman state, where he stayed and assumed the command of an army corps. He then fought the Russians in the Caucasus. There are hundreds of similar examples of Muslims from Russia and the Balkans who preferred, even at the cost of privilege and rank, to live as citizens of a Muslim state.

Abdülhamid's synthesis: the change of identity

Sultan Abdülhamid's first priority, when he came to the throne in 1876, was the maintenance of the six-centuries-old dynasty, and his second was the maintenance of the Ottoman state and territory. His third priority was to strengthen the Islamic creed in whatever way was necessary to assure the mutual survival of dynasty, state, and faith.[9] Through trial and error, an "Islamic policy" gradually emerged.

Proroguing the Parliament and the Constitution in 1878, he sought to silence opposition to the administration at a time when popular dissatisfaction with the government and support for the populist−fundamentalist movement were growing. The populist−fundamentalists did not in fact pose a direct challenge to the throne because they were too heterogeneous and lacked a well-articulated ideology and strong leadership. But Ottoman sultans had always harboured fears of the popular *tarikats*, and tried to neutralise them by bribes or even imprisonment. Abdülhamid rather hoped to win the support of the Muslim masses by co-opting leaders of the Sunni orthodox fraternities, or *tarikats*, of Syria and Iraq − such as the Qadiri and Rafai, which had a mass following.

Although Abdülhamid espoused the Islamist views prevailing initially among the upper classes − which placed emphasis on orthodox Islam and established institutions such as the caliphate, and which were at variance with the views of the populist−fundamentalists − the French occupation of Tunisia (1881) and the British seizure of Egypt (1882) inspired a general change of opinion. Now, after 1882, the leaders of orthodox Islam came closer to adopting the militant, radical anti-European spirit prevailing among the fundamentalists, and the ideological differences between grassroots Islamic fundamentalism and the state-supported Islamic orthodoxy of the upper-class groups seems to have declined. The two streams converged, in fact, into a distinct consciousness that both sides were part of a single Muslim nation. The sultan, becoming the active champion of this consolidated Islamic nationality, eventually emphasised his role as caliph, although not before the issue had been extensively debated in the press and several religious leaders had urged him to do so for the sake of Muslim unity and survival.

A perfunctory look at the textbooks used in Ottoman primary schools after 1880 shows that these were written primarily to foster a sense of Ottoman–Muslim identity in the pupils. It is not surprising that the Greek Orthodox and Armenian patriarchs in 1897 protested against the obligatory use of these textbooks, which extolled the virtues of Ottoman history and glorified its achievements. The two Christian prelates wished to teach only the history of their own ethnic groups, but their protest went unheeded. In order to develop the concept of the Ottoman–Muslim nation, the government was willing to use all the devices at its disposal – many borrowed from Europe. The elementary schools, which expanded rapidly though not extensively into the countryside during the reign of Abdülhamid, assiduously cultivated the idea of a Muslim–Ottoman citizen. That this was bound to develop in these pupils a political identity different from that of their predecessors was evident.

Abdülhamid was soon to incur the opposition of westernised intellectuals, and even some religious officials, for his timid foreign policy and autocratic manner of governing, and was eventually overthrown in 1908–9. But his Islamic policy produced lasting results. Indeed, it is symbolic that many of the founders of the secret association that came to be known as the "Young Turks" and that produced the revolution of 1908 were medical students who were ethnically non-Turks from the peripheral regions of the state. The founder of modern Turkey, Atatürk himself, who was instrumental in the abolition of the sultanate and the caliphate, was an immigrant from Salonica, as were some of the parents of his two successors as president. Moreover, in the rise of Turkish nationalism, Yusuf Akcura and Huseyinzade Ali (from Kazan and Azerbaijan in Russia respectively) and other immigrants, played key roles. Because Abdülhamid managed for most of his reign not to become embroiled in international wars (except for the short but victorious war of 1897 against Greece), he was able to devote himself to the promotion of this Islamic policy and to amalgamate the various elements of the population into a synthesis that was the new Ottoman–Muslim nation, existing on its own territory and demanding impersonal bonds of loyalty.

Conclusion

The migrations and the circumstances that produced them have been shown to be the catalyst for the transformation of the religious and cultural identity of the immigrants into a dynamic new political identity linked to the new concept of a Muslim territorial state. The migrations also triggered changes in the social and occupational structure, demography, settlement patterns, and land tenure system of the Ottoman state. The migrants were well integrated throughout Muslim–Ottoman society – from the lower classes to the elite classes – and were active participants in its affairs at a time when constitutional changes were being made and a European-type market economy adopted.

In order to achieve internal cohesion, Sultan Abdülhamid II used his position as caliph to contain and control populist fundamentalism, and to integrate it with the more orthodox Islamist ideology of the elites. Eventually, this policy also achieved the ideological and cultural amalgamation of the migrants and large segments of the Muslim middle and upper classes – including the Arabs of the urban areas of Syria and northern Iraq – into a relatively cohesive political and social unit that was the new Ottoman Muslim nation.

The individual Muslim citizens gradually came to identify themselves with the new entity, formed of different tribes and ethnic groups but having Islam as its binding ideology and Turkish as its language of administration and communication. This was the territorial state, the motherland, the *vatan*, to which, ideally, all Muslims would pledge allegiance and loyalty. The survival and welfare of the motherland took precedence over those of the sultan. Moreover, the idea that certain conditions within the motherland could be improved so as to strengthen the nation and make life better for the Muslims gained acceptance. Thus, the Muslims now looked upon the *vatan* not only as an arena in which to cultivate virtue and prepare himself for the next world, but also as a place in which to fulfil worldly aspirations. The idea of active participation in political and social affairs espoused by the Naqshbandis was, in fact, an outgrowth of this new worldly outlook. This acceptance of change and material improvement in one's existence – or "modernisation", as it was often called – was implicit in Abdülhamid's Islamic policy.

This new Ottoman–Muslim nation, the results of a dialectical process to which the various elements of the society contributed, had an inner strength that vigorously resisted the forces which, after 1908, pulled it apart: new ethnic nationalisms; the anti-imperial nationalism promoted by the Young Turks; and the threatening military might of the west. Modern Turkey inherited the vital core of this state, and its transformation from a monarchical regime to a republic was but the logical and ultimate result of the interplay of the forces that had earlier transformed the traditional Ottoman state itself.

A personal postscript

Many of the themes that have emerged in this discussion are reflected in my own personal experience of a later period. I was born in Dobruca – a province located between the lower Danube and the Black Sea – in a Muslim–Turkish community that had been part of the Ottoman state from the fourteenth century until 1878, when it was incorporated into Romania. The community, adapting well to the non-Muslim regime, maintained its Islamic communal socio-cultural identity. Although the community consisted of Turks, Tartars, Lazzes, and Kurds, among others, the ethnic differences among the members of these groups were generally superseded by their overall consciousness of themselves as Muslims. Yet there was a striking lack of *political* consciousness within the Muslim community, which appeared interested mainly in maintaining its cultural, religious, and social customs and mores rather than in securing a distinct legal–political or constitutional recognition of its religious status.

The notables and the religious leaders – the *efendis*, *qadis*, and *muftis* – were even more lacking in Muslim *political* consciousness than the ordinary members of the community. Most of these rose to prominence during Romanian rule after 1878 as the representatives of the community. They clung tenaciously to their Muslim denomination (which had secured them their position) while also serving the Romanian administration (whose policies often worked to the detriment of the basic principles of their faith). Individuals in the community – usually younger people with some education, the very poor (who felt stifled as a minority with low class status), or the old *'ulama'* (who did not want to compromise their faith) – looked upon emigration as the only logical way out of their predicament. Those with education had limited opportunity for career advancement, while the poor felt that they were discriminated against and exploited economically by the Romanian officials and the elites of their own community.

Turkey was regarded by both groups as the only country in the world with which they had a cultural affiliation and historical ties, and which offered them hope for social advancement and material betterment. The stories of the secularism and anti-Islamic policies of Atatürk were dismissed by Muslims of all ranks because of the expectation that the basic Islamic identity of the country could not be abandoned, and that the material progress and increased well-being attributed partly to his reforms would compensate for the loss of religious zeal. This was the situation that prevailed in the 1930s, the days of my childhood in Dobruca.

I grew up as a Turkish-speaking Muslim in a community con-sisting of Muslims of various ethnic origins, and non-Muslim Romanians and Bulgarians. I spoke perfect Romanian and many assumed it likely that I would be assimilated sooner or later into the culture of the dominant Romanian majority. However, I found that my early Islamic education within the family had instilled values that distinguished me from both the Romanians and the sub-servient Muslim communal leaders: my sense of loyalty to family and friends set me apart from the former and my sense of equality from the latter. It was in these circumstances that my Turkish identity acquired a new meaning, since it provided me with a solution to my personal problems, which had been created by the encounter of different cultures and political systems. The Turkey of Atatürk, cleansed of religious bigotry, appeared as a haven where my aspirations to attend a university (the graduates of my school in Romania were deprived of this right) could be fulfilled and my identity would no longer excite the derision of my compatriots. From then onwards, even as my interest in Romanian literature and social life remained alive, I began to feel a keenness in being Turkish in addition to being a Muslim, and began to defend and identify myself with everything I considered Turkish. I finally came to the conclusion that it is not possible to live in two worlds with two cultures and decided, on my own, at the age of 18, to emigrate to my "real" country – only to discover that my Turkish identity was different from that of the natives.

I went to Turkey in the 1940s, and, from the very beginning, I was struck by unsuspected differences of identity, that separated both my Muslim community in Dobruca from that in Turkey, and from me as an individual (coming from a different Turkish–Muslim environment) from the natives. I did not feel these differences in the observance of Islamic rites or in any lack of Islamic self-consciousness (which, despite secularism, paradoxically enough was far more intense in Turkey than in Dobruca). Only years later did I realise that what had struck me as being different was the predominance among the Turks of Turkey of a special type of political–national consciousness that stemmed basically from Islam – different opinions notwithstanding – while the consciousness of the Muslims of Dobruca was communal and apolitical, or passive. Living in a state of their own that was Muslim in character but also national, the Turks of Turkey had a political consciousness that derived its strength from the fact that they identified themselves with a national territory. In my community in Dobruca, by way of contrast, the territorial identification was conspicuously absent from the Muslim identity. The community had only limited historical memory, possessed no consciousness of its territorial dimensions, and had no political aspirations as Muslims.

Almost all of the Dobrucan immigrants living in Turkey, while fondly remembering their birthplace and often expressing a profound nostalgia for it, became politically identified with Turkey and what it stood for. To the best of my knowledge, out of the 45,000 to 50,000 Dobrucans who went to Turkey in the period 1934–8, only two or three families returned to Romania. In Ottoman times, peregrination between Anatolia, Thrace, and Dobruca was common, and amounted to a mere change of place rather than of identity. But the migrants of the 1930s remained in Turkey because it gave them a political future and because the Kemalist regime began an intensive programme of Turkification. The overwhelming majority of destitute immigrants also knew that they would not be welcome if they returned to their old country. But, above all, the immigrants felt that their traditional cultural and religious identity was no longer in danger, even though some were aware that the government's view of Islam in the 1930s was substantially different from that of the populace. Perhaps unsurprisingly, it was only when I migrated for the second time – from Turkey to America – that I was able to put my experiences in Dobruca and in Turkey into perspective.

Notes

1 The term "Ottoman" as it appears in the western and Turkish literature originated in the nineteenth century despite the state's official title – *Devlet-i Ali-i Osmani*, "the exalted state of Osman". For five centuries this title was patrimonial, whereas the term in the nineteenth century came to mean a territorial state and body of citizens inhabiting the Ottoman homeland.

2 A great variety of books was issued by Ottoman statesmen and thinkers from the fifteenth century onwards on the subjects of the social order, authority, and the duties of subjects. One can cite among them, for instance, Tursun Bey and Kınalızade Ala'i (AD 1510–72). None of their

works is translated into English. Kınalızade's work, *Ahlak-i Ala'i* was translated into modern Turkish in the *Tercüman* collection, Istanbul *c.* 1970−. Koçibey's famous *risale* of the seventeenth century also belongs to this category of books.

3 See the proceedings of a conference on the "Jews in the Ottoman Empire", to be published by Brandeis University. See also Karpat 1985.

4 Migration matters were placed initially under the General Commission for Migration Administration (*Idare-i Umumiye-i Muhacirun Komisyonu*) established in 1860. Later in the 1880s, as mentioned, the new enlarged commission was headed by the sultan.

5 Although the only land border recognised by medieval jurisprudence was between *dar al-Islam* and *dar al-harb*, as early as the fifteenth century the Ottoman thinker Kınalızade Ala'i pointed out in his *Ahlak-i Ala'i* that the "order of the world" (*nizam-i alem*) was an arena surrounded by the "walls of state" as part of the cycle necessary for the existence of justice − the key ingredient in the "order of the world". The area between the "walls of state" would be considered the territory of the state.

6 These reports are scattered in various collections found in the Public Record Office, London. The FO 78 and 424 collections, covering the period from 1860 and 1880, are particularly relevant. The British government also published several reports on the Circassians. See, for instance, the report presented to the House of Commons, *Accounts and Papers* (1864), vol. 63. See also Karpat 1985.

7 This section draws on my paper presented to the biennial conference on Ottoman and pre-Ottoman Studies, Cuenca, Spain, July 1981, and material obtained from various archival sources which is being amalgamated into a monograph.

8 On Montenegrins and Bosnians, see FO 424, vol. 72, no. 333 and vol. 89, no. 52; see also dispatches in the Archives of the Turkish Foreign Ministry, *Idare*, vol. 269.

9 There is a rich literature in Turkish and European languages on Abdülhamid II, much of which is subjective. The best insight into his thinking is offered by his memoirs published in French and Turkish. The first memoirs, found initially by Ibnulemin Mahmut Kemal in the sultan's private collection in the Ildiz Palace, consist of brief notes related to various issues which came up during his reign. These were published along with new found notes as *Abdulhamit'in Hatıra Defteri* [*Abdülhamid's Notebook of Memoirs*]. The second series of memoirs was written after Abdülhamid was ousted in 1909 and, though defensive in tone, appears to represent a reasonable general view of his opinion on a number of key issues, including Islamism: *Siyasi Hatıratım* [*My Political Memoirs*]. The 5th edition (1987) comprises new additions which do not significantly alter the content of previous editions. The memoirs were also published in French.

Muslim travellers

References

Abdulhamid, Sultan (1960) *Abdulhamit'in Hatıra Defteri*, Selek Yaynevi, Istanbul.

------ (1987) *Siyasi Hatıratım*, 5th edn, Dergah Yaynlar, Istanbul.

Berje, A.B. (1982) 'Vasilenie gortzev s. Kavkaza', *Russkaisstarina*, vol. 36, chapter 7.

Issawi, C. (1966) *The Economic History of the Middle East*, University of Chicago Press, Chicago.

Karpat, K.H. (1976) *The Gecekondu, Rural Migration and Urbanization in Turkey*, Cambridge University Press, Cambridge and New York.

------ (1981) 'The status of the Muslims under European rule: the eviction and settlement of the Cerkes', *Journal of Muslim Minority Affairs*, 2, no. 1, pp. 7–27.

------ (1984–5) 'Ottoman urbanism: the Crimean emigration of 1856–65 and the establishment of *mecidiye*', *International Journal of Turkish Studies*, 3, no. 1, pp. 1–25.

------ (1985) *The Ottoman Population, 1830–1914: Demography and Social Characteristics*, University of Wisconsin Press, Madison.

Lewis, B. and Braude, B., (eds) (1982) *Christians and Jews in the Ottoman Empire*, Holmes & Meier, New York, 2 vols.

Pamuk, S. (1987) *The Ottoman Empire and European Capitalism, 1820–1913*, Cambridge University Press, Cambridge and New York.

Pinson, M. (1972) 'Ottoman colonization of the Circassians in Rumili after the Crimean War', *Etudes Balkaniques*, 3, pp. 71–85.

Chapter eight

Shifting centres and emergent identities: Turkey and Germany in the lives of Turkish *Gastarbeiter*

Ruth Mandel

"For the expatriot, reality is always someplace else"
(Ariel Dorfman, Chilean writer and sometime expatriot)

Introduction

This chapter addresses the cultural expressions of movement in the migration of Turkish workers to West Germany. It suggests that physical movement entails a variety of types of exchange, which in turn contribute to the dynamics of social mobility. Making these relationships explicit sheds light on the dynamics informing social and cultural transformations.[1]

The particular transformations dealt with here bear on the formation and reformulation of migrant identity in the light of concepts and orientations towards centres and peripheries. The centre dealt with in this chapter in some ways follows the notion of centre discussed by Edward Shils. Shils's centre is ideological in nature, and can be understood as representing the institutions of a dominant order. The centre that I am concerned with is geographically located, but also finds salience in the realm of individual perception. This centredness is articulated in terms of a geographic core which becomes, in effect, a metaphor for an ideological core around which one's identity revolves. Eickelman and Piscatori (see Chapter 1 of this volume) discuss the notion of centres in relation to the complexity of Islamic symbols and affiliations. They make the important observation that the notion of centre must be understood in the plural, in order fully to grasp the complexity of a hierarchy of centres. Furthermore, alternate hierarchies not only exist simultaneously, but, as with all social and ideological structures, remain subject to historical change. The introductory chapter of this volume also calls into question "the straightforward distinction between centre and periphery". The material presented here echoes these concerns by illustrating how the relevant centre and periphery of the migrants undergo fundamental transformations in relation to each other.

The past quarter-century has witnessed a migratory movement unprecedented in Turkish history and irreversible in its consequences. Close to two million Turks currently reside in the Federal Republic of Germany and West Berlin, with significant numbers scattered throughout the rest of western Europe. West Germany, commonly joked about as Turkey's sixty-eighth province – Turkey has sixty-seven administrative provinces – has entered into the consciousness even of non-migrant Turks in Turkey. An awareness of the Turkish experience in Germany has penetrated the modern-day folklore, popular songs, literature, television, film, popular newspapers, and the daily and annual life-cycles of many Turks. In some respects, the diaspora has ironically assumed the authority of a legitimate and even desirable "centre" in contrast to an increasingly "peripheral" Turkey. This chapter proposes, first, to explore how the central point of reference is shifting by examining the types of personal encounters between Turkish migrants and Turks who stayed at home; and second, to understand how the relations between the past and present identities of the migrants are shaping a new, emergent identity – one no longer oriented towards a concrete centre, but increasingly towards a necessarily elusive "other place".

To understand the historical, political, and emotional resonance of this migration, we must first analyse such categories as *gurbet* and *gurbetçi*. The *gurbetçi* – one who lives in exile, diaspora, or away from the homeland – lives in a state of *gurbet*. It is a relative term, one that might describe the state of those living in Frankfurt, as well as Turks living in Istanbul, who feel that their primary identification is with their natal village rather than the city. The emergent literature and musical genres produced by Turkish artists in western Europe, although addressing this relatively recent phenomenon, actually draw upon a long tradition of exile and *gurbet* experiences. Throughout history, Turks have known many types of exile and migration. Thus, there is an established paradigm for the cultural structuring of contemporary labour migration. Under current conditions, however, the concentric circles marking distance or proximity from the original centre have expanded, encompassing a new dimension: *Alamanya*, or Germany.

Despite the Turks' familiarity with migration and life in *gurbet* in the past, the German episode marks both a greater distance from the original centre and a transformation of the relationship to the centre itself. Moreover, West Germany, as a "centre" for Turks, threatens to break away from earlier Turkish centres and to establish itself as a rival, alternative one. This seems to be particularly true for Turks of the so-called "second generation" in West Germany.

The changing relations between core and periphery are highlighted in several contexts. One context is the annual summer *izin*, the holiday in Turkey undertaken by the *gurbetçi*. Another context is the experience of the "second generation" (German: *die zweite Generation*; Turkish: *ikinci kuşak*), which can be seen as the repository, or even the creator, of the inherent contradiction between centre and periphery. This generation, often described in melodramatic terms as "caught between two cultures but part of neither", constructs its identity in a social field where the "myth of the final return" serves as a guiding orientation, to be negotiated amidst a host of contradictions.

A third and final consideration is the effect which migration to Germany has had upon explicitly religious beliefs and practices, both for the dominant Sunni majority and the Alevi minority – which in Turkey comprise perhaps 20 per cent of the total population. In particular, the Alevis have significantly changed their modes of self-expression. I look at how Alevi identity and community is differentially constructed in the West German "diaspora" and in Turkey; and how, as a by-product of this particular migration and specific social context, Alevi identity has come to be redefined in relation to the dominant Sunni majority.

Izin and *izinli* (taking leave)

Turkey looms large in the social life of Turks who work in West Germany. For example, Turkish politics not only are discussed, but are often engaged in more actively than in Turkey. At home, Turks prefer to watch Turkish video films on their VCRs rather than the German television programmes which they must struggle to understand because of language barriers.[2] Most socialising is carried out with other Turks[3] in private homes, mosques, public restaurants, and coffee houses (the exclusive domain of men), and on structured occasions such as the large parties frequently held in rented halls to celebrate engagements, weddings, and circumcisions. In nice weather, picnics in several parks in particular are so popular that Germans have nicknamed a couple of parks "Turkish meadow". At many of these gatherings the theme of travel to Turkey dominates the conversation. Both the *kesin dönüş* (permanent return, repatriation) and the *izin* (return, the summer vacation) provide grist for endless discussion. Past trips are compared and future trips are the subject of speculation. The discussions focus on both the actual trip itself and on the state of things in Turkey. The topics discussed include the following: whose car did not make the trip; who was turned back at the Turkish border for what infraction; which side roads are best for avoiding the worst traffic; which alternate frontier crossings have the shortest lines or the most easily bribed customs agents; the European goods most desired by relatives back in Turkey, and how unschooled these relatives are in the real costs of such items; and which travel agents can be trusted to arrange legitimate charter flights. Conversations also include: horror stories of departures from obscure airports, train stations, and bus depots; experiences of those who have recently returned as well as whose investment went bankrupt; who took back his German wife to the village; possible real estate investments; how Turkish compatriots back home try to cheat vacationing migrants; how to smuggle valuable contraband; the devaluation of the Turkish lira; and comparative stories about the relative strengths of different sorts of patronage invoked to weed through the endless, Kafkaesque Turkish bureaucracy.

A great deal of thought, planning, shopping, and arrangements go into the extensive preparations for the trips to Turkey. Much of the preparation is grounded in past experience – what was and was not efficacious on the last trip. Yet the impending journey is also idealised: fantasies are spun, elaborately weaving the texture of the summer to come. Migrants discuss what they will do, eat, see, to whom they will give gifts, which seaside resort they will visit, at what local shrine they will sacrifice a lamb, how they envisage the parties where they will sing, dance, and drink, and how they will add to their new house. Clearly, the ideas of past and future trips to Turkey motivate the physical and psychological energies of migrants while they are *gurbetçi* in Germany. This focus upon trips to Turkey should not be surprising, since the sorrow, isolation, and difficulties associated with the state of *gurbet* cry out to be assuaged. Although the migrants live and work in Europe for eleven months of the year, they do so in order to be able to "really live" during the twelfth month. This attitude is a critical aspect of the Turkish guestworkers' identity as *migrants* rather than *immigrants*: they believe that they are temporary residents and not permanent immigrants, even when appearances seem to indicate the contrary.

The status of *Gastarbeiter* in Germany contrasts with that of foreign workers in other European countries. In Sweden, foreign workers are called "immigrants" and are granted many more rights of political participation; for example, they are allowed to vote in local elections. Moreover, the processes and criteria for naturalisation differ from country to country.

This migrant identity is highlighted in both subjective and objective definitions. The vast majority of Turks in Europe see themselves as temporary denizens who came for a few years and were unfortunately waylaid by any number of things (such as indebtedness or family problems) but who "will soon be returning to Turkey – for good". The migrants' self-definition is consistent overall with the appellation bewstowed on them by Germans – *Gastarbeiter*. Germans and Turks know that to be a guest is to be temporary, and to be a worker is to fulfil, acknowledge, and legitimise only one dimension of "personness". The Turks know painfully well their narrowly delimited status which is shaped daily in colloquial language and behaviour. Therefore, an "immigrant *Gastarbeiter*" would be an oxymoron. Negotiating this paradox on a daily basis surely increases the desire to identify with a place other than the one that refuses legally and socially to accept them, even if it has long since managed to do so while turning a blind eye. Thus the image of Turkey in *Gastarbeiter* consciousness is a bright one; now distant, now fleetingly close, but always the legitimising, defining referent of their absence.

This idealised view of Turkey infuses the preparations for the annual holiday return trip with a mystique. As migrants prepare for the return to Turkey, they often complain about the huge expenditure that they feel obliged to make. A relatively secure worker's family, only moderately in debt, might spend up to DM 5,000 (equivalent to US$3,000 in 1987) for summer preparations, including replenishing the family's wardrobe and filling requests of all sorts – from sports shoes to electronic appliances and silk headscarves. In fact, it has become so costly to return for a summer vacation that some families I met claimed that they could not afford it more frequently than once every several years. They went instead to Spain or elsewhere in Europe where they could ultimately spend far less than they would by returning to their own houses in Turkey.

The long, hot, and uncomfortable trip to Turkey by car is fraught with difficulties, hassles, and often day-long delays at international frontiers. In addition, it becomes an aggressive, competitive race amongst the tens of thousands of Turkish drivers. In spite of this, as they leave western Europe behind and approach the Balkans – signalling the proximity to Turkey – the travellers' spirits lift and expectations mount. The stresses associated with driving worsen as they go along the roads through the Balkans, but moods lighten in direct proportion to the distance from western Europe. Yugoslavia and Bulgaria feel familiar to Turks, who are aware of the close historical connections between these countries

157

and their own.[4] The travellers note the similarity of the Balkans – people, food, architecture, ambience, and landscape – to Turkey. They also express great pleasure each time they manage to speak a bit of Turkish with Serbs, Albanians, or Bulgarians along the way, while being amused by the accents.[5]

The marked difference that can be discerned once the Turks leave German-speaking lands behind them is felt and expressed in terms of a burden having been lifted – in their words *"nihayet, Almanya'dan kurtulduk!"* (at last, we're rid of, freed from, Germany!). Sometimes *"Gavuristan"* is substituted for *Almanya*, Germany becoming the "land of the infidels". In addition, Turks feel a comfortable ease and relaxation with the local people, something that rarely occurs when they are *Gastarbeiter*. Here, in the Balkans, they are foreigners, but not as foreign as they are in Germany; they still are "other" *vis-à-vis* the Balkan populations, but, to apply Arjun Appadurai's phrase slightly out of context, "it has always been true that some others are more other than others" (Appadurai 1986: 357).

The emotional pitch heightens as the returnees approach Kapıkule, Europe's largest international frontier station, at the Bulgarian–Turkish border. Inevitably, a long line awaits the weary, anxious returnees. It is the first shock of many to come; the next will most certainly be the obstacle course at the checkpoints, manned by a series of surly civil servants who provide a baffling set of foils and hurdles which seem to be designed to impede a smooth homecoming. Some of the returnees find themselves caught in a bureaucratic nightmare. They may be informed that their car's papers are out of order, they might be found with contraband (perhaps unknown to them), or they may have neglected to update a visa. Finally, assuming a family of returnees passes relatively unhindered through the checkpoints, they still may face another 24 hours of driving before setting sight on their natal village, for many of the migrants come from south-east Anatolia, not far from the Syrian border.

Once the initial excitement of homecoming begins to wane, the *izinli* returnees find that the privileged treatment which they have received – as esteemed, long-lost relatives – evolves into something quite different: they have become, willy-nilly, *Alamancılar* – German-ish, or German-like. Implicitly derogatory in its markedness, in its explicit differentiation from a non-emigrant Turk, the label bears witness to a combination of difference, lack of acceptance, and rejection. It is a distancing mechanism, expressing the ambivalence contained in the same outstretched arms which greet the returning vacationers, and accept the prestigious gifts, but which also keep them at a socially safe distance. A poem, written by an anonymous Turk in Germany, succinctly expresses this identity conundrum:

Yabancılar derler bize burada
Alamancılar derler bize orada
Anadolum biz kalmışız arada
Bağrımıza hançer vurma ne olur

Here they call us strangers, foreigners,
There, they call us German-like.
Oh, my Anatolia, we're caught in between,
Just don't stab us through the heart.

Their stay in Germany is thought to have fundamentally changed the *Gastarbeiter*, rendering them unlike the compatriots left behind. Exposure to luxuries is believed to have spoiled them and they might now have become accustomed to running water, bathing facilities, automobiles, punctuality, business-like relations with people, efficiency, and cleanliness of a western sort. These attributes are expected of the returnees, and the relatives and neighbours back in the village often respond with defensively apologetic tones. Eventually the novelty of returning and being home wears thin. As frequent comparisons are made with Germany (e.g. "in Germany it's cleaner; more efficient; more modern; the civil servants actually work and are honest"), annoyance and tensions rise in the daily interactions with friends and relatives. Hierarchically, the *izinli* often find themselves having advanced a notch upwards. By virtue of their extended residence in the "First World",[6] the returnees are expected to take on the role of providers, patrons, and philanthropists, as well as to be exhibition-ists, financially successful, and "Europeanised". As such, they are effectively barred from returning to their former identities and relationships.

The symbolic efficacy of objects in the process of constructing and reconstructing personal relations is of paramount importance during the *izin* vacation return. The awareness of the expectations of their compatriots back in Turkey exerts a strong pressure on the migrants, and, accordingly, there are many ways in which the *Gastarbeiter* attempt to fulfil these expectations. For example, they might drive to Turkey in a new car every summer, thus reinforcing the image of the foreign, rich uncle. The poor relations back in the Anatolian village, or in the *gecekondu* shanty town, sufficiently impressed with the great wealth, only see what is conspicuously con-sumable. They have no idea about debts, bank loans, hours worked

159

overtime, unhealthy living conditions, or the social stigma shading the lives of the supposedly wealthy relatives abroad. The demands placed upon the returnees have undergone a rapid and steep inflation.

In the village house of one *izinli* returnee family, I watched a steady stream of neighbours trickle in, ostensibly to pay their respects and welcome them back to the village. Elderly widows seemed especially eager to stop by for tea; a few came back to read the Qur'an to the family. In each case the visitors left with a gift of some sort, either a German trinket, a scarf, or some cash in Deutschmarks. On the day of the emotionally charged festival of *Kurban Bayramı* (Feast of the Sacrifice), this family sacrificed three lambs: one for the elderly, sickly grandmother; one for her returned daughter, who was guilt-ridden for "abandoning" an invalid parent; and one for the car and the journey. Blood from this latter sacrifice was smeared on the front of the car. Some of the meat from this animal was brought back illegally to Berlin for neighbours and friends unable to make the journey.

As *Alamancılar* (i.e. German-like) the *izinli* returnees suffer from disorientation. Some are convinced that the physical ailments that afflict them in northern Europe can be cured with a trip to Turkey.[7] They have returned home to drink the water, feel the sun, and breathe the air. They have come home to reaffirm their Turkishness, yet they find themselves unaccepted as "normal" Turks. They have become irrevocably marked by virtue of their extended absence from Turkey. Feeling misunderstood and less than appreciated by their compatriots in Turkey, they seek others like themselves. On quite a few occasions in Turkey, I saw individuals and families travel considerable distances to visit friends whom they had made in Germany. With each other they were able to relax, tell jokes in German, and compare experiences. They could relate to one another without the constraints of material and social expectations and obligations demanded by an uncomfortable hierarchy.

The social asymmetry to which the *Alamancılar* return is a newly forged structure, one not yet free of burdensome scaffolding. The returnees enter a defined set of social relations in which extensive expectations, primarily financial, are foisted upon them. In order to maintain the prestige that they feel is rightfully theirs by virtue of long, arduous years lived in *gurbet*, toiling to improve the family's lot, they must live up to the role of spendthrifts and benefactors. This is clearly not without serious consequences, essentially reproducing the necessary conditions for extended residence in *gurbet*. On the one hand, their "Turkishness" marginalises the migrants in the German context; on the other, the markedness of being *Alamancılar* in Turkey, the inability to merge back into the Turkish mainstream, entraps Turkish *Gastarbeiter* in a circular quest for an increasingly elusive identity. More and more often, the returnees look northward, turning to the symbols, persons, and identifications associated with their lives in Germany in order to find comfort and meaning.

The second generation: disorientations

The disorientation of returning migrants proves disillusioning and disappointing because their expectations based on past, often romanticised memories remain unrealised. Their children's experience of Turkey is slightly different, however, since many of the children, although born in Turkey, have lived there only as small children and are unschooled in its history and norms, geography and civics, military and civil servants, and codes of gender segregation. Though many of them grow up in closed, ghetto-like enclaves in West German cities, they still are often unprepared for what they find when they return. For example, a girl who in Stuttgart is accustomed to travel alone to school or work on public transportation may suddenly find herself shamed and embarrassed for leaving her family's village house without a male relative to escort her. Alternatively, parents who are protective of their daughters in Germany, and unwilling to allow them much liberty, may give them free rein to socialise with other young people once they are in the safety of their natal village. In one Anatolian village where the Turkoman population was sedentarised two generations ago and approximately 25 per cent of the population now lives in Germany, it is common to see teenage girls and boys openly socialising in the streets, riding motorcycles together, and holding unchaperoned dances until early morning hours. This situation – which is admittedly rather exceptional – contrasted sharply with a town not ten kilometres away, where even a middle-aged, respected, married woman (to say nothing of an unmarried girl), reluctant to expose herself to any unnecessary public scrutiny, will send a 6-year-old neighbour boy to the local oven to buy her bread.

Predictably, young people who return experience painful and disturbing cognitive and behavioural dissonance. For instance, a 15-year-old boy related how shocked he was when he was beaten by male relatives of female schoolmates with whom he had been seen chatting. Teenagers have a particularly difficult time adapting to the mores and rigid hierarchical system prevalent in Turkish schools. They are punished for infractions unknowingly committed – such as not wearing their prescribed uniform properly, leaving a hand in a pocket when a teacher walks into the room instead of

161

standing to attention, or using the informal *sen* ("tu") form of address with a teacher instead of the mandatory *siz* ("vous"). Older girls complain of being ostracised, since their peers assume they are not virgins by virtue of their connections with Germany – a land associated with infidels, immorality, and promiscuity.

Whereas their parents have many and specific expectations of Turkey, the children's notions are few and vague. Most of the second-generation children in Germany can recite by rote: "We are in *gurbet*; we will soon be returning to Turkey, things are better for us in Turkey, we are foreigners here, and it is always best to live in the father/motherland, the *vatan*". Even children whose concrete memories of the *vatan* are hazy at best, grow up hearing these collocations constantly, and repeat them. Yet despite the lip service acknowledging their exiled existence, they have been socialised in Germany, albeit as Turks. For them, Turkey is a distant memory, almost a myth. Increasingly, Turkey is acquiring the status of a vacation land for them, the holiday spot which it is for the thousands of Germans who travel there each year.

In the past several years, many *izinli* returnees have altered the itineraries of their summer visits, and now include holiday villages and resorts on Turkey's spectacular Aegean and Mediterranean coasts. Some of the financially more secure *Gastarbeiter*, after completing retirement homes for themselves in villages, towns, or cities, have invested in holiday homes. Therefore, migrants – and their children – come to see an added dimension of Turkey, and see it now as a spot for amusement, fun, vacationing, and spending money. Many have never travelled within Turkey before, for the concept of *izin* only meant seeing and spending time with relatives. A vacation in the European sense has until recently been an alien concept for them. With the advent of their new European- or German-style vacations, they are in effect beginning to appropriate the German concepts of time, work, place, and leisure. Since vacation *time* is peripheral to the work year, it follows that the *place* of vacation is marginal to the work-place, which assumes centrality in the lives of workers.

Migration and Islam

In recent years, the so-called "Islamic revival" has come under scrutiny in western Europe. Public and private monies are being allocated in order to identify the extent, types, and nature of what is commonly misperceived as a monolithic, nascent, European Islam. For the Turks, well-entrenched networks sustain and regulate the international movement of personnel through whom often competing Turkish and Islamic identities are fostered and kept alive abroad. A bilateral agreement permits the Turkish Ministry of Education to send Turkish teachers to the Federal Republic of Germany to teach public-school courses in Turkish history, culture, and civics. (Turks already living abroad also teach.) These teachers have generally tended to be staunch supporters of the military regime and Kemalism. By definition, they are laicists.[8] A lively competition for control of the indoctrination and education processes of the second generation has thus ensued, compounded in 1987 by a major scandal that broke in Turkey. Saudi Arabian money was linked to key officials in the Turkish government, specifically intended to support the export of religious education to West Germany.[9]

Indeed, many Turks in West Germany were already observant Muslims in Turkey prior to their migration. For many, however, it is the foreign, Christian, and German context that provides the initial catalyst for active involvement in religious organisations and worship. One interpretation of this increased identification with Muslim symbols and organisations is that the popularity of Islamic groups and identifications is a form of resistance against prevailing norms of an alien society, a society commonly perceived of as dangerous, infidel, and immoral. In this view, the migrants' distance from Turkey and their feeling of marginality – not only with regard to Turkey but also to mainstream German society – provide the context for these newfound religious sentiments, which might not have been relevant had the migrants remained with the mainstream in Turkey.

Questions of legality, power, and authority also enter into the picture, if we consider that a great deal of the organisational, preaching, and educational modes that are widespread in West Germany would be clearly illegal in Turkey.[10] For Turkish Sunnis in West Germany, the distance from Turkey ensures freedom from legal constraints, while Turkish Alevis also find in the diaspora an environment conducive to expressing their Alevi identity free from what they perceive as the pressures of a Sunni-dominant, repressive, hegemonic order in Turkey. Thus, embedded in the process of the dual marginalisation – both from Turkish and German societies – of migrant Turkish Alevis and Sunnis are the seeds from which may be observed the blooming of alternative expressions of "re-imagined" (Anderson 1983) Islamic identities.

Turks in western Europe take great care to prevent the moral contamination that they believe threatens them, particularly in the form of *haram* (forbidden) meat – i.e. pork. The Islamic dietary laws, nearly forgotten in Turkey, have moved to the forefront of

163

concerns in *gurbet*. Clever entrepreneurs have used the fear of *haram* to their advantage, and have had great success with their *helal* industries, which sell everything from *helal* sausage to *helal* bread. The explicit association which many Turks make between pork consumption and promiscuity lends still greater fervour to the conspicuous avoidance of German food, restaurants, grocery stores, and butchers.[11] In a country such as Germany, where pork products are an important dietary staple, the adamant Turkish avoidance of pork is sometimes interpreted negatively by German natives as a type of social and cultural rejection, a refusal to integrate and to accept prevailing norms.

Moreover, the overt anti-Muslim sentiment prevalent among Germans is, naturally, resented by religiously observant Turks. This sentiment is manifested in a variety of ways – from the forcible removal of girls' headscarves by public-school teachers, to public mockery or ridicule, to the various strategies employed to oppose and undermine Qur'anic schools. The *kopftuch* (headscarf) debate continues as a heated issue, more among Germans than Turks. Many Germans feel offended by seeing Turkish women and girls with their heads covered. Ironically, the left (particularly feminists) and the right have united in their categorical opposition to the wearing of scarves. Though articulated and rationalised differently – it is variously described as "ugly", "backward", "un-German", "sticking out", or symbolic of sexist, patriarchal dominance and repression – the message is the same. In a self-consciously blatant Christian society, albeit dually denominational, it is not surprising that non-Christians may react by feeling un-accepted and marginalised (see Mandel, 1989).[12]

Although Turkish parents (particularly Sunni) commonly feel threatened by the encompassing Christian, permissive society and its potentially corrupting influence on their children, the reactions of the second-generation children can take different forms. For some, years of intensive indoctrination at Qur'an schools and the mosque outweigh other forces and influences. But teenage girls in particular often respond to the religious resistance of their parents with a counter-resistance of their own. For instance, as soon as they are out of sight of their own homes, they may shed the "Islamic" garments that their fathers force them to wear, and adorn themselves at school with make-up, fashionable mini-skirts, and the like.

In interviews with repatriated migrants in Turkey, I was told a number of times by informants that it was in Germany that they became religious; only there did they begin wearing *baş örtüsü* (the headscarf) and attending mosque. Many Sunni informants also related how they met their first Alevi in Germany. Anti-Alevi prejudices migrate along with the Sunni *Gastarbeiter*, and although in some instances these prejudices may be overcome by direct contact, these are generally thought of as exceptions and are not applicable to the general group. The deeply ingrained Sunni beliefs about the alleged immorality, ritualised incestuous practices, and impure nature of the Alevis determine a significant dimension of patterns of differentiation and affiliation within the Turkish community. This is most evident in the marriage partners chosen by second-generation young people, who rarely marry outside sectarian boundaries.

For centuries in Turkey the Alevis have been the underdogs, often perceived as a fifth column in the Ottoman Empire, as they occasionally sided with the Shi'i Safavis.[13] In Republican times, Alevis have had more than their share of massacres, oppression, and deportations. This extends to the present day, when to identify oneself as an Alevi is an unambiguous identification with the political left – a difficult and dangerous position since the 1980 military *coup d'état*. The problems that the Alevis face in Turkey are reflected in their disproportionate over-representation in the migrant diaspora. Moreover, the tense, repressive state of martial law in several largely Alevi and Kurdish provinces in eastern Anatolia makes itself felt in the lower incidence of repatriation of Alevis to Turkey compared with Sunni migrants.

Within and between Alevi communities various patterns of movement among members of holy lineages have long been an expected way of life. The itinerant holy man, the *pir* or *dede* (spiritual leader, descended from a holy lineage) typically wandered much of the year, travelling from one group of his *talip* followers to the next, and leading *ayin-i cems* (the secret communal Alevi–Bektaşi ritual of solidarity and "collective effervescence", involving song, music, and dervish trance dancing, as well as a re-enactment of the martyrdoms of 'Ali and Hüseyin [Arabic, Husayn]). In addition, the *pir* can legitimately demand tribute from the *talip*, which may assume many forms. Historically, we know that the *pir* served as the locus of intra- and inter-regional communication and was at key times a crucial link in political networks. Often a central figure in opposition movements, he was able to rally followers due to his legitimacy and success as a *pir*, and to convey information.

In the context of contemporary migration, this practice of the itinerant priest, travelling to Alevi communities to conduct the *ayin-i cem* and collect tributes, is maintained, transformed, and might even become the locus of serious intra-Alevi tension and

165

controversy. Elsewhere I have written about an Alevi–Bektaşi *cem* in West Berlin that fell apart in its final moments (Mandel 1986). In that case, the schism ostensibly stemmed from a disagreement between most of the participants and the officiating *dede* over the appropriateness of a particular song's inclusion at the end of the *cem*. The *dede*, who had been flown in from Ankara, wanted to forbid the song, written by Pir Sultan Abdal, on the grounds that it was "political".[14] For the majority of the Alevis there, already alienated from the *dede* for what they felt to be other offensive behaviour, this was the final, backbreaking straw, inciting the minor rebellion that followed.

Migrant Alevis have in many ways successfully reversed their hierarchically subordinate position to the Sunni Turks. They point to what they see as their more "democratic, tolerant, and progressive" stance. While steadfast in their "Aleviness", they identify with and admire many aspects of West German society that the Sunnis interpret as threatening. Modelling themselves on certain German, western modes, they pride themselves on how modern they are, as opposed to the "backward" Sunnis. They point to the village clothing which many Sunni women wear, such as their flowing *şalvar* pants and headscarves. Also, the Alevi practice of not attending mosque, perhaps along with some of the aspects of the practice of *taqiyya* (dissimulation) which characterise them, together serve to raise their status in the eyes of Germans. Finally, Alevis tend to be more politically engaged in leftist politics than Sunnis, and through such activities have greater contact with Germans. Though still peripheral with respect to Sunnis, the Alevis might be slightly *less* marginal (i.e. more integrated) than Sunnis with respect to mainstream German society.

The Alevis, in their consistently heterodox (from the Sunni perspective) stance, have always been inherently "political", even though it was not until the 1970s that the Alevis consciously began to identify themselves as a group, and organise themselves as a formal political party – now outlawed (Mardin 1980: 186–7). Today in western Europe several Alevi groups conceive of themselves in explicitly political – and national – terms. Perhaps the most extreme, a group calling itself "Kızıl Yol" (or Red Path), advocates the founding of "Alevistan" (or a nation of Alevis). Taking its model from the struggles of Kurdish separatists for the establishment of an independent Kurdistan, these followers of the Red Path are criticised by some on the grounds that *Alevilik* (Aleviness) is a religion, not a nationality. Most Alevis would surely not support this nationalist expression of *Alevilik*, and Kızıl Yol is far from representative. None the less, the notion of "Alevistan" is compelling, for it suggests the emergence in the diaspora of a consciously discrete identity (here influenced by the discourse of western nationalisms) which gravitates around a fantastic centre.

While the Alevis abroad are doubly marginal with respect to both Germans and Sunni Turks, their relative position *vis-à-vis* Sunnis has undergone a transformation. In West Germany, the reference point of Sunni dominance becomes less and less relevant. Alevis, who had defined themselves primarily in opposition to Sunnis, and always in reference to them, have in some respects gradually replaced the latter with Germans in the process of identity construction. Furthermore, Alevis in Germany have the freedom to adopt a more inward, communal orientation, unfettered by past political and social constraints.

Displaced centres, emerging identities

Among other things, this chapter has shown how the experience of migration affects different articulations of Islam among expatriate Turks. Not only do Alevis and Sunnis confront the foreign context in very different ways, but their relations to each other are undergoing a transformation in the light of their respective interactions with German society. To a large extent, the separate Sunni and Alevi value systems and histories are reproduced in the second generation, reflecting the different patterns of socialisation in each group. These different patterns of socialisation influence the overall future orientations of Sunni and Alevi youth towards Turkey and Germany.

Migrant parents soften the daily blows of *gurbet* by telling stories to their children, painting for them the contours and shades of a land that they will never see since it does not exist apart from in their stories. They sweeten the bitter present with the elusive saccharin future, which is, to be sure, a revisionist, romanticised projection of a past. A vicious circle of sorts reflects the migratory cycle itself and eventually results in a situation in which the centre finds itself wherever the migrant is not, be it Turkey or Germany. No given locus can be the totalising centre for long. The migrant's marginality in both Turkey and Germany precludes his or her full identification with either place. This displacement is exacerbated by the fact that in either place migrants partially define themselves in relation to the values and symbols of the other locale, which are ubiquitous even in its absence.

The *izin* vacation trip to Turkey is the event that crystallises this conundrum. In the idealisation of Turkey and in the drive there, the crescendo of a southward identification builds up, only to be foiled by the anti-climatic reception in the homeland. From the vantage point of Turkey, Germany then becomes the salient place of reference – that is, until the trip back. Thus, an undercurrent of disaffection and dissatisfaction informs the migrant's experience.

Ultimately, the annual *izin* trip home neither provides an opportunity for collective solidarity with compatriots, nor offers an infusion of the stuff that reinforces identity. Rather, it furthers the alienation resulting from the absence of an attainable centre in the lives of *Gastarbeiter*. In a twist to Benedict Anderson's call for a rethinking of our tendency to reify nations and nationalisms in our act of imagining them (Anderson 1985), here it seems that the *Alamancılar* have been imagined by their compatriots back home, objectified and distanced by the latters' expectations and projections. Yet the annual circular choreography that patterns the migrants' lives contributes to reproducing the *Alamancı* identity of marginality. Thus, as *Gastarbeiter* in Germany they cannot escape their Turkishness, and, conversely, they become *Alamancılar* ("German-like") in Turkey, where they had hoped to be Turks.

Acknowledgements

I would like to acknowledge the valuable suggestions and editing generously offered by Mariane Ferme during the writing of this chapter. Also I would like to thank Robert Dankoff for his advice in the Turkish translations. The remaining faults or errors remain, of course, my responsibility.

Notes

1 This chapter is based on research data gathered in Turkey, West Germany, and West Berlin. Between the years 1980 and 1986, I spent over two years in Turkey and eighteen months in the Federal Republic of Germany, conducting research as a participant observer on several aspects of the migration cycle.
2 With the exception of one forty-minute programme, called "Türkiye Mektubu" ("Turkey Letter"), broadcast each fortnight as part of a Second-Channel weekly programme, "Nachbarn in Europa" ("Neighbours in Europe"), there have been no Turkish television programmes in West Germany. On the rare occasions when Turkish movies are shown on television, they, too, are out of linguistic reach of most Turks, since they are dubbed into German rather than sub-titled. It is the exceptional Turkish migrant family that does not have a VCR, and the Turkish video industry abroad is booming; West Berlin boasts perhaps seventy Turkish video shops. However, the recent introduction of cable television may change the viewing habits of Turkish families, and there is now a nightly Turkish cable-radio broadcast from Cologne.

3 Not only is most socialising carried out with other Turks, but preferably with Turks who, if not relatives, identify with the same region of the country, speak the same language (many of the migrants speak one of two Kurdish languages), and affiliate with the same expression of Islam – be it Sunni, Alevi, or one of the many *tarikats* (religious orders) active in Germany.

4 Due to recent unfortunate incidents affecting the Turkish minority in Bulgaria (ostensibly of an anti-Muslim nature), some Turks have felt apprehensive about driving through the country. However, the apprehension was not serious enough to warrant any change of plans. No one with whom I spoke was willing to opt for the alternate route through Turkey's adversarial NATO ally, Greece, despite the fact that the road through northern Greek Macedonia and Thrace passes through the heartland of Greece's Turkish minority.

5 Turkish still serves as a *lingua franca* in many parts of the Balkans that were under Ottoman rule.

6 I use this term with reservations, following Carl Pletch's criticism of the three-world theory. However, in the present case the informants themselves perceive Turkey as backward and underdeveloped in contrast with the west, which is always the point of reference. Their perception of the hierarchical relations is expressed as an unambiguous Eurocentricity.

7 A new field of medicine, *Gastarbeiterkrankheit*, has emerged in West Germany. In western Europe, Turks claim to experience physical and emotional ailments never known before migration – a complex series of what we would call psychosomatic and psychological illnesses (see, for example, Edinsel 1984).

8 Not all European host countries follow West Germany's example. The Netherlands, for instance, has had altercations with Turkey over this issue, since Holland refuses to admit Turkish textbooks and teachers into its school system. Instead, in an effort to address the migrant situation, Holland has commissioned its own, custom-tailored texts, which are taught by resident Turks. The Dutch object to the pedagogic content and level in the material from Turkey, and claim that through the official books and teachers sent from Milli Egitim (the Ministry of Education), Turkey is merely exporting political propaganda with which the Dutch government does not wish to be associated. West Berlin commissioned and has recently instituted a new, controversial set of Turkish textbooks for grades 1 through 8. They were written and illustrated by Turkish intellectuals residing in West Berlin and contain a great deal of literature and references that are banned in Turkey.

9 Not unrelated are findings that trace massive amounts of presumed Saudi money entering Turkey via Germany to support popular religious orders in Turkey whose social, economic, and educational networks operate by means of an elaborate patronage system. Some sociologists in Turkey have been conducting research on the links and functioning of this sophisticated and highly efficacious patronage system.

10 For example, the maps and pictures decorating the walls of a well-

established Qur'anic school in West Berlin are of the Ottoman Empire and the Ottoman sultans; none represents the Turkish Republic or Mustafa Kemal Atatürk. Much of the preaching that takes place in mosques in Germany is of an explicitly political nature, prohibited in Turkey.

11 I became aware of this after having been asked by Turks on numerous occasions if I ate pork. The intensity of their concern led me to pursue the issue, and in many cases the act of eating pork or abstinence therefrom served as the demarcation line between acceptance as one of "us" and rejection of "them". The way it is often phrased, *"domuz kıskanmaz"* ("pigs are not jealous") euphemistically signifies that pigs are promiscuous animals, not monogamous, and that therefore those who partake of pork also become promiscuous, shameful, lacking in honour and virtue. It is the moral extension of "you are what you eat".

12 A parallel battle is raging in Turkey conducted by Muslims who would like to see the wearing of the headscarf legalised in the schools (it has been banned since the time of Atatürk). This issue has become highly politicised and has been the source of intense strife, strikes, and protests. A scandal involving the former prime minister's brother revolved around bribe money paid to women university students if they agreed to wear the scarf.

13 The Alevis are not a homogeneous, monolithic group. They fall into at least four different language groups – Turkish, Arabic, Zaza, and Kurmançı. The latter two are Iranian and Kurdish languages. In western Anatolia most Alevis are formerly transhumant Turkoman; many in the east call themselves Kurds, or are labelled Kurdish by others.

14 Pir Sultan Abdal, a sixteenth-century *pir*, is revered today as an Alevi folk hero. The eloquent, mystical, politically charged poetry and music he wrote, in the *semah* dervish style, has been kept alive by Alevis since his death. Considered a threat to the Ottoman regime, he died by hanging in 1560 during the reign of Süleyman the Magnificent. The power of the songs has not diminished through the centuries, as the Berlin *cem* incident made clear.

References

Anderson, Benedict (1983) *Imagined Communities*, Verso, London.

Appadurai, Arjun (1986) 'Theory in anthropology: center and periphery', *Comparative Studies in Society and History*, 28, pp. 356–61.

Castles, Stephen and Godula Kosack (1973) *Immigrant Workers and Class Structure in Western Europe*, Oxford University Press, London.

Edinsel, Eser (1984) *Die Psychosoziale Situation Türkischer Kinder und Familien in West-Berlin*, Freie Universität, Berlin.

Mandel, Ruth (1986) 'Sectarian splits: interpretations of Turkish Muslim identities and history', paper delivered to the American Anthropology Association, Philadephia.

—— (1989) 'Turkish headscarves and the "foreigner problem": constructing differences through emblems of identity', *New German Critique*, no. 46, pp. 27–46.

Mardin, Şerif (1980) 'Centre–periphery as a concept for the study of the social transformation of Turkey', in R.D. Grillo (ed.), *'Nation' and 'State' in Europe: Anthropological Perspectives*, Academic Press, London, pp. 173–89.

Piore, Michael (1980) *Birds of Passage: Migrant Labor and Industrial Societies*, Cambridge University Press, Cambridge and New.York.

Pletsch, Carl (1981) 'The three worlds, or the division of social scientific labor, circa 1950–1975', *Comparative Studies in Society and History*, 23, pp. 565–90.

Rahman, Fazlur (1979) *Islam*, University of Chicago Press, Chicago.

Shils, Edward (1961) *Centre and Periphery: The Logic of Personal Knowledge*, Routledge & Kegan Paul, London.

Part four

Saints, scholars, and travel

Chapter nine

Pedigrees and paradigms: scholarly credentials among the Dyula of the northern Ivory Coast

Robert Launay

The Hijaz in particular and the Arabic-speaking Middle East in general have always constituted points of reference for Dyula Muslims.[1] At the most basic level, Arabic is the obligatory language of prayer and the *hajj* an obligation for those who have the means to peform it. Not only the Qur'an but the vast majority of commentaries, legal texts of reference, and personal prayers are written in classical Arabic – an entirely foreign, quintessentially written language, totally unrelated to the Manding language spoken by the Dyula. The ability to read and to write Arabic were necessary conditions for accession to the status of *karamogo*, or "scholar". Travel for the purposes of study was a common means of acquiring knowledge of Arabic as a language and of written texts.

Indeed, the Dyula of the northern Ivory Coast have always valued travel positively. The word *dyula* also means "trader". Formerly the Dyula, as a Muslim minority living amongst "pagan" Senufo, enjoyed an ethnic monopoly over various sectors of both intra-regional and long-distance trade. For individuals involved in commerce, travel was an integral part of the process of making a living. As for religious learning, it was by no means remarkable for younger scholars to travel outside their home communities to pursue their education with more knowledgeable or prestigious teachers. Likewise, scholars from established centres of learning travelled to smaller or more distant communities where they might outshine potential rivals and establish a firm and profitable local reputation.

It is hazardous, however, to make an *a priori* assumption that travel and study in the Arabic-speaking Middle East was the most prestigious form of travel – for study or for the dissemination of ideas. Just as Dyula traders were anxious to maintain control, if not a monopoly, over access to trade goods, so Dyula scholars were concerned to maintain control over access to knowledge – the equivalent of goods in the spiritual and intellectual realms.

175

Knowledge, in this sense, is not simply that which one knows. More crucially, it is the authority with which one speaks or writes. Such authority depends in part on what one has studied and with whom. Claims to superior knowledge, on the grounds that one has studied directly in the Middle East, may constitute a challenge to the authority of local traditions of scholarship. In the last resort, the exercise of intellectual authority is just as much a question of legitimacy as the exercise of political authority. Like political authority, one can attempt to monopolise it, but the success of such attempts depends – even more than in politics – on the attitudes of one's constituency.

The authority of scholars ultimately derives from their expertise in religious matters. The scholar's role in Dyula communities thus hinges first of all on notions of what Islam is and what it means to call oneself a Muslim. Since the nineteenth century, these notions have changed in important ways, and even in the nineteenth century were subject to debate. Controversies about the legitimacy of locally-trained as opposed to foreign-trained scholars are also controversies about different conceptions of Islam and of "being Muslim". In order to evaluate and understand these controversies, it is necessary to establish an historical baseline, albeit a tentative one.

The Suwarian tradition among the Dyula

Until the mid-twentieth century, Islam among the Dyula was predicated on the notion that all Dyula were Muslim and that, locally, most others (particularly Senufo) were *bamana*, "pagans". Supra-locally, the Dyula were in regular contact with other West African Muslim communities, usually Manding-speakers like themselves. Local Dyula were divided into two hereditary categories: *tun tigi* and *mory*. *Tun tigi* were associated in principle with warfare and with the exercise of political power. Adolescent males were initiated into *lo* societies, involving masquerading and blood sacrifices (*jo*) to various spirits. *Tun tigi* were not expected to abstain from alcoholic beverages, to fast throughout the month of Ramadan, or even to pray regularly five times a day. *Mory*, on the other hand, were expected to conform with reasonable diligence to the strictures of the *shari'a*, and adolescent males often received at least rudimentary instruction in reading and writing Arabic. Ideally, the occupations of *mory* were trade and scholarship rather than warfare and politics. These categories, it must be stressed, were hereditary; they applied to entire clan wards (*kabilas*) and not to individuals. Individuals could and did engage in occupations that were more typically associated with the opposite category. Religious practices might also vary on an individual level, at least among the *tun tigi*; since all Dyula were Muslims, it was meritorious, but hardly obligatory, for individual *tun tigi* to emulate *mory* standards of piety.

The common religious identity of all Dyula, *mory* and *tun tigi*, was most fully expressed in certain rituals: the slaughter of sheep on Tabaski, the annual sacrifice during the month of the *hajj*; singing and dancing during Ramadan and on *donba* (the Prophet's birthday); and the manner of observing various life-crisis rituals – naming, weddings, and funerals. Performing these rituals on the required occasions in the proper manner was one central feature of "being Muslim", although the authority for performing them in this manner did not necessarily rest in the prescriptions of written religious texts. On the other hand, outward signs of piety – prayer, fasting, abstaining from alcohol and from blood sacrifices – were not in and of themselves hallmarks of a Muslim identity. At one level, such manifestations of piety were typical only of *mory*, and not of all Dyula Muslims, although at another level they represented an ideal standard of behaviour which all Muslims might choose to emulate. Scholars were responsible for establishing these standards of piety – obligatory in principle for all *mory* and to some extent ideal for *tun tigi*. Their command of Arabic provided them with access to the written texts, which furnished the necessary guidelines for behaviour. They were also expected to set a personal example of piety for others to follow.

There was a tendency for scholarship to be a hereditary occupation. Whole clan wards, or a section of a large clan ward, might specialise in scholarship in any given community. In this way, each village tended to have a few, usually quite small, specialised scholarly families. None the less, any Muslim man might choose at any time to pursue his studies at an advanced level and accede eventually to the status of *karamogo*.

Both the extent of a person's religious learning and the degree to which he was expected to demonstrate this learning in his own pious behaviour corresponded ideally to the circumstances of his birth – as a *tun tigi* or *mory* (i.e. a member of a scholarly lineage or not). However, accession to the status of scholar involved the conferring of a second pedigree, intellectual rather than hereditary. This *isnad* was very much like a genealogy. The Dyula words for teacher and pupil are *karamogo fa* and *karamogo den*, literally "scholar father" and "scholar child". The authority of a scholar ultimately derives from his possession of such a pedigree, which places him in a line of teachers and pupils. If one examines any

177

such *isnad*, one notices that the line of teachers extends literally all the way to God, the ultimate source of knowledge and moral authority. Beneath God, a number of angels are also listed as teacher and pupil before this knowledge is transmitted to humankind in the person of the Prophet. The name of Malik ibn Anas (AD 715–95) is also on every such list among the Dyula, as they all belong to the Maliki school of jurisprudence. More important, the Dyula *isnads* all converge on the name of al-Hajj Salim Suware, who lived in the fifteenth century.[2] The line of transmission from Malik to al-Hajj Salim is clearly abbreviated, as it contains only six names, including two identifiable ninth-century scholars: 'Abd al-Rahman ibn al-Qasim of Cairo and 'Abd al-Salam Sahnun of Qayrawan (Wilks 1968). The convergence of *isnads* on the person of al-Hajj Salim is by no means a peculiarity of the Dyula of the northern Ivory Coast; his influence was so decisive, in a belt that runs from Guinea (Hunter 1977; Sanneh 1979) to northern Ghana (Wilks 1968), that it is perfectly reasonable to speak in terms of a "Suwarian tradition"[3] in West African Islamic scholarship.

This widespread convergence of *isnads* conveys a symbolic message about the nature of knowledge and the authority derived from its possession. God and the angels are the ultimate source of knowledge and moral authority. However, in terms of "this-worldly" geography, knowledge stems first and foremost from the Hijaz (from the Prophet to Imam Malik), then derivatively from Arabic-speaking northern Africa (Cairo, Qayrawan), and finally from the person of al-Hajj Salim, before diverging into various lines. In short, if the Arabic-speaking world is the ultimate earthly source of knowledge, access to this knowledge is mediated by a regional tradition of scholarship; it is not acquired directly at, or closer to, its source.

The Haidara scholars of Kadioha and Boron are a case in point. The Haidara are universally acknowledged in the region as *sharifs*, direct descendants of the Prophet. A putative Middle Eastern origin is not at all unusual among the Dyula. Various clans privately claim descent from one companion or another of the Prophet, admittedly without providing any genealogical evidence, or have oral traditions about the dealings of their "ancestor" with the Prophet, and how in one way or another they were loyal Muslims from the very beginning. Such claims symbolically anchor the clans in space (the Hijaz) and time (the Prophet's lifetime), but they are not socially relevant for regulating inter-clan relationships. Unlike such stories, the Haidara claim falls into the domain of common knowledge. Even so, the Haidara *isnads* also converge on al-Hajj Salim; although they can effectively claim a direct hereditary link to the

Prophet, their intellectual pedigree, like that of everyone else, hails from West Africa and from al-Hajj Salim.

Al-Hajj Salim's scholarly activity was centred on the town of Jagha in western Sudan, but his influence was greatest along the southern fringes of the Manding trade network, and corresponds to the period of the disintegration of the old Malian empire. This was a region in which such Manding-speaking Muslims as the Dyula lived as a minority among various groups of "unbelievers". The tradition of scholarship founded by al-Hajj Salim stressed the religious co-existence of these two categories – Muslims and unbelievers – with the attendant separation of religion and politics. No active attempts were made to proselytise unbelievers, and militant *jihad* was avoided. It would be a serious misconception to label this tradition as "pacifist", however. Warfare, whether with Muslims or unbelievers, remained a distinct possibility. Rather, the Suwarian approach was neatly mirrored in the Dyula distinction between the hereditary categories of *tun tigi* and *mory*, those whose business was ideally warfare and politics and those whose business was ideally religious scholarship. Relations between the Dyula and their "pagan" neighbours might range from open hostility to active alliance, but in no case was religion a deciding issue. The Suwarian tradition not only fostered the development of relatively peaceful co-existence between Muslim minorities and their neighbours, but also sanctioned the existence of different hereditary categories within the Muslim community itself – making outward piety an obligation for some Muslims (especially scholars themselves), but only an ideal for others.

The first challenge: militant *jihad*

In short, the Suwarian tradition incorporated a number of basic distinctions between politics and religion, hereditary and intellectual pedigrees, the Hijaz as the ultimate source of knowledge and moral authority and a local tradition of scholarship. Beginning in the late eighteenth century, comparable traditions of Islam and Islamic scholarship were subjected to challenges in much of West Africa in the form of militant *jihad* movements. Several of these movements attempted to draw their legitimacy from direct study in the Hijaz as opposed to local scholarly traditions. 'Uthman dan Fodio's teacher, Jibril ibn Umar, studied in the Hijaz (Hiskett 1973), as did al-Hajj Umar Tall (Robinson 1985). It would be far too simplistic to explain the *jihad* movements exclusively in terms of the diffusion of ideas from the Middle East to West Africa. The *hajj* itself, especially combined with study in the Hijaz or elsewhere

179

in the Middle East, constituted a different principle of legitimacy, an alternative source of intellectual and moral authority. Under certain circumstances, it could be explicitly opposed to the authority of local scholarly traditions.

The *hajj* has always been a powerful Islamic symbol among the Dyula. Until recently, the journey itself was exceedingly long, hazardous, and difficult. Indeed, I know of no individual at all from the Korhogo region who successfully completed the journey before the twentieth century. On the other hand, I was shown a manuscript list of various illustrious Manding scholars who had accomplished the *hajj*. Twelve scholars are cited in all, hailing from various communities in Mali and particularly in Guinea and the western Ivory Coast. Not surprisingly, al-Hajj Salim Suware headed the list. This list hearkens back to a sort of "golden age" of Islamic scholarship in the region, when scholars were in direct contact with the Hijaz and when the Suwarian tradition itself came into being. After this era, the *hajj* became an ideal rather than a reality. For example, the Cisse of Kadioha relate that their ancestor, Mammadu, left his native town of Bakongo in Guinea to undertake the *hajj*. Along the way, he stopped in the village of Kadioha, where he was finally persuaded to abandon his pilgrimage and to settle instead. Whether or not the story is true, the ancestor is remembered for his piety, not because he accomplished the *hajj*, but rather because of his intention to perform the journey. The *hajj*, situated in the distant past or in terms of intentions rather than accomplishment, constituted a symbolic link between the Dyula and the ultimate source of their faith, much as did the claims of various clans to descent from companions of the Prophet. But it did not necessarily represent an alternative source of moral authority.

This is not to say that the *hajj* was never used as a challenge to the authority of the Suwarian tradition. The career of al-Hajj Mahmud Karantaw among the Kantossi of the Volta Basin, to the east of Korhogo, provides an interesting example.[4] The Kantossi, like the Dyula, were a Muslim minority of Mande origin living in the midst of "unbelievers". Mahmud studied with local teachers and was trained in the Suwarian tradition before undertaking the pilgrimage. During his journey, he stopped to study in Syria with a Qadiri teacher, Shaykh 'Abd al-Rahim, who persuaded him to undertake a *jihad* on his return. This *jihad* against neighbouring "pagans" was launched in the mid-nineteenth century. Al-Hajj Mahmud attracted some support, both among his fellow Kantossi and in the nearby town of Wa, a major centre of Muslim learning in the region (Ivor Wilks, personal communication). With this army, he was able to conquer some of the surrounding area and to found the polity of Wahabu. However, Muslims in the area were strongly divided over support for the *jihad*, with the majority opposing Islamic militancy and favouring the maintenance of friendly relations with neighbouring "pagans" – whether on moral, political, or commercial grounds. Ultimately, the movement was a very limited success, and Wahabu was limited to a small cluster of villages.

Al-Hajj Mahmud's movement demonstrates, first of all, that peoples like Dyula belonging to the Suwarian tradition were aware of and not always impervious to the *jihad* movements that swept through much of West Africa. Second, like a number of other *jihad* leaders, al-Hajj Mahmud sought legitimacy through a direct appeal to study in the Arabic-speaking world, effectively attempting to supersede the mediating role of local scholarly traditions. Finally, this attempt, though not entirely a failure, did not win the support of the vast majority of local Muslims, both scholars and ordinary believers, who continued to affirm their loyalty to the Suwarian tradition. Such loyalty was hardly surprising. Not only were they outnumbered ten to one by their "pagan" neighbours, but they were also more heavily involved in local as opposed to long-distance trade, and they relied on their Senufo neighbours both as customers for their wares and as suppliers of food for purchase in the market place. A *jihad* movement would have been a dangerous gamble, calling into question their relations of co-operation with their neighbours, which the Suwarian tradition legitimised. However, the Dyula were well aware, not only of the existence of *jihad* movements, but also of the religious issues involved in either supporting or opposing them. The absence of such movements in the Korhogo region cannot be taken as a sign of inertia, of an unquestioning respect for the force of religious tradition, but rather as a deliberate confirmation of the principle that religious authority, though it might stem ultimately from the Hijaz, was to be mediated by established local lines of scholarship rather than by a direct appeal to contemporary teachings in the Arabic-speaking world.

The second challenge: the "Wahhabi" movement

The imposition of French colonial rule was to lay the groundwork for the redefinition of what it meant to be Muslim among the Dyula. Consequently, they had new grounds for calling the Suwarian tradition into question. French rule in and of itself did not constitute a major problem within the Suwarian tradition.

Before the colonial period, the Dyula had accommodated them-selves quite well to being ruled by non-Muslims. Given the principle of the separation of politics and religion, it was expected that scholars would profess outward loyalty to whatever regime was in place, although other individuals were free to support or to oppose it as they saw fit. Rather, the social, political, and economic changes that ultimately accompanied French rule were to transform society and consequently the place of scholars within it. In the first place, the *pax colonia* abolished pre-colonial patterns of warfare and rendered the warrior functions of the *tun tigi* obsolete. At the same time, it opened new avenues for trade in the south of the Ivory Coast – not only for the Dyula but also for other trading groups, who were often better able to exploit these new possibilities. Dyula from Korhogo began to migrate in substantial numbers to the south – where kola nuts (a major trade good) were grown, and where there was a ready market for livestock, cloth, and other commodities. At the same time, the village of Korhogo was chosen as the major administrative centre for the entire northern region of the Ivory Coast, eventually attracting a stream of migrants in its own right. The development of rail and motor transport, by revolutionising patterns of African trade, marginalised the strategic importance of communities along trade routes in favour of those situated directly near centres of production or consumption, and also concentrated trade in the hands of large-scale traders. In the towns of the south, the Dyula immediately found themselves in direct contact – and in competition – with Muslim traders from elsewhere. As a plantation economy developed in the south, the north, and Korhogo in particu-lar, became important as a source of both migrant labour and staple foods. Korhogo began to attract ever more substantial numbers of immigrants, mainly Senufo from outlying areas but also individuals from neighbouring countries, many of them Muslim and often Manding-speakers like the Dyula.

By the middle of the twentieth century, the Dyula of Koko, des-cendants of the original Dyula inhabitants of the town, found that their situation had altered radically in a number of respects. First of all, they had lost all pretensions to a monopoly over trade in the region. Second, they were no longer in a position to assimilate new Muslim immigrants to Korhogo, as they had in the past. While they retained the "ownership" of the town's Friday mosque, they no longer enjoyed a monopoly over Islam. Formerly, trade, Muslim identity, and membership in the Koko Dyula community all coin-cided in Korhogo. Now, these three features became dissociated. A Muslim identity remained a pre-condition for entering the sector of local trade. However, the relationship between trade and Islam changed in a crucial if not immediately obvious manner. In the past, Muslims, defined in terms of their Dyula ethnic identity, had monopolised trade. Now, non-Muslims could enter the trade sector by converting to Islam. Growing numbers of Senufo "pagans", beginning with the chief of Korhogo himself, converted to Islam, especially within town.

These conversions were partly responsible for changing the symbols of Muslim identity in Korhogo. In the past, a Muslim was one who belonged to a Muslim community and affirmed this identity by participating in the performance of communal rituals on Muslim calendar holidays and at the time of life crises. Now, new converts might adopt Islam individually without renouncing their membership in communities which also included unbelievers. Their newfound Muslim identity was most conveniently expressed through the adoption of outward forms of piety – praying, fasting, etc. – once typical of Dyula *mory* but not of *tun tigi*. Such forms of piety were recognisable signs of an Islamic identity anywhere, outside as well as within the region. Consequently, Dyula *tun tigi* were increasingly attracted to *mory* forms of piety. Their former role as "warriors" was obsolete. Initiation into the *lo* societies constituted a drain on the time and financial resources of younger men – who, during and just after the Second World War, refused *en masse* to participate. The *lo* societies were abandoned, and the *tun tigi/mory* distinction ceased to be socially salient. Calendrical and life-crisis rituals continued to be of importance, but they ceased in and of themselves to constitute the signs of Muslim identity – giving way to observances which were more globally identifiable as "Muslim".

The immediate consequence of this shift was to reinforce the leadership role of scholars in the Dyula community. Their personal behaviour was expected to set a standard, not only for the *mory*, but for the entire community. They were responsible for explaining to the entire community the kinds of behaviour that were proper or improper, forbidden, or enjoined. The guidelines which they set had to be acceptable, not only to Dyula Muslims but to Muslims from other communities as well. Before the Second World War, the public preaching of homilies was not a major activity of scholars, and was usually left to students. Now, *karamogos* – the younger ones at first – began to deliver sermons on a regular basis, as part of the ceremonials associated with Muslim calendar holidays as well as funerals. The sermons found ready and avid audiences, admittedly because they were a form of entertainment, but also, as one friend of mine explained, because Islam is a complex matter and it is the ordinary believer's responsibility to make himself aware of the rules so that he may observe them properly.

In the short run, this new found *"shari'a*-mindedness"*, to use Hodgson's (1974) term, provided Dyula scholars with more moral authority in the community than ever before. In the longer run, however, it provided a basis for challenging, rather than reinforcing, the legitimacy of scholars trained in the Suwarian tradition. Islam among the Dyula had formerly been predicated on the notion that different kinds of religious behaviour were appropriate for different categories of persons: *tun tigi*, *mory*, and *karamogos*. By the 1950s, a single standard of piety was held to apply, not only to all Dyula but effectively to all Muslims. Once the principle is established that all Muslims throughout the world ought to conform to the same norms of piety, perceived discrepancies appear as problematic. Indeed, if there is a universal standard of piety, the status of a local tradition of scholarship is effectively altered. Islamic knowledge has universal applications, and there ceases to be any *a priori* reason why a local pedigree, anchored in the Suwarian tradition, is necessarily preferable to any other.

Discrepancies are only a problem if they are perceived as such. However, the *pax colonia*, by favouring the freer movement of individuals from place to place, broadened the contact of Dyula with other Muslims (though the Dyula, as traders, were never isolated from such contacts) and increased the likelihood that individuals might perceive discrepancies of various kinds. In particular, it became easier to accomplish the *hajj*, though as long as the pilgrimage remained an overland journey, it remained long and hazardous. Few individuals from Korhogo actually undertook such a journey. It involved leaving one's family for years on end and finding odd jobs from place to place along the way in order to pay for each leg of the trip. Those who made the trip are remembered as having accomplished something remarkable, but not for returning with new ideas, new conceptions of Islam, or "being Muslim". However, the very fact that such journeys were actually made was itself significant. Al-Hajj ceased to be a title which was applied only to names on a list going back to the remote past, but became a contemporary reality. The journey to the Middle East and to the Hijaz – to the ultimate source of religious knowledge and authority – was no longer an ideal which for all intents and purposes was almost unrealisable, but a real possibility, even if beyond the means of most.

While the overland *hajj* did not have a direct intellectual impact on Islam among the Dyula of Korhogo in the first half of the twentieth century, it did for other West African Muslim communities with whom they were in touch. Towards the end of the Second World War, when the Dyula of Korhogo were in the process of abandoning the *lo* societies, a number of Manding-speaking pilgrims returned from the *hajj* with a different set of ideas. After a prolonged sojourn in the Hijaz and the Arabic-speaking world, al-Hajj Tiekoro Kamagate returned to Bouake, the second largest town in the Ivory Coast, and began to preach against various practices associated with the Suwarian tradition. Roughly at the same time, a small cadre of young *hajjis* from Guinea and the Gambia – notably al-Hajj Kabine Kaba and al-Hajj Muhammad Fode – returned from several years of study at al-Azhar in Cairo, where they had chosen to remain as students on their return from the Hijaz. During their stay, they were exposed to the reformist ideas of Muhammad 'Abduh and his disciples. On their return, most members of this group ultimately chose to settle in Bamako, a more central and cosmopolitan location than their home communities. These individuals in Bouake and Bamako were disparagingly labelled "Wahhabis" by the French colonial authorities, who took a dim view of their activities.[5]

In both towns, they directly challenged the authority of established scholars. First of all, they criticised the formalism of the Sunni legal schools, and attacked the Sufi orders. Although Sufism is a relatively peripheral feature of Islam among the Dyula, most *karamogos* belong to the Qadiriyya or the Tijaniyya. The Hajjis denounced all forms of saint worship as illegitimately positing the existence of intermediaries between God and the ordinary believer. Like Sufism, saint worship is not a central feature of the Suwarian tradition, but the tombs of certain founders of scholarly lines are considered legitimate objects of veneration. By challenging this notion, they called into question the legitimacy of such lines of scholarly authority, and, by implication, the intellectual pedigrees of Dyula scholars. They attacked all forms of magic as illegitimate: for example, the manufacture of written amulets – which constituted a part of the earnings of scholars. Last but not least, they denounced aspects of life-crisis and calendrical rituals, particularly the distribution of prestations – called *saraka* ("charitable donations") by Suwarian scholars and their followers. These, the Wahhabis argued, did not constitute charity at all and so conferred no religious merit.

The Wahhabi criticism went considerably further than the challenge of nineteenth-century *jihad* movements. Adherents of *jihad* movements had appealed directly to the sources of knowledge in the Hijaz and the Middle East, without necessary recourse to the scholarly tradition of al-Hajj Salim Suware. The Wahhabis argued that such a direct appeal was not only possible but necessary, that the Suwarian tradition as a whole was corrupted and characterised by *bid'a* ("innovation"). It is not hard to understand why the French colonial authorities were openly hostile to the movement. They had, after long years of suspicion (Triaud 1974), come to terms with and accepted the Suwarian tradition. The Suwarian distinction between "religion" and "politics" encouraged Muslim scholars to come to a *modus vivendi* with the French, and even at times to proffer active declarations of support. Having reached the conclusion that established Muslim scholars were their allies, the French were alarmed about direct attacks on their legitimacy. Worst of all, the direct appeal to the Middle East as a source of knowledge and authority laid open the gates for the spread of pan-Islamic (and anti-French) nationalism, which, given the climate of emerging African nationalism at the time, was the last thing the French wanted to see. Indeed, some scholars have stressed the link between the Wahhabis and the Rassemblement Démocratique Africain (RDA), the major nationalist party in West Africa.[6] However, although most Wahhabis were sympathisers, if not militants, of the RDA, both movements chose to distance themselves from one another. In Bamako, some of the wealthiest and most prominent Wahhabis chose to support the French (Amselle 1977); on the other hand, RDA support for the Wahhabis would have alienated Muslims loyal to the Suwarian tradition, many of whom also gravitated to the RDA. Despite French fears, the Wahhabiyya in West Africa was never a proto- or even a pro-nationalist movement in religious garb. The Wahhabi leadership took no official stance against the French but concentrated their attacks on local scholarly traditions.

This Wahhabi attack split Muslim communities throughout Ivory Coast and Mali. There were anti-Wahhabi riots in Bamako in 1957, and scuffles in Sikasso – just across the border from Korhogo. In communities with a large Wahhabi presence, including Bouake in Ivory Coast, control over the main mosque was a major issue, and the secession of the Wahhabis a frequent outcome. In general, the Wahhabis symbolically expressed their separation from the masses who continued to follow the lead of Suwarian scholars. The Wahhabis made a point of praying with their arms crossed instead of outstretched in the Maliki fashion. They also embarked on a programme of educational reform, establishing religious schools of their own. Such schools were partly modelled on western forms of secular education, with separate classrooms and an emphasis on language instruction as opposed to rote memorisation. Such schools were intended as an alternative not only to traditional Qur'anic instruction but also to the rapidly expanding state-run secular school system which Wahhabis – and also many anti-Wahhabi Muslims – accused of undermining Islamic values.

Korhogo avoided the violent clashes between Wahhabis and their opponents that plagued other West African communities. None the less, the town was by no means isolated from the split between Wahhabis and Suwarian loyalties. The Wahhabis succeeded in making a few converts among the Dyula of Koko – notably among those living in Bouake – but also several who remained in Korhogo. In 1972–3, I was repeatedly witness to impassioned anti-Wahhabi arguments. Supporters of the Suwarian tradition of scholarship were on the defensive, eager to castigate their opponents as dangerous and ignorant innovators. Naturally, local scholars were all militantly anti-Wahhabi, as their own credentials were at stake. However, anti-Wahhabi sentiments were by no means limited to scholars; in this matter, they had the firm backing of the vast majority of Koko's Dyula community.

At stake was the relationship of Islam – of being Muslim – to community identity. The Suwarian tradition had not only tolerated but legitimised distinctions of status within the Dyula Muslim community. In the past, *tun tigi* and *mory* were allowed two different standards of religious behaviour. While this no longer held true, communal Muslim rituals gave expression, not only to ethnicity, to membership in neighbourhood or village communities, but also to clan ward membership, elder or junior status, and even to slave or free origins. The Wahhabis, on the other hand, denied the religious importance of such distinctions. For them, there were only "pure" Muslims – themselves – and ignorant Muslims. For this very reason, others perceived their behaviour as a form of exclusiveness. Implicitly or explicitly, the Wahhabis constituted a new kind of community, distinct from traditional bases. The Dyula stereotype of typical Wahhabis was of wealthy merchants, often relatively recent converts to Islam: Senufo for example, but also groups of traditional "caste" status like the Kooroko (Amselle 1977), or even slaves. In short, the Wahhabis were particularly successful in recruiting converts from among those groups and individuals who, during the initial years of the *pax colonia*, had moved into such new towns as Bouake or Bamako, converted to Islam, and wrested trade monopolies from groups such as the Dyula. They represented, in effect, the *nouveaux riches* among Manding-speaking Muslim traders. The danger remained, however, that they might also woo away the loyalties of successful merchants from communities such as Koko, who might be tempted to throw in their lot with wealthy colleagues of heterogeneous origins rather than acknowledge their obligations to less prosperous kin and neighbours.

Within the Suwarian tradition, intellectual pedigrees and hereditary statuses, while they were kept distinct, were nevertheless
closely related. Access to knowledge was mediated by one's place in
a locally anchored line of scholarly transmission; one's identity as a
Muslim was mediated by one's hereditary membership of a local
Muslim community. The Wahhabis denied the legitimacy of both
of these criteria. Knowledge and moral authority came directly
from al-Azhar and the Hijaz; indeed, some Wahhabis have recently
begun veiling their women, a practice unknown until now in the
Korhogo region. True Muslims are to be known not from their
birth, but rather from their behaviour which sets them apart from
the mass of ignorant believers.

In 1972–3, although the Wahhabis made few converts in Koko,
they attracted a number of sympathisers and seemed to be gaining
ground in the community. When I returned some twelve years later,
I found to my surprise that the issue had ceased to become controversial. To be sure, individuals were willing, in response to my
questions, to list the multifarious errors into which the Wahhabis
had fallen, but no one bothered to raise the subject on his own. The
Wahhabi presence in the town as a whole was actually more conspicuous than before, if only because one could not help noticing
the presence of women (even in small numbers) wearing the veil.
However, among the Dyula of Koko, Wahhabi influence was on
the decline. The example of one prominent Wahhabi – a prosperous trader living in Bouake – may demonstrate why. By 1984, he
had acceded to the headship of a section of a large clan ward, and
was now a prominent elder. As such, he was responsible for
organising life-crisis rituals such as weddings and funerals,
involving himself in the distribution of *saraka* prestations, and
inviting scholars to preach sermons – the very kinds of activities
that the Wahhabis vocally condemned. Though a Wahhabi, he was
respected and well liked in Koko; the price he had to pay was public
behaviour that flagrantly contradicted his Wahhabi ideas. Ultimately, the exclusiveness and dogmatic rigidity of the Wahhabis
precluded their winning many converts in Koko. One could not
simultaneously behave like a Wahhabi and like a prominent elder.
Risking mild ridicule, one could privately hold Wahhabi beliefs and
publicly behave like everyone else. Hard-line Wahhabis, uncom-
promising in their behaviour, were not tolerated in Koko. Such a
stance would cut one off from one's kin, and no one I knew from
Koko was prepared to go to such lengths. On the other hand, the
kind of compromises necessary to remain simultaneously a
Wahhabi and an active member of the Koko Dyula community
tended in the long run to discourage further conversions.

The third challenge: the new literacy

Paradoxically, whereas the Wahhabis themselves continued to be rejected by the Koko Dyula community, many of the ideas central to their conception of Islamic reform have become increasingly attractive. More than anything else, the spread of western-style secular education has been indirectly responsible, but western education came very late to Koko. The northern Ivory Coast – far removed from the capital and particularly impervious to missionary influence – had always lagged considerably behind the rest of the country. Only after the Second World War did any children from Koko attend western schools, and only because they were recruited by force. Such force quickly ceased to be necessary, as it became clear that western-educated youths had access to relatively lucrative salaried employment, but the north continued for a long time to lag far behind the Ivory Coast as a whole. As late as 1963, a survey of the Korhogo region indicated that only 17 per cent of school-age children were enrolled in primary school (SEDES 1965: I, 60). As a result, the first generation of educated males in Koko are only now in their fifties. They are old enough to be considered elders, though not senior elders, but a few are quite wealthy, and others relatively well-to-do, giving them a far greater influence than their age would normally merit. Partly as a result of their example and their influence, the number of educated – among women as well as men – has increased steadily, although the employment prospects for the educated have proportionally diminished at an even faster rate.

The spread of western education has altered Dyula perceptions of Arabic literacy. The Suwarian tradition of scholarship stressed rote learning. Texts, beginning with *suras* from the Qur'an, were memorised. The written word functioned partly as an aid to memory, as a means of assuring that texts were properly learned, and as a corrective to faulty recall. Even among *karamogos*, knowing a text meant in the first place knowing it by heart, as well as understanding the meaning of particular words and passages. I was constantly impressed by the facility with which scholars could reproduce Arabic texts from memory, rather than relying on the books in their libraries.[7] It must not be forgotten that the Suwarian tradition developed at a time when copying was the only means of procuring a text, when paper was a scarce and valuable commodity, and when libraries were highly perishable. Nowadays, when printed books in Arabic are readily available in the marketplace, human memory is not the only means of storing knowledge. Western education furnished another model for acquiring literacy. Of

189

course, western education also involved considerable amounts of rote learning, but children were from the very beginning introduced to the alphabet, to the meanings of specific words, and to basic principles of grammar. French, moreover, was also a spoken language in Korhogo, and could be used to communicate not only with French administrators but with Africans from other parts of the Ivory Coast. In the Suwarian tradition, the first use to which reading was put was the recitation of texts; in secular education, reading allowed the literate both to speak French and to understand various kinds of written texts at their disposal.

One of the first actions of the Wahhabis in Bamako had been to establish Arabic schools modelled to some extent on the western secular school system – not a surprising idea from individuals trained at al-Azhar and fluently literate in Arabic. The idea of a *madrasa* – a school which taught Arabic literacy in the same way as French – did not remain a Wahhabi monopoly. Such schools constituted an alternative to a purely secular education. The idea spread late to Korhogo, precisely because of Korhogo's lag in the field of western education, but in 1971 the first such school, the Ecole Franco-Arabe, was founded in town. The purpose of the school was to educate children, both in the standard, primary-school curriculum – French, mathematics, history, etc. – and in the Arabic language and Islam. Pupils were prepared for the primary-school certificate as a means of entry to modern employment, but in a way that would reinforce rather than conflict with religious values. However, such schools were not officially recognised by the government, and thus could not furnish an official transcript, required for admission to secondary school. Initially, this discouraged most parents from enrolling their children, but as employment prospects for secondary-school leavers became more bleak the benefits of such a combined system of education seemed more attractive. The Ecole Franco-Arabe has not only survived, but has spawned a host of imitators in Korhogo. In 1973, it was common to pass groups of boys sitting outside, reciting texts from writing boards under the watchful eye of an adolescent, poised over their head with a rod ever ready to strike the pupil whose memory faltered. By 1984, two scholars from Koko had opened their own *madrasas*, complete with schoolrooms, blackboards, and French-as well as Arabic-language instructors, and the old system of Qur'anic education was virtually defunct in town.

The hope of such students and their parents is that they may pursue their education in the Arabic-speaking world. Various Arab countries offer scholarships to such students from time to time. The head of the Ecole Franco-Arabe keeps in constant touch with various embassies in the capital, hoping each year to extract promises for a few reserved slots. In 1985, for instance, he was offered three scholarships from Egypt, and graduates from that year's class were urged to travel to the capital in order to take a competitive examination to determine who would go. In past years, I was told, Saudi Arabia, Kuwait, various Gulf emirates, and even Syria offered scholarships. (Admittedly, the Syrian case was a fiasco, since almost no parents were willing to send their children. This reluctance may have stemmed from the fact that Lebanese traders, who are either Christians or Shi'i Muslims, used to be known as "Syrians". As a result, African parents may have felt that "Syria" was hardly the place to procure a worthy Sunni Muslim education.) The winners of such scholarships might even obtain a university education in the Arab world, either in religion or in some secular subject. One could never be sure in any particular year which countries, if any, might offer scholarships, but as long as some pupils were chosen from time to time the hope remained.

I do not know what has happened to individuals from Korhogo who left for study in the Middle East, as this is such a recent development. However, other communities in the Ivory Coast – most notably Abidjan and Bouake – as well as in other African countries, began sending students rather earlier. Such students, if they do not return with a marketable technical skill, are prime candidates to teach in the new *madrasas*. They have first-hand experience of classroom teaching in Arabic, and they have achieved a considerable degree of fluency in spoken as well as written Arabic. Those who study in Saudi Arabia have a particular advantage, as the Saudi government has apparently been interested in underwriting some of the costs of such *madrasas*. According to the director of the Ecole Franco-Arabe, two Saudi teachers were originally sent to a school in Bouake, but they suffered from severe culture shock and had to be recalled. Since then, the Saudi government has preferred to pay the salaries of African-born teachers, trained in Saudi Arabia, as a form of assistance. One such teacher, a young man from Sierra Leone, was on the staff of the Ecole Franco-Arabe in 1985.

Aside from classroom teaching, individuals trained in the Arab world may choose to become full-fledged Islamic scholars. One such young man passed through Koko in 1985 and delivered a sermon. Local Dyula, particularly those educated in French, were impressed. It was pointed out to me that he could pronounce Arabic in the way that Arabs do (the mass media have familiarised Dyula with "Arab" Arabic pronunciation), and not with the heavy

191

accent of locally trained scholars. He read texts fluently out loud (rather than reciting them from memory) and could comment readily on the meanings of different words, glossing them in Dyula with greater ease, in the opinion of his audience, than could local scholars.

Locally-trained and foreign-trained scholars thus possess two distinct styles of Arabic literacy. For Suwarian scholars, knowledge is first and foremost memorised knowledge of a relatively standard-ised corpus of texts; as one of them commented to me quite explicitly, "It's what's in my head, not in my library, that counts". Foreign-trained scholars have a conception of knowledge that more closely resembles western notions. Knowledge consists in large measure in the ease with which information can be retrieved from written texts, as well as the fluency with which individuals can write and speak – as well as read and understand – Arabic. Literacy, in short, is a skill rather than a mastery of a relatively fixed body of texts. For western-educated Muslims, study in the Middle East is valued for the new style of Arabic literacy to which it gives direct access.

Fluency in Arabic, however, is not the only quality that attracts the western-educated to this new generation of Arab-trained scholars. Among students in the secular school system, there is a revival of interest in Islam, associated with the emergence of the *Association des Elèves et Etudiants Musulmans de la Côte d'Ivoire* (AEEMCI) – the Muslim Students' Association of the Ivory Coast. The AEEMCI is officially recognised, and indeed partly funded, by the national government. It broadcasts a popular weekly pro-gramme on state-run television, and organises study sessions for students, as well as an annual national conference. Indeed, the con-ference was held in Korhogo in 1985, and was heavily attended by local residents as well as by delegates from around the country. Significantly, the association has links with the Arabic-speaking world and with Africans trained there. For example, the director of the Ecole Franco-Arabe in Korhogo is active in the local chapter, and the guest speakers chosen for its television show are frequently young scholars trained in the Middle East. The association and its Arab-trained scholars represent, like the Wahhabiyya, a "reform-ist" style of Islam. It preaches above all an Islamic morality – against drugs, alcohol, delinquency, prostitution, and premarital sex, stressing the importance of prayer, fasting, and the *hajj*. In itself, such moralising does not conflict with the Suwarian tradition of scholarship; local scholars preach on much the same issues. The difference lies in what the AEEMCI and the Arab-trained scholars choose to ignore and, in subtle ways, to devalidate – i.e. those rituals, typical of local Islamic traditions, which are associated with life crises and Muslim calendar holidays.

This devalidation – one television show, for example, warned against overly ostentatious funerals – is consistent with the attitudes of a younger generation of western-educated Dyula Muslims. Unlike the first generation of school graduates, they are not assured of lucrative employment. Many of them can hope for a reasonably cosy living, but hardly for senior appointments in the foreseeable future. They are neither old enough nor wealthy enough to have much voice in local community affairs, but many of them are (or can aspire to be) prosperous enough to attract demands from their kin, particularly on such occasions as funerals and weddings. Their attitude towards such rituals can be summed up by a comment made privately to me by a young military technician during his grandmother's funeral: "*Ça pue le fric*" ("It stinks of cash"). These young educated Muslims feel attached in important ways to their home communities, but in other respects wish to distance themselves, and feel unconcerned by many local goings-on. The Suwarian tradition, which places great emphasis on the importance and obligations (monetary and otherwise) of community membership, is associated in their minds with the heavy demands that the home community makes on them. The kind of Muslim identity advocated by the AEEMCI still permits them to express their solidarity with their home communities – Islam is after all a minority religion in the Ivory Coast – without making the same kind of demands on their resources.

Like the Wahhabiyya, the AEEMCI and the younger Arab-trained scholars thus constitute an ideological alternative to the local scholarly tradition. However, unlike the Wahhabis, the AEEMCI rigorously avoids confrontation. On the contrary, individuals active in the AEEMCI make every attempt to maintain cordial relations with locally-trained scholars: for example, inviting them to the graduation ceremonies at the Ecole Franco-Arabe. This policy is dictated in the first instance by the national government, which underwrites some of the association's expenses and without whose co-operation a weekly television show would be unthinkable. Indeed, the government is quite willing to foster the association's co-operation with conservative Muslim countries such as Saudi Arabia and Egypt, and in this way counteract the possible appeal of the "radical" ideology of states such as Libya or Iran. However, the association's conciliatory stance towards local scholars is not simply dictated by the state. Unlike the Wahhabiyya, the association does not reject Maliki "formalism" nor does it seek to distinguish itself doctrinally from the Suwarian scholars. The differences are primarily those of style and emphasis. This allows the association to seek the support of local scholars for some of its goals, and gives scholars no legitimate grounds for denouncing its activities. Ordinary Muslims are thus not faced with choosing definitively between local scholars trained in the Suwarian tradition and Arab-trained scholars associated with the AEEMCI.

Individual preferences for one or the other group are not the subject of controversy and consequently do not split the Muslim community. Paradoxically, this peaceful co-existence of two scholarly styles is the greatest threat yet to the survival of the Suwarian tradition. More and more Muslims now own television; a novelty in Koko in 1973, they are now a common sight, even in relatively poor households, and villages in the north are beginning to receive electricity, which will permit villages to own their own sets. The younger Arab-trained scholars' access to television is a considerable boost to their prestige. Their new style of literacy in Arabic is intuitively perceived as superior – not only by Muslims with western secular education but also by those educated in the *madrasas*. The fact that the Arab-trained scholars distance themselves morally from the practice of ostentatious prestations during life-crisis rituals without denouncing such practices vocally attracts younger Muslims – particularly educated Muslims living away from their home communities, who privately resent the demands on their resources that such practices entail but do not wish to make a public stand against them that might alienate their older kinsmen.

In short, the spread of new forms of education – in both French and Arabic – have led to a certain disenchantment with the Suwarian tradition and its scholars. To possess an *isnad* that traces one's intellectual pedigree directly back to al-Hajj Salim Suware is no longer a *sine qua non* for being acknowledged a Muslim scholar, since training in the Middle East now constitutes a universally accepted alternative. This is not to say that the Suwarian tradition is defunct. *Karamogos* are still being trained in the Suwarian tradition, although these are usually older men, villagers, or scions of locally established scholarly families. However, as more and more generations of educated Dyula Muslims accede to elderhood, it seems likely that the Suwarian tradition, once the only legitimate scholarly tradition in the region, will become more marginal.

Conclusion

The Hijaz, and, more generally, the Arabic-speaking world, have always constituted a source of origins for the Dyula: origins conceived both in terms of heredity (when different clans trace their origins to the Hijaz during the Prophet's lifetime) and in terms of the transmission of knowledge and moral authority (as expressed in *isnads*). Until the twentieth century, these origins were largely situated far away in space and time. Appeal to these origins was mediated by the presence of local scholarly lines of transmission of knowledge. This principle of mediation, and legitimacy which it conferred on local scholars, was always subject to possible challenge – to the notion that it was possible to acquire knowledge directly from its geographical source and thus to short-circuit the Suwarian pedigrees. Such challenges have occurred in three sets of circumstances: in the mid-nineteenth century, with the rise of militant *jihad* movements; after the Second World War, with the emergence of the Wahhabi movement; and in the past decade, in the form of an Islamic revival among educated Muslim youth. These instances were not accidental. Individuals did not simply happen to study in the Middle East and then attempt to bring back new ideas to their home communities. Until relatively recently, the trip itself was a formidable one, and even now is by no means easy. Study in the Middle East represented a quest for an alternative and superior source of knowledge, and consequently an implicit, if not explicit, calling into question of the local scholarly tradition.

These challenges all revolve around the issue of legitimacy – of the respective moral authority of a direct as opposed to a mediated appeal to the original sources of knowledge. The question of whether direct study in the Middle East does or does not supersede the authority of local lines of transmission is ultimately decided in the home community by individuals who for the most part are not themselves scholars. The fact that such issues have repeatedly split local communities, often violently, suggests that a great deal more is at stake than the reputations of individual scholars trained in one tradition or another. For this very reason, such challenges are not made lightly, and the circumstances in which they occur are highly significant. In each case, the underlying issue was the nature of the Muslim community itself. The *jihad* movements called into question the status of Muslim communities as minorities living in the midst of unbelievers. The Suwarian tradition held that different hereditary categories of persons might legitimately observe different religious practices. While it might be meritorious for anyone to emulate "*shari'a*-minded" standards of behaviour, only certain hereditary categories of individuals were under an obligation to do so. Unbelievers, provided they were not apostates and did not interfere with the religious practices of Muslims, were not necessarily to be fought, much less converted. In this way, Suwarian scholars legitimised patterns of relations between Muslim minorities and their "pagan" neighbours; proponents of *jihad*, on the other hand, dictated that such relationships be jeopardised. Such movements advocated the creation of a new political and economic, as well as religious order. In communities such as Koko, where most individuals stood to benefit from the status quo, such ideas were not received with a great deal of enthusiasm.

By the end of the Second World War, the nature of the Muslim community in Korhogo had changed substantially. For reasons which lay largely outside the control of the Koko Dyula community, "Muslim" had ceased to be a hereditary category. Korhogo was full of new converts, both from within and outside the region. However, the Koko Dyula community continued to exist as such, and membership in it or in its constituent parts was continually expressed through rituals presided over by local scholars, who thereby implicitly asserted its legitimate existence in Muslim terms. Wahhabi leaders, invoking both their experience of the *hajj* and their training at al-Azhar, denied the legitimacy of both the Suwarian tradition, and, more crucially, of traditionally constituted communities within the larger community of Islam. They denied the salience of ethnic, local, slave, or caste origins in favour of the distinction between a truly Islamic community and the mass of believers who remained in ignorance, and mingled – in their eyes – Islamic and extra-Islamic practices. Dyula were effectively asked to choose between loyalty to their home community or to the new community of Wahhabi believers. Confronted with such a radical choice, the vast majority were unwilling to renounce their membership in their local communities, and Wahhabi influence was limited.

The growth of western secular education was again to alter the nature of the community and to provide the basis for yet another challenge to the authority of traditional religious leadership. A new social category is in the process of emerging, consisting of young educated men (and increasingly women), often living outside their home communities, relatively well-to-do but hardly wealthy. These individuals are subjected to demands from their relatives, often in the context of life-crisis rituals which express both community membership and the status of individuals within it. While these demands are often resented, such persons are not financially or socially well enough off to wish to sever themselves from their kinfolk. Their situation differs from that of the Wahhabis in one crucial respect. Wahhabis are mainly merchants, involved in a sector largely dominated by Muslims, and so they can reasonably aspire to the constitution of a new, largely mercantile, Muslim community. The western-educated, on the other hand, find themselves in a category dominated by non-Muslims from other parts of the Ivory Coast, and so cannot express their social identity – i.e. class position – in religious terms. They can, however, look to younger Arab-trained scholars – individuals of their own age-category – for religious leadership.

These scholars and their followers are careful not to contest the authority of older local scholars or of the community rituals over which they preside, but they emphasise those aspects of Islam which stress the universal nature of the community of believers as opposed to those which implicitly validate traditional social categories. In this way, recourse to the Middle East as a direct source of knowledge and moral authority does not constitute a radical challenge to the Suwarian tradition of mediated knowledge, but rather poses itself as an alternative. However, for these very reasons, Suwarian scholars are left with no grounds for objection, nor can members of their home communities accuse their younger, educated kinsmen of wishing unequivocally to renege on their obligations.

Underlying these three sets of challenges to the Suwarian tradition of scholarship is a single issue: does Islam recognise, and by implication legitimise, hereditary social distinctions of any kind? The Suwarian tradition has always acknowledged the salience of hereditary categories – initially in the form of differences in religious practice, more recently in the modified recognition that it accords to community rituals. Within this tradition, *isnads*, while they are never assimilated to genealogies, perform an analogous function: scholars are attached to a local line of transmission of knowledge in the same way that ordinary believers are attached to local ethnic, political, and kin units. The appeal to direct, unmediated contact with the Hijaz – or, more generally, with the Arabic-speaking world – provides a model for a different kind of Muslim community that in principle ignores all hereditary distinctions and focuses exclusively on religious practice as the criterion for inclusion in the Muslim community. Study in the Middle East frees the aspirant scholar from dependence on the local religious elite in the same way that newly-constituted Muslim communities liberate their adherents from dependence on hereditary chiefs and clan elders. The Suwarian emphasis on the principle of heredity was attractive to the vast majority in the Korhogo region when the Dyula constituted the sole Muslim community – enjoying various economic, political, and social monopolies. With the erosion of these monopolies, however, control lay increasingly outside the community, and this emphasis on hereditary principles appealed less and less to those individuals who were relatively successful, but whose age or social origins relegated them to a subordinate position in traditional terms. Those who found new sources of wealth, power, or prestige were also attracted to sources of knowledge and moral authority which, in a sense, were also new (in that they lay outside the local community). Moreover, as they were geographically located at the wellsprings of religious knowledge, these new sources of authority simultaneously enjoyed the aura of venerability – of a return to tradition rather than a departure from it.

In short, the spread of influence from the Middle East to West African Muslims like the Dyula has not simply been a question of diffusion, of a radiating outwards from a "centre". Rather, it has been part of a quest by groups and individuals for a set of religious principles which might call into question the importance of locally-anchored, hereditary, social distinctions, and might ultimately re-evaluate the relationship between the local Muslim community and the global community of Muslims. Such quests have led individuals to seek knowledge outside their home communities, specifically in the Arabic-speaking world. Of equal importance is the fact that others in their communities have, for the same reasons, looked to these foreign-trained scholars for leadership.

Notes

1 This paper is based on research carried out in and around the neighbourhood of Koko in the town of Korhogo, the largest in the northern Ivory Coast, in 1972–3 and in 1984–5. The second trip to the field was funded by both the National Endowment for the Humanities and the National Science Foundation. Except where othewise specified, observations in this paper about the "Dyula" refer specifically to those Dyula living in Koko quarter. For a detailed account of the Dyula of Koko, see Launay 1982.
2 Sanneh (1979) argues for an earlier, thirteenth-century date for al-Hajj Salim Suware.
3 The phrase was used by Ivor Wilks, to whom I am heavily indebted for his discussion of al-Hajj Salim and the Suwarian tradition.
4 For the career of al-Hajj Mahmud Karantaw, see Levtzion (1968: 147–51) and Hiskett (1985: 168–70).
5 For a history of the "Wahhabi" movement in West Africa, see Kaba 1974.
6 For example, see Kaba (1974). Hiskett (1985: 290) goes so far as to label them "the religious wing of the Rassemblement Démocratique Africain in West Africa".
7 On the role of rote memorisation in other traditions of Islamic learning, see Eickelman (1985) and Santerre (1973).

References

Amselle, J.-L. (1977) *Les negociants de la Savane*, Anthropos, Paris.
Eickelman, D. (1985) *Knowledge and Power in Morocco*, Princeton University Press, Princeton, N.J.
Hiskett, M. (1973) *The Sword of Truth*, Oxford University Press, New York.
—— (1985) *The Development of Islam in West Africa*, Longman, London and New York.
Hodgson, M. (1974) *The Venture of Islam*, University of Chicago Press, Chicago.
Hunter, T. (1977) 'The development of an Islamic tradition of learning among the Jakhanka of West Africa', unpublished PhD thesis, University of Chicago.
Kaba, L. (1974) *The Wahhabiyya*, Northwestern University Press, Evanston, Ill.
Launay, R. (1982) *Traders without Trade*, Cambridge University Press, Cambridge.
Levtzion, N. (1968) *Muslims and Chiefs in West Africa*, Oxford University Press, London.
Robinson, D. (1985) *The Holy War of Umar Tall*, Clarendon Press, Oxford.
Sanneh, L. (1979) *The Jakhanke*, International African Institute, London.
Santerre, R. (1973) *Pedagogie Musulmane d'Afrique Noire*, Les Presses de l'Université de Montréal, Montreal.
SEDES [Société d'Etudes pour le Developpement Economique et Sociale] (1965) *Région de Korhogo: Etude de Developpement Socio-Economique*, vol. I, Paris.
Triaud, J.-L. (1974) 'La question musulmane en Côte d'Ivoire (1893–1939)', *Revenue Française d'Histoire d'Outre-Mer*, 61, pp. 542–71.
Wilks, I. (1968) 'The transmission of Islamic learning in the Western Sudan', in J.R. Goody (ed.) *Literacy in Traditional Societies*, Cambridge University Press, Cambridge, pp. 161–97.

Chapter ten

Between Cairo and the Algerian Kabylia: the Rahmaniyya *tariqa*, 1715–1800

Julia A. Clancy-Smith

Introduction

The organised Sufism of the Islamic religious orders *turuq* (singular: *tariqa*) often had its origins in the travels of individuals driven by an intensely personal desire to acquire knowledge and to fulfil religious duties. The emergence of the Algerian Rahmaniyya order in the last quarter of the eighteenth century illustrates how the perigrinations of one man, in this case Muhammad ibn 'Abd al-Rahman, contributed to the restructuring of socio-religious bonds in a particular Muslim community as well as the reaffirmation of ties between that community and the wider Islamic *ecumene*. Thus, a study of the activities of such an individual joins three strands in historiography: biography; world history; and the sociological and social historical study of mass movements aiming at religious renewal and reform. Together, these approaches can isolate the types of social transformations that constitute sea changes in any society, Muslim or otherwise.

At some time in the 1760s or 1770s, the kinds of popular expressions of piety that frequently signal the rise of a new saint or mystic began to occur in the Kabylia of north-eastern Algeria. Crowds gathered, miracles were proclaimed, and religious savants from other areas travelled to the Jurjura mountains to hear the preaching of a *hajji* and *'alim* (Muslim scholar) who had recently returned from the eastern Arab world. By 1777 Sufi *zawiyas* (religious lodges) had been created in the region, pilgrimages were organised, and local religious notables or disciples were authorised to assume certain functions within the *tariqa* (Sa'adallah 1981: i, 514–16; al-Hifnawi 1982: 457–60). At the same time, a cult of saints had already coalesced around the figure of Sidi 'Abd al-Rahman, whose intercession was sought by the faithful because of his *baraka* (supernatural blessing) and ability to work miracles (Rinn 1884). Several features of this cult and the emerging Sufi network were viewed with alarm by political and religious authorities in the capital of the Turkish regency of Algiers, in particular the institution of the *ziyara* or pilgrimage. Even the saint's death did not necessarily remove the perceived threat. Sidi 'Abd al-Rahman's burial and the popular ceremonials tied to his *qubba* (shrine) triggered more struggles to control the privileged places (and remains) associated with extraordinary beings.

The emerging cult in honour of Muhammad ibn 'Abd al-Rahman and the elaboration of a new *tariqa* (brotherhood) were interrelated. Both of these were the product of earlier phases in Sidi 'Abd al-Rahman's life, before he became a saint or the founder of a new Maghribi Sufi order, and thus a menace to entrenched elites in his own country. Before examining the political nature of the *ziyara* in Turkish Algeria, a brief summary of Muhammad ibn 'Abd al-Rahman's life demonstrates one dimension of movement in Islamic societies – the connection between travel for pious purposes and socio-religious mobility. This in turn will help to explain how popular cults develop and why a conflict erupted over Sidi 'Abd al-Rahman's earthly remains in AD 1793–4.

Shaykh 'Abd al-Rahman's career was divided between the urbane, erudite world of the Cairene *'ulama'*, extensive missionary activity in *dar al-Islam*, and the Berber Kabylia with its tribal social structure. Through his efforts at *tajdid* (religious reform and renewal), and those of other like-minded Sufi scholars, the purified and the popular were recombined to produce what some scholars have called a neo-Sufi revival – "Sufism reformed on orthodox lines and interpreted in an activist sense" (Rahman 1979: 206; Voll 1982: 37–8). The Berber saint is thus representative of a whole class of energetic, itinerant Sufis and scholars whose activities in the late eighteenth and nineteenth centuries more closely linked distant parts of the Muslim world. This created the conditions of "critical mass" which led to populist movements of reform and renewal in Africa, the Middle East, and Asia (Voll 1980, 1982; Martin 1976).

Nothing in Shaykh 'Abd al-Rahman's family background predisposed him to a career that brought him within the inner circle of leading Egyptian *'ulama'* and Sufis. In fact, the inhabitants of the Kabylia were not generally among those Maghribi groups that lingered for years in established communities in the Mashriq (Raymond 1959). Muhammad ibn 'Abd al-Rahman's missionary activities, his attainment of spiritual perfection, and his advanced education (acquired in Cairo) transformed a local *talib* (religious student or scholar) into a member of the Muslim elite. Thus, the matrix of the saint cult and Sufi order associated with Sidi 'Abd al-Rahman during his lifetime and after his death lay as much in Cairo and the *Haramayn* (the holy cities of Mecca and Medina) – and elsewhere in *dar al-Islam* – as in his native Kabylia.

From the Maghrib to the Mashriq

Muhammad ibn 'Abdal-Rahman al-Azhari Abu Qabrayn was born sometime between 1715 and 1729 into the Ait Isma'il tribe of the Qashtula. This large confederacy was located at the margins of central government authority in the Kabylia, a mountainous area in the Algerian Tell that is heavily forested and densely populated. Its inhabitants are mainly Berbers or Arabised Berbers.

Independent, enterprising, and rebellious, the Kabyles maintained their traditional political and administrative institutions under Turkish rule. Before the French conquest, the region was composed of semi-autonomous village republics, estimated at some 1,400 settlements (Hanoteau and Letourneux 1872–3; Daumas 1853).

Sidi 'Abd al-Rahman was from a locally prominent family claiming descent from the Prophet through Morocco's Idrisi *shurafa'* (descendants of the Prophet). His father, a scholar of somewhat modest stature, sent his son to a nearby *zawiya*, controlled by another saintly lineage, for religious instruction. Muhammad ibn 'Abd al-Rahman then studied at the Great Mosque in Algiers prior to his departure for the Mashriq around 1739 or 1740 to perform the *hajj* and complete his education. After a period of time in the Hijaz, he settled in Egypt to acquire advanced learning at the Azhar mosque–university in Cairo, then the undisputed centre of Islamic learning. There the aspiring Berber scholar immersed himself in both jurisprudence and the mystical sciences (Rinn 1884; Giacobetti 1946).

Sidi 'Abd al-Rahman's sojourn in the east lasted almost three decades. During that time he studied with a number of leading Muslim scholars. The most important and influential was Muhammad ibn Salim al-Hifnawi (1689–1767/8), the leader of the Egyptian Khalwatiyya and rector of al-Azhar from 1758 until 1767 (Bannerth 1964: 1–74). Shaykh al-Hifnawi was a charismatic Sufi leader who, like many of his contemporaries, was not only in touch with developments throughout the Muslim world, but was also aware of the political inroads made by European powers into *dar al-Islam*. Muhammad ibn 'Abd al-Rahman eventually became one of Hifnawi's favoured students and closest associates (Martin 1972; de Jong 1978).

At some point, Shaykh al-Hifnawi ordered his Algerian disciple to travel to Dar Fur in the eastern Sudan to instruct the ruler there. Muhammad ibn 'Abd al-Rahman's instructions were to teach Khalwatiyya doctrines in the Sudan and to "render service to humanity" (al-Niyal 1965: 337). He spent some six years in Dar Fur, where his efforts met with success, and may have subsequently travelled as far as India to preach. Some writers mention Turkey and the Hijaz as sites of his missionary activity as well (André 1956; Haas 1943). Upon his return to Egypt, Muhammad ibn 'Abd al-Rahman was again instructed by Shaykh al-Hifnawi to embark upon more travels; this time he was to travel to the Maghrib to proselytise. Before the disciple left Cairo, al-Hifnawi conferred upon Muhammad ibn 'Abd al-Rahman the *khirqa*, a ritual garment signifying the attainment of spiritual perfection (al-Hifnawi 1982). It was with great reluctance that the Algerian Sufi and *'alim* left his master's side; he was not to see him again.

The fact that al-Hifnawi ordered Muhammad ibn 'Abd al-Rahman to propagate the Khalwatiyya doctrines in Algeria is significant. Although Algeria, unlike Dar Fur at the time, was decidedly not a frontier region of Islam, the coastal region of the province of Oran was still occupied by the Spanish, who only abandoned their presidio in 1792. Moreover, because Egypt and the Ottoman Regency of Algiers were alike in terms of the oppressed condition of their local populations under Turkish rule, al-Hifnawi may have regarded Algeria as suitable territory for neo-Sufi reforming activities (Julien 1964, 1970).

After an absence of nearly thirty years, the Berber *shaykh* and his family returned to the Jurjura at some time between AH 1177–83/ AD 1763–70 (Rinn 1884; Delpech 1874). By the 1770s a school and *zawiya* were in existence among the Ait Isma'il. From this outpost, Sidi 'Abd al-Rahman taught, performed miracles, and initiated the Kabyles into the *tariqa*. Before long, it commanded a substantial following. News of his teachings and of the new ideas brought back from the Mashriq soon spread beyond the Jurjura, and attracted learned men from Algiers, Constantine, and Bougie to the Kabylia to hear him preach (al-Hifnawi 1982; Sa'adallah 1981). The founder of the important Tijaniyya order was first initiated into the Khalwatiyya way by Sidi 'Abd al-Rahman himself, perhaps during Ahmad al-Tijani's journey from Fez to Mecca via northern Algeria in 1772–3 (Martin 1972: 303). Diplomas conferred by Sidi 'Abd al-Rahman in the 1770s upon local religious notables in the region indicate that the brotherhood was in full expansion less than a decade after his return from the east. By the 1790s, the Khalwatiyya-Rahmaniyya *zawiya* in the Jurjura had evolved into a prestigious centre of learning (Delpech 1874).

While the *tariqa* was being established in the Kabylia, its Sufi membership grew steadily elsewhere in Algeria. Muhammad ibn 'Abd al-Rahman's reputation as a savant and saint soon spread among urban notables in eastern Algeria. At some time in the late 1770s, Muhammad Bash Tarzi, a member of an eminent religious family from Constantine, travelled to the Jurjura *zawiya* to hear Shaykh 'Abd al-Rahman's words. Impressed by Bash Tarzi's erudition and virtue, and perhaps by his family's prominence, Sidi 'Abd al-Rahman made him a Sufi *muqaddam* (representative), and enjoined him to proselytise in his native city to combat the "worldliness of its inhabitants" (Cherbonneau 1852: 517). Bash Tarzi's affiliation with the Rahmaniyya worked to increase his clan's fortunes and clientele, in addition to aiding greatly the expansion of the nascent *tariqa* in eastern Algeria and in north-western Tunisia. Particularly in the Biskra and Awras regions, the rise of local religious families to regional importance can be directly traced to their membership in the Rahmaniyya in this period (Clancy-Smith 1988: 41–3). Thus, the prestige of certain families became tied to Muhammad ibn 'Abd al-Rahman's own rising status; indeed, the two were intimately connected.

Sidi 'Abd al-Rahman's order encountered little, if any, opposition in Constantine, either from Maliki and Hanafi officials or from secular families of ancient notoriety. Perhaps these religious notables did not view the emerging Rahmaniyya *tariqa* as a threat precisely because they were so firmly embedded in the city's social fabric (Vaysettes 1869; Mercier 1903; Nouschi 1955, 1961). However, Muhammad ibn 'Abd al-Rahman's activities aroused considerable enmity among some high-ranking *'ulama'* and local maraboutic lineages in other parts of Algeria. The antipathy of saintly clans to Sidi 'Abd al-Rahman's reforms is revealing. The expanding Sufi order posed an unambiguous challenge to vested interests, particularly since it drew rural clients away from maraboutic leaders. This eroded their prestige, authority, and material resources, which were measured by popular followings and expressed in the idiom of the *ziyara* (Rinn 1884; Robin 1901). The annual or periodic *ziyara* to local saintly figures was both a visit which reaffirmed ties of religious patronage and an occasion for various sorts of exchanges (symbolic and material), since an offering was invariably made to the marabout for his intercession or blessing.

Early in the 1790s, Sidi 'Abd al-Rahman began publicly to preach Khalwatiyya doctrines in Algiers, an activity that soon encountered opposition from some *'ulama'*. Although denounced as a heretic, he was found innocent and allowed to continue preaching. In the aftermath, Shaykh 'Abd al-Rahman established a Khalwatiyya-Rahmaniyya *zawiya* – not in the heart of Algiers but in the adjoining suburb of al-Hamma (Margoliouth 1924; Rinn 1884). He possibly chose this spot to temper any lingering hostility on the part of the city's *'ulama'* and to distance himself from the central government. As will be seen, however, the political centre would subsequently seek to appropriate the populist movement associated with the Berber saint to its own ends.

Roughly six months prior to his death, Sidi 'Abd al-Rahman journeyed back to his native Kabylia to resolve the critical matter of his successor. The saint–founder did not select any of his countrymen to succeed him. Instead, he named his closest disciple and spiritual son, Sidi al-Hajj 'Ali ibn 'Isa, originally from the Sus in Morocco, to lead the Rahmaniyya after AH 1208/AD 1793–4, the year most generally accepted for Sidi 'Abd al-Rahman's death. Sidi 'Ali, who inherited his Sufi master's *baraka* and the administration of the order's *hubus* (*waqf* or religious endowment) properties, directed the *zawiya* in the Jurjura for some forty years without opposition (Rinn 1884; Depont and Coppolani 1897).

Towards the end of Sidi 'Ali's tenure in office, the French army landed in Algeria, causing the precipitous collapse of Turkish rule. During the two decades or more of military pacification following the 1830 invasion, membership in the Rahmaniyya appears to have increased. By the last decade of the nineteenth century, the *tariqa* commanded the largest popular following of any single Muslim brotherhood in Algeria and had important branches in Tunisia, the Sahara, and the Ottoman regency of Tripoli (Depont and Coppolani 1897).

Religious and political centres and peripheries

The issue of the "why" of Rahmaniyya growth is related to the issue of the "how" of its grass-roots mobilisation. The spiritual lessons composed by Sidi 'Abd al-Rahman were evidently very popular. Moreover, his lessons distinguished the North African order from its eastern Khalwatiyya parent. Part of the Rahmaniyya's ordinary ritual were the so-called "seven dreams", inspired by the Prophet's appearance to Muhammad ibn 'Abd al-Rahman on seven different occasions. In the dialogue between the saint and the Prophet, the brotherhood's orthodoxy is affirmed by Muhammad, and Shaykh 'Abd al-Rahman's virtues are enumerated for the edification of the faithful. The recitation of these seven dreams appears to have become part of popular lore and was recited during weekly Sufi meetings, rural religious festivals, and pilgrimages (Rinn 1884: 466–71).

Ritualised, collective visits to the shrines of saints and Sufis not only held forth the promise of supernatural favours, but were also important social events. They brought participants a large measure of emotional and psychological comfort, and, like the annual *hajj* to the *Haramayn*, local pilgrimages served commercial purposes since they frequently occurred within the context of *mawsims* or rural markets and fairs. Moreover, saints' tombs and *zawiyas* were considered *haram* – sacred spaces whose inviolability was normally respected by Muslim rulers (Trumelet 1881, 1892; Dermenghem 1954). As such, they provided asylum for those fleeing tax collectors, political repression, or tribal vendettas. Later, under the colonial order, collective pilgrimages to saintly intercessors sometimes were the prelude to revolt or a forum for passive resistance to foreign rule, a fact recognised by French authorities who attempted to limit or even prohibit the *ziyara* in Algeria (Boyer 1977; Ageron 1968).

In Rahmaniyya doctrine, the founder-saint's blessings were not limited only to members of the order; a visit to his *zawiya* sufficed to channel grace to the supplicant (Giacobetti 1946). For this reason, the Rahmaniyya can be characterised as an inclusive organisation because adepts were permitted to belong to other *turuq* concurrently, and non-affiliates could receive spiritual rewards. This contrasts with the Tijaniyya which was more exclusive in terms of membership. This may have limited the Tijaniyya's appeal to specific social "classes" and prevented it from becoming the mass association that the Rahmaniyya did in eastern Algeria (Abun-Nasr 1965).

This popular appeal initially inspired official hostility to Muhammad ibn 'Abd al-Rahman towards the end of his life, and specific objection would have been made had he espoused Wahhabi doctrines. We know that the Kabyle scholar had spent time in the Hijaz during the middle of the eighteenth century and was a contemporary of Muhammad ibn 'Abd al-Wahhab, the puritanical Najdi reformer. However, according to Sa'adallah, there was little, if any, Wahhabi influence in Rahmaniyya doctrine (1981: I, 516). Thus, other explanations must be sought for the elite's distrust of the new saint and Sufi from the Kabylia.

Muhammad ibn 'Abd al-Rahman was not only an outsider to Algiers by virtue of his village–maraboutic origins, but also as a Berber. He was thus regarded with disdain by the predominantly Arab and Arabo-Turkish *'ulama'*, who, out of social prejudice, did not mix with the Kabyles (Valensi 1969: 52). In addition, his substantial popular following was undoubtedly viewed as a menace by both the religious and the political notables of the capital, whose interests were intimately intertwined. Moreover, in contrast to the situation in Constantine, the *'ulama'* of Algiers occupied a much more precarious niche *vis-à-vis* secular political authorities. Above all, he probably antagonised the traditional men of religion, or part of them, by espousing "novel" ideas learned in Cairo – although the Egyptian Khalwatiyya's insistence upon the strict observance of the Qur'an and the *sunna* would scarcely seem heterodox (Rinn 1884). Perhaps working in his favour was the fact that the city's *majlis* and *'ulama'* were divided into warring camps, with the Malikis pitted against the Hanafis (Boyer 1963). On the other hand, envenomed relations among religious factions may have provoked charges of heresy in the first place, with one group attempting to outmanoeuvre the other by making Sidi 'Abd al-Rahman's preachings into a *cause célèbre*.

The role played by Turkish officials in the incident was characteristically equivocal. Some writers state that Shaykh 'Abd al-Rahman was cleared of the charges of heterodoxy after the authorities intervened on his behalf (Margoliouth 1924). News of the saint's internment in Algiers had sparked violent demonstrations in the Kabylia, and the government sought to appease the bellicose Kabyles who were upset by the persecution of their countryman. Other sources maintain that central authorities induced the *majlis* to level charges against Sidi 'Abd al-Rahman because his nascent movement threatened to group around the semi-independent Qashtula tribal dissidents situated at the margins of state control (Rinn 1884; Doutté 1900). In all probability, both interpretations are accurate since these kinds of strategies were traditionally employed by the Turkish regime to rule Algeria (Boyer 1966). Here it can be posited that opposition by secular, ruling elites to Sidi 'Abd al-Rahman was based more upon the saint cult associated with him rather than the establishment of a new Sufi *tariqa*. Yet the clumsy meddling from political authorities, seeking to dampen popular fervour attached to the Kabyle holy man, had the opposite effect.

What did not transpire in the period immediately after the saint's release in Algiers was as significant as what actually occurred. Given Sidi 'Abd al-Rahman's following in both the capital and the Kabylia, one might have expected a showdown between the saint and his detractors. Nevertheless, Muhammad ibn 'Abd al-Rahman chose not to capitalise upon his victory, either by forcing concessions from the authorities or by forming a party of militant resistance to Turkish rule. Instead, leaving the city for the countryside, he returned to the Jurjura mountains and his *zawiya* there.

The man with two tombs

Sidi 'Abd al-Rahman's death in 1793–4 placed him once more at the heart of a controversy which demonstrates the intersection between the social meaning of sainthood in the Maghribi context and the interests of the state. Public rituals, whether rural or urban, in veneration of holy persons might pose a threat to public order. Particularly worrisome were the festivals connected with the *ziyara*, or pilgrimage, which gave expression to collective beliefs about *baraka*, regarded as most potent in the vicinity of the saint's tomb (Doutté 1900).

While all the European accounts and some of the Arabic versions mention the tug-of-war that erupted over Sidi 'Abd al-Rahman's corpse, there are two slightly different interpretations of the primary motives behind the theft. De Neveu and Trumelet portray the struggle, which ultimately resulted in two bodies and two tombs, as a purely devotional clash – two groups of spiritual clients desiring to possess what remained of the great Sufi and saint (de Neveu 1845; Trumelet 1892). However, among others, Depont and Coppolani (1897) and Rinn (1884) attribute a leading role to the central government, which seems plausible in the light of what happened earlier. Obviously, the two versions are not mutually exclusive; rather, the motives of secular authorities and *tariqa* brothers were different in inspiration.

Upon learning of Sidi 'Abd al-Rahman's death in the Jurjura, the authorities in Algiers became alarmed at the prospect of his burial in the Kabyle centre. This would attract large crowds of pilgrims to the shrine seeking divine favours through the saint's intercession, something which could spark rebellion in an unruly population only imperfectly governed by the political centre. Several authors suggest that Turkish officials, out of "diplomatic" concerns, encouraged Rahmaniyya adepts in Algiers to visit the Kabylia with the express purpose of repatriating the deceased to the capital by whatever means (Depont and Coppolani 1897; Gouvian and Gouvian 1920). Rinn (1884: 455) explicitly states that the government sought to end popular pilgrimages based in the Jurjura through the tactic of body-snatching.

Three days after Sidi 'Abd al-Rahman's death, his followers in Algiers learned of the event; particularly distressing was the fact that his tomb was a considerable distance from al-Hamma. Realising that neither pleas nor force would convince the Jurjura populations to relinquish the saintly remains of their spiritual mentor, the adepts in Algiers decided to employ a ruse. Three clandestine groups of Rahmaniyya brothers from Algiers went to the region, determined to steal the recently entombed corpse of Sidi 'Abd al-Rahman from its resting place. One group hid near the tomb; the other two sought to distract the Kabyles by joining with them in mourning the departed master. The plan succeeded. The mourners from Algiers kept the Kabyles sufficiently off-guard, while the others opened Sidi 'Abd al-Rahman's tomb, placed his corpse upon a mule and transported the stolen saintly goods under cover of darkness to the capital (de Neveu 1845).

Figure 10.1 Shrines are also important among the Shi'a. A Turkish post-card (*c.* 1980) depicting the carrying of a coffin to a shrine associated with the mosque in Kufa, southern Iraq. The main inscription in Arabic, which is translated into Turkish on the reverse side of the card, reads, "There is no youth equal to 'Ali and no sword equal to Dhu al-Fiqar ['Ali's sword]". (From the collection of Lois G. Beck.)

At daybreak, news that the stones and earth covering the burial site had been disturbed reached the assembled mourners; a bitter quarrel immediately erupted between the remaining Rahmaniyya brothers from Algiers and the Kabyles. As might be expected, the Kabyles suspected the outsiders and reproached them for their untoward behaviour. Seeking to exonerate themselves, the visitors from Algiers suggested that they inspect Sidi 'Abd al-Rahman's tomb. The corpse was still in the *qubba*, much to the relief of the Kabyles and the astonishment of the others; a miracle was in the making (de Neveu 1845; al-Hifnawi 1982).

In the meantime, the third group had reached the capital, and soon arranged for Sidi 'Abd al-Rahman's burial in the al-Hamma *zawiya*. The struggle over the saint's body was only resolved when each side proclaimed a miracle. The disputed corpse had been reduplicated, and both shrines – one in Algiers, the other in the Jurjura – contained the *baraka*-producing remains. The news of the miracle spread rapidly throughout the Kabylia and elsewhere. The title *Abu Qabrayn* ("the man with two tombs") was immediately bestowed upon Muhammad ibn 'Abd al-Rahman by his followers, who from that day forth never invoked him without affixing the sobriquet to his name (Rinn 1884). The faithful explained this miracle by saying that the Almighty had reproduced the saint's remains to prevent further conflict between brothers of the same *tariqa* (de Neveu 1845). Thus, a peculiar sort of miraculous movement was attributed to Sidi 'Abd al-Rahman in order to maintain religious cohesion and avoid dissension. It was, moreover, in the political self-interest of the Kabyles to promote the legend because it raised one of their countrymen to "national" religious stature (Rinn 1884: 456).

Because of the remarkable duplication of the Berber saint's body, the reigning *dey*, Hasan, had a magnificent mausoleum and a mosque built for Sidi 'Abd al-Rahman at al-Hamma, with much pomp and circumstance. Not content with the erection of a building, surmounted by a long, pious inscription extolling Sidi 'Abd al-Rahman's virtues, Hasan Dey made arrangements for his own burial beside the *wali* (saint) (de Neveu 1845; Colin 1901). Like many of his Muslim (and Christian) counterparts, the *dey* was striving to bring the rural cult of a saint as well as the organisational matrix of a ramified Sufi order into the city. There he hoped to exercise more effective control over popular religious sensibilities, and obtain spiritual benefits from the company of the "very special dead" (Brown 1981: 69).

The memorial inscription of the al-Hamma shrine is revealing as well. The dedication recalled Muhammad ibn 'Abd al-Rahman's participation in "holy war, the great and small *jihad*". The reader was told that whoever performed the *ziyara* to his shrine would find happiness in this world, and salvation in the next (Rinn 1884: 456). Thus, the individual supplicant's redemption was assured by physical presence at the tomb-shrine, something requiring spatial movement, and by the saint's spiritual odyssey between two worlds, itself paralleled and confirmed by his body's miraculous doubling.

Twice a year a great pilgrimage was held in veneration of Sidi 'Abd al-Rahman, attracting the pious from all over Algeria and as far away as Morocco. The pilgrims reaffirmed their ties to the Rahmaniyya order as well as imploring the founder-saint for his blessings and intercessions in matters pertaining to this world and the next. While these pilgrimages took place at both of the saint's tombs, the Jurjura shrine was popularly regarded as the more authentic of the two; its physical remoteness from Turkish authorities made it all the more attractive (Trumelet 1892).

The French conquest of Algeria in 1830 naturally increased the popularity of the mother *zawiya* in the Jurjura precisely because of its distance from the infidel's contaminating presence, which was much greater in the al-Hamma suburb of Algiers. Nevertheless, by the end of the nineteenth century, a large cemetery had grown up around the al-Hamma *qubba*; each Friday, women gathered there for weekly visits to the deceased, and enjoyed the shade offered by the garden of olive, pistachio, and Barbary fig trees (Trumelet 1892). The *zawiya* in the Jurjura was closed in 1857 and again in 1871 after anti-French insurrections inspired and led by Rahmaniyya *shaykhs*. Despite – or because of – colonial restrictions upon the pilgrimage, the two tombs of Sidi 'Abd al-Rahman remained the object of veneration even as late as 1900. *Mawsims*, organised by Rahmaniyya centres in the south of Algeria, continued until the eve of independence (Rinn 1884; Depont and Coppolani 1897; André 1956; Despois 1957).

Conclusions

Clusters of relationships, sacred and profane, tend to converge around holy persons, whether living or dead. The cult of saints is socially constructed and reconstructed over time and space, resulting in new and multiple centres of piety and devotion – or "new saint maps" to borrow Alex Weingrod's (Chapter 11 of this volume) expression. The same is true of the growth of new Sufi *turuq*. In the case of the Rahmaniyya, the system of rituals organised in veneration of Sidi 'Abd al-Rahman engendered the Sufi order that emerged in late eighteenth-century Algeria during a time of troubles.

The *tariqa* established by Muhammad ibn 'Abd al-Rahman brought social order and the promise of salvation to urban elites, city masses, and rural peoples in North Africa. Yet only after years spent in Cairo or in missionary activities far afield in *dar al-Islam* did he acquire the knowledge, spiritual perfection, and individual piety that made him a cult figure by popular acclaim in his own land. The birth of the new saint and Sufi in Algeria was produced and confirmed by the movement of various groups, popular and learned, to his side after the 1760s or 1770s. The social recognition of his personal piety and learning, together with his earlier eastern travels, thus transformed him from a rustic scholar of unpretentious social origins to a leading member of the Muslim elite and Sufi establishment.

Islamic saints and mystics shared with their Christian counterparts the task of "joining heaven and earth" (Brown 1981: 1). Rather than belonging either to the "learned" tradition or to the "popular", the Berber holy man combined both traditions in his work and teachings. The emergence of Sidi 'Abd al-Rahman's cult and the *tariqa* bearing his name demonstrate the complex interplay between particularistic expressions of belief in the village or tribe and the universal dimensions of Islam as a world religion.

Movement for Muhammad ibn 'Abd al-Rahman, moreover, did not end with the grave. A conflict between state authorities and the very special dead resulted in a man with two tombs. Political elites have always and everywhere sought to appropriate religious symbols, rituals, and movements to their own ends. But the story of Sidi 'Abd al-Rahman and the Rahmaniyya shows how the masses exercise a kind of popular sovereignty over public expressions of belief. The Turkish regime's effort to organise a counter-cult around a stolen corpse and a state-sponsored tomb did not entirely succeed. The Kabyles fended off the attempt to expropriate their saint by collaborating in a miracle and by withholding their patronage of the al-Hamma shrine, located near the political centre.

Finally, in the work initiated by neo-Sufi reformers like Sidi 'Abd al-Rahman, can we detect any evidence of an "important temporal shift in cultural understandings", to use Eickelman's phrase (1976: 20)? Affiliation with the expanding Rahmaniyya order meant that a somewhat parochial group of provincial holy men or saintly lineages became religious leaders, attracting followers from much wider areas by the end of the eighteenth century and the early decades of the nineteenth century. Their social and cultural horizons were no longer circumscribed by the modest outposts of Islam in the countryside that their ancestors had controlled for generations. This was true both in the Kabylia and elsewhere in Algeria and Tunisia, particularly in the pre-Sahara and Sahara.

The older ideology of maraboutism, which harked back to the

Moroccan Sus or the maraboutic diaspora of centuries earlier, was thus overlaid by another ideology. Cosmopolitan neo-Sufism, with its profound commitment to renewal and reform, especially through instruction, was oriented more towards the eastern Muslim world – above all, Cairo and Mecca and Medina. The Muslim East has always been important to the religious life of the Maghrib's inhabitants. Nevertheless, the elaboration of brotherhoods, like the Rahmaniyya, suggests a vital shift in the relative cultural emphasis given to various sources of socio-spiritual legitimacy, although not a total break with the past.

This shift, I suggest, occurred at some time in the last quarter of the eighteenth century and appears to have continued unabated until approximately the middle of the nineteenth century, when the apparatus of French domination in northern Algeria was more or less firmly in place. Colonial authorities and institutions, whether wittingly or unwittingly, imposed forms of social and political control over Algeria's Muslim population which gradually worked to reduce the extra-local nature of the Sufi *turuq* and the trans-regional relationships upon which those orders depended.

As far as eastern Algeria – the seat of Rahmaniyya influence – was concerned, a series of colonial laws was enacted from 1850 onwards. These laws restricted public gatherings and the movements of Muslims, particularly for purposes of religion. Many of these measures were the direct consequence of anti-French insurrections, often backed by Sufi or saintly leaders, and of France's discovery of the existence of the Muslim *turuq* and their significance to Algerian society (Ageron 1968, 1979; Clancy-Smith 1989). The North African orders depended to a large degree upon the free movement of leaders and clients to maintain followings, religious centres, revenues, and contacts with notables in other parts of the Maghrib and Mashriq. From roughly the middle of the nineteenth century, these intricate social and religious networks were increasingly prey to obstacles imposed by the colonial order. By the end of that century, many Sufi leaders and other members of the Algerian religious establishment had emigrated, been exiled, or were transformed into pillars of the regime, thus effectively ending the trajectory of the neo-Sufi movement of a century earlier. Other sorts of sea changes were in the making.

Muslim travellers

References

Abun-Nasr, J.M. (1965) *The Tijaniyya: a Sufi Order in the Modern Word*, Oxford University Press, London.
Ageron, C.-R. (1968) *Les Algériens Musulmans et la France, 1871–1911*, 2 vols, Presses Universitaires de France, Paris.
—— (1979) *De l'insurrection de 1871 au déclenchement de la guerre de libération* (1954), vol. 2 of *Histoire de l'Algérie Contemporaine*, Presses Universitaires de France, Paris.
André, P.J. (1956) *Contribution à l'étude des confréries réligieuses musulmanes*, Maison des Livres, Algier.
Bannerth, E. (1964) 'La Khalwatiyya en Egypte, quelques aspects de la vie d'une confrérie', *Institut Dominicain d'Etudes Orientales du Caire*, 8, pp. 1–74.
Boyer, P. (1963) *La vie quotidienne à Alger à la veille de l'intervention française*, Hachette, Paris.
—— (1966) 'Contribution à l'étude de la politique réligieuse des Turcs dans la Régence d'Alger', *Revue de l'Occident Musulman et de la Méditerranée*, 1, no. 1, pp. 11–49.
—— (1977) 'L'administration Française et la réglementation du pèlerinage à la Mecque (1830–1894)', *Revue d'Histoire Maghrébine*, 9, pp. 275–93.
Brown, P. (1981) *The Cult of Saints, Its Rise and Function in Latin Christianity*, University of Chicago Press, Chicago.
Cherbonneau, A. (1852) 'Sur le Catéchisme des Rahmaniens', *Journal Asiatique*, 20, pp. 515–18C.
Clancy-Smith, J. (1988) 'The Saharan Rahmaniyya: popular protest and desert society in southeastern Algeria and the Tunisian Jarid, *c.* 1750–1881', unpublished PhD dissertation, University of California, Los Angeles.
—— (1989) 'In the eye of the beholder: the North African saints and Sufis and the colonial production of knowledge, 1830–1900', *Africana Journal*, 15, pp. 220–57.
Colin, G. (1901) *Corpus des inscriptions arabes et turques d'Algiers*, Algiers.
Daumas, E. (1853) *Moeurs et coutumes de l'Algérie, Tell-Kabylie-Sahara*, Hachette, Paris.
de Jong, F. (1978) 'Khalwatiyya', *Encyclopaedia of Islam*, 2nd edn, Brill, Leiden and London, vol. IV, pp. 991–3.
Delpech, A. (1874) 'Un diplôme de *mok'eddem* de la confrérie religieuse Rahmania', *Revue Africaine*, 18, pp. 418–29.
de Neveu, E. (1845) *Les Khouan, Ordres religieux chez les Musulmans de l'Algérie*, Guyout, Paris.
Depont, O. and Coppolani, X. (1897) *Les Confréries Réligieuses Musulmanes*, Jourdan, Algiers.
Dermengham, E. (1954) *Le Culte des Saints dans l'Islam Maghrébine*, Gallimard, Paris.
Despois, J. (1957) *Le Djebel Amour*, Presses Universitaires de France, Paris.

Doutté, E. (1900) *L'Islam Algérien en l'an 1900*, Mustapha, Algiers.

Eickelman, D.F. (1976) *Moroccan Islam: Tradition and Society in a Pilgrimage Center*, University of Texas Press, Austin, Texas.

Giacobetti, A. (1946) *La Confrérie des Rahmaniya*, Maison Carrée, Algiers.

Gouvian, M. and Gouvian, E. (1920) *Kitab Aayane al-Marhariba*, Imprimerie Orientale, Algiers.

Haas, W. (1943) 'The Zikr of the Rahmaniyah order in Algeria', *Muslim World*, 33, pp. 16–28.

Hanoteau, A. and Letourneux, A. (1872–73) *La Kabylie et les Coutumes Kabyles*, 3 vols., Challamel, Paris.

al-Hifnawi, M. (1982) *Ta'rif al-Khalaf bi-Rijal al-Salaf*, al-Maktaba al-'Atiqa, Tunis.

Julien, C.-A. (1964) *La conquête et les débuts de la colonisation (1827–1871)*, vol. 1 of *Histoire de l'Algérie Contemporaine*, Presses Universitaires de France, Paris.

—— (1970) *History of North Africa*, Praeger, New York.

Margoliouth, D.S. (1924) 'Rahmaniya', *Encyclopaedia of Islam*, 1st edn, Brill, Leiden and London, vol. III, pp. 1104–5.

Martin, B.G. (1972) 'A short history of the Khalwati order of dervishes', in N.R. Keddie (ed.), *Scholars, Saints, and Sufis; Muslim Religious Institutions since 1500*, University of California Press, Berkeley and Los Angeles, pp. 275–305.

—— (1976) *Muslim Brotherhoods in Nineteenth-Century Africa*, Cambridge University Press, Cambridge.

Mercier, E. (1903) *Histoire de Constantine*, Marle, Constantine.

al-Niyal, M. (1965) *al-Haqiqa al-Ta'rikhiyya li'l-Tasawwuf al-Islamiyya*, al-Najjah, Tunis.

Nouschi, A. (1955) 'Constantine à la veille de la conquête française', *Cahiers de Tunisie*, 11, pp. 371–89.

—— (1961) *Enquête sur le niveau de vie des populations rurales Constantinoises de la conquête jusqu'en 1919*, Presses Universitaires de France, Paris.

Rahman, F. (1979) *Islam*, 2nd edn, University of Chicago Press, Chicago.

Raymond, A. (1959) 'Tunisiens et Maghrébines au Caire au dix-huitième siècle', *Cahiers de Tunisie*, 26–7, pp. 336–71.

Rinn, L. (1884) *Marabouts et Khouan, étude sur l'Islam en Algérie*, Jourdan, Algiers.

Robin, N.J. (1901) *L'Insurrection de la Grande Kabylie en 1871*, Lavauzelle, Paris.

Sa'adallah, A. (1981) *Ta'rikh al-Jaza'ir al-Thaqafi*, 2 vols, Société Nationale d'Edition et de la Diffusion, Algiers.

Trumelet, C. (1881) *Les saints de l'Islam. Légendes hagiologiques et croyances Algériennes*, Didier, Paris.

—— (1892) *L'Algérie Légendaire. En Pèlerinage ça et là aux Tombeaux des principaux Thaumaturges de l'Islam*, Jourdan, Algiers.

Valensi, L. (1969) *Le Maghreb avant la prise d'Alger, 1790–1830*, Flammarion, Paris.

Vaysettes, E. (1869) *Histoire de Constantine*, Constantine.
Voll, J.O. (1980) 'Hadith scholars and tariqahs: an *'ulama'* group in the 18th century Haramayn and their impact in the Islamic world', *Journal of Asian and African Studies*, 15, pp. 264–73.
—— (1982) *Islam: Continuity and Change in the Modern World*, Westview Press, Boulder, Colorado.

Chapter eleven

Saints and shrines, politics, and culture: a Morocco–Israel comparison

Alex Weingrod

Emigration and immigration movements provide rare opportunities to examine changes in the making. Social scientists can sometimes observe and trace the small, incremental acts that are the stuff from which larger-scale trends and processes subsequently grow. This chapter concentrates upon one such series of acts: the mass migration of Jews from North Africa to Israel, and particularly the ways in which new North African Jewish saints and shrines have been created in the fertile soil of the Holy Land. Compressed within a brief span of years, this latter process is packed with irony, volatility, and paradox. It is one of those occasional "ripe events" that invites a clearer glimpse into the dynamics of culture.

The problem: explaining the message

Each year since the early 1960s, late in the spring season, large crowds gather to take part in the pilgrimage to the grave of a new Jewish saint (or *zaddik*) – Rabbi Chayim Chouri. This pilgrimage takes place in the municipal cemetery of the city of Beersheba, located in Israel's southern (or Negev) region. By any reckoning, it is an extraordinary "multivocal" event, of which only the bare outline can be described here.

Rabbi Chouri was born in 1885 in the Tunisian island of Jerba, and was for many years the chief rabbi of Gabes. He was a popular figure within the relatively small Tunisian Jewish community: throughout a long and productive life he sponsored the publication of many religious texts, revived community activities, and, not least, successfully guided the Jews of this rural region when the Germans invaded Tunisia during the Second World War. Following the establishment of the state of Israel in 1948, and with the emigration of most of the Tunisian–Jewish community to Israel, Rabbi Chouri left for Israel in 1955, joining his wife and children

217

in the town of Beersheba. Soon thereafter, in 1957, he died at the age of 72. He was buried in a simple grave in a corner of the Beersheba cemetery.

As is customary among Jews, the following year on the anniversary of his death, members of the Chouri family and a small band of friends gathered beside his grave; several spoke briefly recollecting their rabbi, and the eldest son recited the memorial *kaddish* prayer. There was nothing unusual about this family ceremony; a year later it was repeated with a slightly larger number of participants. However, in the years following, this small family gathering grew enormously and became transformed into a great pilgrimage. By the early 1960s, hundreds and soon thousands of persons gathered at the cemetery on the occasion of Rabbi Chouri's *hillula*, or memorial celebration. They crowded around the rabbi's grave; lit candles and recited prayers; spread themselves across the cemetery with its graves and memorial stones in order to eat and drink the traditional meal, visit with friends, sing and dance – all in an outpouring of spontaneous gaiety and thundering power.

This tradition of a yearly pilgrimage has gained in popularity over the years, so that by the 1980s as many as 15–20,000 people gather annually to celebrate the event. Rabbi Chouri has become a saint, or *zaddik*, and many of the thousands who crowd around his grave pray for his intercession in matters relating to their health, good fortune, or problems of love and business. Tales are told and retold that celebrate the rabbi's miraculous powers – how he appeared in dreams and offered direction and guidance to the ill, or how in time of war and peril he mysteriously presented himself to soldiers and guided them to safety. Within a brief span of approximately twenty years, Rabbi Chayim Chouri has been transformed from being a relatively obscure Tunisian rabbi to becoming the "saint of Beersheba".

Although Rabbi Chouri was Tunisian, many of the celebrants in his *hillula* – as in many others – are Moroccan Jews who have, in effect, adopted the new *zaddik* as their own. In a recent article, Harvey Goldberg (1983: 68) makes the point that, in Morocco, the Jewish *zaddikim* were a close parallel "to the elaborate culture of maraboutism characterizing Moroccan Islam". Goldberg goes on to say (1983: 68) that the widespread belief in the powers of saints in fact served as a "conceptual bridge which allowed Jews and Muslims to communicate . . . Jews and Muslims could enter into social exchange because of a shared set of notions and symbols defining the mundane and supernatural worlds". The point is well-taken: one can see a kind of semiotic message of commonality in which the saints were markers in a discourse between the Moroccan Jewish minority and the Moroccan Muslim majority. But here lies the puzzle: if, in Morocco, the traditions of the *zaddik* and *hillula* were expressions of common understandings, then what meanings are being conveyed by new Jewish saints and memorial celebrations in Israel, where the majority of Jews are secular in orientation and disapproving of merriment and feasting in the cemetery and of the reputed magical powers of old rabbis and their graves? Why do tens of thousands of Moroccan and Tunisian Jews, now living in Israel, flock to these festive events?

Historical background: *zaddikim* in Morocco

In order to understand the growing popularity of these celebrations within their new and different Israeli setting we must first consider the historical context. Fortunately, recent studies of the Maghrib, referring both to Muslims and Jews and to the relationships between them, are in many respects comprehensive, authoritative, and detailed.[1] Comparatively small communities of Jews were for hundreds of years distributed throughout North Africa: Jews commonly resided in their own separate quarters (*millah*) in the principal cities and towns, and in the extensive rural areas they lived in their own small hamlets or were concentrated in a corner of Berber and Arab settlements (Eickelman 1983; Goldberg 1983; Shokeid 1985b). As was the case everywhere throughout the Muslim world, the Jews were defined as belonging to the political– legal category of *dhimmi*, or non-Muslim "protected people". As *dhimmis* they were permitted to live alongside Muslims and to maintain their own internal community organisation. At the same time, they were required to pay special taxes to the reigning power, faced numerous social and economic restrictions, and were especially vulnerable to periodic plunder and physical attack (Chouraqui 1952; Lewis 1985). Although the overall fortunes of the Jews improved considerably under French rule, during the period of the Protectorate they were in a separate (unequal) political and social category and typically maintained their distinctive minority identity (Abitbol 1986: 12–13). It should nevertheless be emphasised that, however inferior and peripheral they were to the society's centre, the Jewish minority was tightly knit within the local social, economic, and political landscapes. For example, in rural regions (both Berber and Arab) the Jews supplied the tribesman as traders or artisans and were bound to them as their clients, and they also entered into wide-ranging economic and other exchanges with the town-based Arab elites and merchant families (Eickelman 1983; Geertz *et al*. 1979; Rosen 1984).

In addition, Arabs and Jews throughout the Maghrib also shared a broad array of common cultural features (Geertz *et al*. 1979; Goldberg 1983). To cite several examples from among many, they spoke the same language and dialects, seem to have shared sets of understandings regarding how society was to be organised, and drew upon similar beliefs and practices. This latter point is documented by the prevalence and importance for both Arabs and Jews of saints, their holy shrines, and the frequent pilgrimages made to them. Belief in the miraculous power of saints and holy men (*walis*), as well as the tradition of making a pilgrimage (*ziyara*) to their presumed grave or some other physical marker, has a wide distribution practically everywhere among Muslim populations throughout the Middle East and North Africa (Eickelman 1976; Goldziher 1971). Indeed, these practices are undoubtedly ancient and pre-Islamic, and they were shared by the numerous tribal or religiously-defined groups that spread throughout this large region. Within Islam, which itself originated from a composite of different religious orientations and world views, the belief in the miraculous power of saints is linked (although certainly not identical) with Sufism – that more mystical, emotional current of Muslim thought and practice.

As Islam evolved in the Maghrib, it developed a special emphasis upon saints and their powers, both spiritual and temporal. Maraboutism was, as Geertz and others have shown, a major motif and generating power within Moroccan Islam (Geertz 1968; Westermarck 1926). Eickelman's study of a Moroccan pilgrimage centre clearly summarises its main contours.

> The most striking feature of North African Islam is the presence of marabouts . . . They are persons, living or dead, to whom is attributed a special relation towards God which makes them particularly well-placed to serve as intermediaries with the supernatural and to communicate God's grace (*baraka*) to their clients. On the basis of this conception, marabouts in the past have played key religious, political and economic roles in North African society, particularly in Morocco . . . A concrete indication of this is the proliferation of maraboutic shrines throughout the Maghreb . . . In Morocco's rural areas, one rarely loses sight of the squat, whitewashed, and – in the case of the more popular ones – domed maraboutic shrines. In towns, more lavish shrines with green-tiled roofs are often found.
>
> (Eickelman 1976: 71)

The themes underscored here – the marabout's *baraka*, his role as intermediary, the proliferation of shrines – are basic elements in the pattern. The shrines served as pilgrimage points, and the more important among them grew into pilgrimage centres: the believers came there often to pray for the saint's intercession in various problems of daily living, and during the yearly festival dedicated to the saint (*musim*) entire groups made the pilgrimage to the holy shrine, where they received the blessing of the living saint. A few of these pilgrimage centres grew into small towns, replete with a market, numerous shrines, a religious lodge (*zawiya*), and various accommodations for pilgrims (Eickelman 1976). To be sure, the belief in saints was frequently attacked by the more orthodox Muslim theologians – yet, for many North African Muslims, maraboutism continued to be a vital part of their religious belief system.

There is, finally, another important dimension to maraboutism: in the Moroccan Muslim tradition *baraka* might be passed continuously along the generations, and saintly lineages played crucial political as well as ritual roles. In fact, the marabouts were frequently at the centre of local and regional political intrigue, and the long-lasting Moroccan pattern of periodic conflict between the central authorities, or *makhzan*, and the peripheral but powerful Berber tribes typically focused upon the ambitions of the living saints (Eickelman 1976; Gellner 1969, 1981).

Given this context of ideas and practices, it is not at all surprising that the traditions of saints (*zaddik*) and pilgrimages (*hillula*) were also extremely powerful among the Jewish minority. Deshen locates the genesis of the *zaddik* in the spiritual setting of the fifteenth- and sixteenth-century kabbalists of Safad and other Palestinian towns; among these Jewish mystics the tradition of prayer at the graves of rabbis and sages apparently began to take root (Deshen 1977). Grave sites became holy, powerful places – shrines – and the legendary Talmudic sages and rabbis who were buried there took the form of the *zaddik* – a pious, righteous man, and, ultimately, a saint. Moreover, a tradition developed of making a pilgrimage to the grave of the saint on the anniversary of his death. These periodic gatherings were known as *hillulot*, or memorial celebrations. Deshen describes the process in the following terms:

> The *hillulot* originally focused upon the death of especially pious men, a death that was seen to be a mystical union between the soul of the deceased and the God-head . . . According to popular thought the belief developed that the *zaddik* (saint) in

whose memory the celebration was held would intervene with God on behalf of his followers. Accordingly, persons who suffered from physical or mental illnesses might undertake a pilgrimage to the site of the *zaddik* in the hope and belief that their suffering would be lessened.

(Deshen 1977: 110–11)

The rabbinic authorities typically condemned and sought to discourage these enthusiastic outpourings, but they continued to have widespread popular support, even spreading from Palestine to the other small Jewish communities located throughout the Middle East and North Africa.

These traditions found a particularly sympathetic, not to say, luxuriant, environment in the Maghrib. What Ben-Ami, the Israeli folklorist who has done the major documentary work on *zaddikim* in Morocco, calls "saint veneration", can be found throughout the North African Jewish communities (1984: 4). Indeed, his compendium of Moroccan Jewish *zaddikim* lists more than 600 saints and their shrines, including dozens that were equally claimed and revered by both Muslims and Jews. Virtually each Jewish community had its "own" *zaddik*, and in some places several local saints and shrines were worshipped. The *zaddikim* were typically deceased Moroccan rabbis, although, in other cases, the shrine and the *zaddik* were named after Palestinian rabbis who had visited North Africa and died there. In still other instances the shrine was named after a famed rabbi; the best known case is the Moroccan shrine of Rabbi Shimon bar Yochai, the Palestinian sage who was the reputed author of the Zohar – a book of mystical-religious teaching. These shrines were often located within the Jewish cemetery, although in some instances "they were not in the cemetery proper, but in a special spot, for example, a cave, at some distance from it" (Goldberg 1983: 65). A *zaddik*'s grave was usually covered by a simple roof in order "to distinguish it from other graves", but these decorations were nowhere as elaborate as among the tombs of famed marabouts. The fact that these shrines were located within the Jewish cemetery is itself important: Goldberg (1983: 65) suggests that, symbolically at least, the Jews were in this way making a "claim to exercise rights in the territory on an equal basis with that of the Muslims".

In addition, a number of the shrines became particularly famous, and these periodically attracted large crowds of pilgrims from various parts of the country; the best example is the grave of Rabbi David u'Moshe, located near Agouim in the High Atlas. Thus, as Ben-Ami (1984: 219) shows, not only were the graves of *zaddikim* to be found in practically every Jewish community, there was also a kind of hierarchy of saints in which certain of them attained regional and almost national levels of importance.

In common with the Muslim marabout, the Jewish *zaddik* also possessed *baraka*, or grace and holy power. The *zaddik* was believed to be able to act as an intermediary with God – prayer at the shrine and vows (*neder*) might result in the positive outcome desired by the supplicant. Beyond prayers, the true mark of a *zaddik* was his ability to perform miracles – heal the sick, bring about good fortune in love and business, cure barrenness in women or provide male offspring, and, in addition, protect the weak exposed Jewish communities from their enemies. As Stillman (1982: 496) points out, however, there also were important differences between *zaddik* and marabout – for example, the miraculous acts attributed to the latter were often "of a more spectacular kind". With notable exceptions, moreover, there were no families or lineages of Jewish *zaddikim*; on the contrary, the saint was typically recognised after his death, and his descendants were not necessarily involved with his shrine. In comparison, the marabouts seem to have played much more active and critical political roles than did the *zaddikim*.

Believers and persons in despair or need visited the *zaddik*'s grave throughout the year. However, the yearly *hillula*, performed on the anniversary of the saint's death, typically brought together a large popular outpouring of persons. Based upon his Israeli informants' recollections of *hillulot* in Morocco, Goldberg describes these celebrations in the following terms:

> Descriptions of the local pilgrimages stressed how they involved the whole community. "Men, women and children" went, it was frequently said. It was commonly stated that everyone participated equally, "rich and poor alike". The pilgrimage involved visiting the grave, lighting candles, and slaughtering animals (cattle or sheep), after which the meal would be served. The meal might take place in the cemetery, or just outside it. Sometimes, after the visit to the cemetery, the meal would be organized in the village proper. Descriptions of the eating patterns also stressed equality; everyone was given the same size or kind of portion . . . Even allowing for an idealization of the equality that characterized these gatherings, it is unmistakable that they were Durkheimian high points in the celebration of communal life.
>
> (Goldberg 1983: 67)

In keeping with their fundamentally different social and political positions, the green-tiled Muslim maraboutic shrines shone across

223

the countryside, whereas the graves of the Jewish *zaddikim* were simpler and plain. Yet, as has been shown, there was also a broad range of overlap in belief and practice between the Muslim and Jewish traditions. Finally, even though the French colonial presence produced a series of rapid changes – migration to the central cities, the spread of French language and culture, growing secularisation – traditions of the *zaddik* and his *hillula* remained vibrant, so much so that new Jewish saints continued to emerge during the 1930s and 1940s (Ben-Ami 1984: 225).

The *zaddik* in the Israeli setting

While small numbers of North African Jews had immigrated to Israel prior to 1948, the establishment of Israel precipitated what ultimately became a virtual transfer of population. This immigration characteristically developed in several waves and ripples – a great initial movement to Israel in the period between 1948 and 1956, then a pause, followed by smaller waves later in the 1950s and mid-1960s. In the process, probably as many as 200,000 Jews left such ancient Jewish communities as Fez and Jerba, as well as such newer urban population centres as Casablanca and Tripoli, and began making a new life in Israel. Numerous studies have shown that their Israeli experience during the first decade or two was at best "bittersweet", and often plainly bitter (Bar Yosef 1959: 249; Weingrod 1965: 39–40). In common with other immigrants then flocking to Israel, the North Africans needed to learn new occupations and skills, a new language and cultural styles, as well as adapt to what was for many a new, centralised, western political–administrative system. Their high hopes and optimistic dreams were frequently dashed by the harsh realities of life in their new, relatively poor country. Moreover, many North African Jews found themselves dispatched by government planners to new development towns and agricultural villages (*moshavim*) then being built in the outlying northern and southern zones of Israel. This is an important point: new towns such as Beth Shean and Kiryat Shmonah in the north, or Dimona and Kiryat Gat in the south, were mainly composed of North African – primarily Moroccan – immigrants.

It was a difficult, frustrating experience, and the Moroccans in particular soon acquired a reputation for being hot-headed and aggressive; they were angered not only by the meagre conditions of daily life but also (and perhaps mainly) by the fact that the society's dominant social roles were monopolised by Ashkenazi Jews, the European-born (or bred) Israelis, and that they were expected to conform to the cultural norms espoused by this elite group (Marx 1976: 24; Shokeid 1985b: 281; Weingrod 1965: 40). The pressures for cultural assimilation and divesting one's self of previous beliefs and traditions were extremely powerful. The Moroccans also resented the discrimination and prejudice that were often levelled against them (a study of a mixed housing estate in the mid-1950s showed that the Moroccans were the least liked group). Not surprisingly, the two major incidents of rioting among Jews – the demonstrations in Wadi Salib in 1958 and the Israel Black Panther protests of the early 1970s – primarily involved Moroccan youngsters who protested violently against the dominant Jewish society and culture.

These were critical, formative features in the experience of many North African immigrants. But there were additional elements that became no less significant. Gradually, many of the immigrants mastered the new skills that had been thrust upon them: they became more fluent in Hebrew and at home in their new surroundings, and in common with other Israelis their living standard climbed steadily upwards. Although memories of prejudice remained close to the surface, the newer generation of youngsters appeared to be more confidently attached to their society. For example, together with other Israelis they fought in several wars, and, as further evidence of their newfound, upwardly-mobile status, a significant proportion married members of other Jewish ethnic groups (Peres 1985). Now entrenched in certain portions of the country, they have become the "veterans", instructing newer groups into the mysteries of life in Israel.

Partly as a consequence of these processes, during the 1970s a new ideology of ethnic pluralism began to typify the Israeli cultural outlook. The previous pressure to conform to European cultural norms lessened (or, putting it differently, the Ashkenazic hegemony weakened), while ethnic cultural differences were pronounced legitimate and even celebrated. The most vivid example of this shift was the late-1960s re-creation of the *mimuna* festival, a minor Moroccan Jewish festivity that has rapidly been elevated into an Israeli national holiday (Goldberg 1978: 75; Weingrod 1979: 63). The Israeli *mimuna* festival is fundamentally secular – its designers have successfully combined the old-country traditions of a springtime gathering that included family outings, feasting, and communal gaiety, with new Israeli political and cultural motifs. Significantly, this Moroccan event became the model for other Jewish ethnic groups – the Kurds, Persians, Georgians, and others – who have subsequently organised their own Israeli ethnic festivals (Goldstein 1985).

Needless to say, ethnic politics began to thrive in this new cultural climate. The recent prominence of North African (mainly Moroccan) political leaders has been striking: several hold important positions at the national levels of government, and, what is more, the "North African caucus" in the Israeli Parliament includes more than twenty members (of a total of 120) who are themselves divided between the different, competing political parties. In these and other ways, Moroccan and Tunisian Jews have become markedly more integrated within Israeli society.

Following this brief review, we can now ask: What factors explain the emergence in Israel of new Jewish saints and pilgrimages? How can we account for the phenomenal growth of Rabbi Chouri's *hillula*? What "message" is being sent by the thousands who gather yearly to celebrate in the Beersheba cemetery?

Several previous interpretations of the newfound popularity of the *hillulot* have been suggested. For example, Ben-Ami takes the view that it was to be expected that Moroccan Jews would adopt or create new saints in Israel. He believes that since the *zaddikim* were so vital an element in their religious traditions in Morocco, they were bound to revive these beliefs in the new, fertile climate of the Holy Land (Ben-Ami 1981: 302). He goes on to suggest that this process unfolded in three steps. At first, during the initial period of mass immigration (the early 1950s), Moroccan Jews sometimes made trips to several already established shrines, such as the Cave of the Prophet Elijah near Haifa. Later, in the second stage (the early 1960s), small celebrations in memory of famous North African saints were held in private homes and in synagogues. During the third stage (the mid-1960s), several new *hillulot* began to take "place on a national scale, and to this people came from all over the country" (Ben-Ami 1981: 303). To cite a different explanation, Deshen (1977: 120) has proposed a somewhat more complex set of reasons. Viewing these pilgrimages in the broader religious context of an overall trend towards secularisation, he argues that their popularity stems from the fact that "they are especially suited to the needs and problems of persons who have lost a large measure of their traditional culture and social moorings". The revival of the *hillulot* is, according to this view, a response to a major cultural change or crisis in identity.

Both of these explanations have a certain logic and power. However, I want to propose a different avenue of analysis, one that focuses more squarely upon the political and cultural processes described previously.

The point can be stated as follows: Rabbi Chouri's *hillula* and others like it are, among other things, statements of a new North

African, and particularly Moroccan, presence in Israel. This is a statement of the possibility of cultural difference or separation: in sharp contrast with the previous Moroccan context, the message sent by the new saints and their pilgrimages is the legitimacy in Israel of a separate, different, cultural and political organisation. Indeed, if, as Goldberg suggests in the passage cited earlier, the Jewish cemetery and its shrines were a symbolic statement of the Jews' equal claim to legitimacy in Morocco, then how much more emphatically (and successfully) this is stated by Moroccan Jewish saints buried in Israeli cemeteries. The message that emanates from the municipal cemetery in Beersheba is not "how much we are like other Israelis", but rather, "since we are Israelis we can also celebrate publicly according to our own particular traditions".

What attracts thousands of Moroccan and Tunisian Israelis to this *hillula* is that it is an occasion for them to celebrate publicly *on their own terms*: this is "their holiday", commemorating "their Rabbi", and it is performed in a grand style according to "their own traditions". This is a powerful motivation: it is now possible for them, Israelis all, to assemble and celebrate the anniversary of the death of a Tunisian *zaddik*. They gather together normally and proudly with no hint of crisis in their social or cultural identity of belonging. This is a true sea change, although it is the result of a gradual process. As was emphasised previously, North African Jews have had a series of difficult experiences as immigrants in Israel. Looking back, they can point to the harsh, trying years when they were *declassé*, thrust into outlying places where they were somehow expected to manage. At the same time, however, they can also proudly claim to have become adjusted and even to have mastered their new Israeli environment, and – at least for some – to have climbed upward on the socio-political and economic ladder.

The movement from a kind of self-hate to a newer "ethnic pride" is an important facet of this process. Indeed, it helps to explain why, following Ben-Ami, it was only in recent years that the *hillulot* were publicly celebrated on a massive scale. The Israeli emphasis upon "immigrant absorption" and against separate cultural organisation had previously stigmatised ethnic cultural as well as political organisation, and it was only later – as in the case of Rabbi Chouri – that these and other festivities attracted ever-widening audiences. This is the "other side" to social mobility and heightened social integration: as these immigrants became more accustomed to life in Israel and more adept at moving upwards in the society, they also gained the confidence and strength enabling them to organise their own public festivals. The emergence of ethnic celebrations is therefore not a sign of the failure to assimilate, but the reverse: large public events such as Rabbi Chouri's *hillula* are legitimate because the participants have become more thoroughly absorbed within their new milieu.

Saints, politics, and culture in contemporary Israel

Attention has thus far been given to new saints and pilgrimages as a focus for ethnic group revival and mobilisation. There is, of course, an array of other topics arising from the emergence of new *zaddikim* in Israel. Some of these issues can best be understood by continuing the Morocco−Israel comparison, whereas others are better analysed within the particular contexts of contemporary Israeli society. What they have in common, as we shall soon see, is a certain paradoxical, unexpected quality.

Before turning directly to these topics, however, it is necessary to get a better sense of the scope of the process itself. Rabbi Chouri is not, of course, an isolated case: a new "saint map" replete with yearly festivities is rapidly being engraved upon the landscape. During the past twenty or so years pilgrimages have been initiated or greatly enlarged to a series of old and new holy shrines (Ben-Ami 1981: 301−2). These older shrines include the giant pilgrimage to the grave of Rabbi Shimon bar Yochai, located near Safad, that yearly draws upwards of 150,000 participants; or the *hillula* of Honi Hameagel, a Talmudic sage whose grave near the northern town of Hatzor has also become a local pilgrimage site. Two new shrines are especially fascinating. Within a Safad neighbourhood, a Moroccan immigrant developed a new shrine devoted to the famous Moroccan *zaddik*, Rabbi David u'Moshe: in this case the *zaddik* is believed to have been mysteriously transported from the Moroccan Atlas to his new shrine in northern Israel, where thousands of believers now light candles and pray for the saint's intervention in matters of health or good fortune (Bilu 1987).

Another case of a new saint is that of Rabbi Israel Abouhatzeira, or, as he is popularly known, the Baba Sali. In certain respects this *zaddik* is similar to Rabbi Chouri. Like Rabbi Chouri, he too was a contemporary rabbi (in this case Moroccan) who has become a *zaddik*. Rabbi Abouhatzeira was a member of the most distinguished Moroccan Jewish rabbinic family and famed for his erudition and healing powers; his home and *yeshiva*, or religious seminary, near the southern town of Netivoth, drew crowds of believers who came to him for his counsel and blessing. Indeed, the Baba Sali had already become a *zaddik* during his lifetime, and it was therefore not surprising that following his death (at the age of

94) his grave immediately became a holy shrine. He is undoubtedly the most famous of the new *zaddikim*, and his photograph – icon-like – can now be seen hanging in countless homes and shops spread throughout Israel.

Needless to say, the sites on this new "saint map" are primarily frequented by North African Jews: the periodic *hillulot* draw large crowds of older and younger Moroccans and Tunisians who expend considerable time and substantial resources in taking part in these festive occasions. To be sure, the giant celebration to the grave of Bar Yochai also includes thousands of Ashkenazic religious zealots, and the Baba Sali also attracted followers from within this group. None the less, North African Jews have given the major impetus to this saintly revival.

One of the striking features of both the new and older shrines is that they are situated in outlying marginal zones: while the majority of Israel's population resides in three large central urban areas – in and around Tel Aviv, Jerusalem, and Haifa – saints and pilgrimages are centred in peripheral small towns in the north and south, places like Hatzor in the Galilee or Netivoth in the Negev.[2] How can this be explained?

Several interpretations may be suggested. First, these peripheral areas are precisely the places to which large numbers of North African immigrants were directed when they first arrived in Israel, and, as was pointed out previously, these zones continue to have a large Moroccan–Israeli population. This somewhat skewed population concentration is a major reason why the new *zaddikim* and their shrines have developed there: the new saints, all of whom are of North African provenance, thrive close-by to their followers and believers. Second, as suggested in a recent article (Ben-Ari and Bilu, 1987), the new shrines are an expression of the immigrants' growing ties and attachments to their new locale. Ben-Ari and Bilu (like Ben-Ami) also emphasise the fact that new *zaddikim* are a recent trend, and argue that this is a part of the process through which "the residents' sense of belonging to the locality acquires a wider meaning".

A third reason may also be suggested. For a variety of reasons saints typically are to be found in more remote, peripheral areas. This was certainly the Moroccan pattern (true for both Moroccan Muslims and Jews), and it also extends to saints' shrines and pilgrimages in other civilisations (Brown 1981: 43; Gellner 1981). If anything, saints seem to thrive away from the more refined, cosmopolitan, urban centres. It is not that urban residents are less prone to search for saintly inspiration or do not have a need for saintly intermediaries – an unlikely hypothesis – but rather that urban-based religious theologians tend to oppose or denigrate the worship of saints. To a considerable degree this has been the case in Israel, where the religious authorities have tended to oppose or frown upon the "discovery" of new *zaddikim*.[3] This helps to explain why, for example, new *zaddikim* have thus far not emerged among the substantial North African populations that reside in or around Jerusalem and Tel Aviv. The greater likelihood is for shrines to develop in rural areas, and for town and city residents to undertake pilgrimages to these distant locales.

Beyond their physical location, the process of new saint formation is closely tied to a number of recent Israeli political and cultural currents. If, as was pointed out previously, there were no families or lineages of "living *zaddikim*" among Jews in Morocco, this may be changing in the new Israeli environment. There appears to be emerging, to some extent at least, a Moroccan–Israeli version of "maraboutism".

This development has to do with "religion" and "politics", and the curious ways in which they sometimes intersect in contemporary Israel. Two of the famed new *zaddikim* – Rabbi Chouri and the Baba Sali – can serve as cases in point. To begin with, family members and close kin of both of these saints have lately plunged into politics: one of Rabbi Chouri's grandsons is a rambunctious member of the Beersheba City Council, and one of the *zaddik*'s sons was mentioned as a candidate for election to the Israeli Parliament (or Knesset) on a new, mainly North African religious political party list. Similarly, the Baba Sali's son and erstwhile "spiritual heir", himself a controversial personality, has also become involved in local and national politics, and one of his cousins is Knesset member. Thus it would appear that the saintly mantle and its *baraka* are not far removed from political party as well as personal ambition and power.

There has also been a rapid expansion of activities around both of these new *zaddikim*. Several years ago an already existing small Beersheba *yeshiva* was named after Rabbi Chouri: located in a modest building, the *yeshiva* has become the centre of activities designed to spread the Rabbi's fame. A small core of devoted followers (including one of the Rabbi's sons) take the leading roles in these endeavours. Like other religious seminaries, the Chouri *yeshiva* receives government financial support, and private supporters and believers have also contributed to its activities. Thus, in effect, the new *zaddik*'s charisma and following has produced a linkage with a state-sponsored religious institution that, as a consequence, has resources placed at its disposal.

A similar process has been under way at Netivoth, the "home" of the Baba Sali, but there the institution-building is on a more lavish scale and the resources are considerable. The saint's tomb was elaborately built and decorated in a style reminiscent of the Maghrib: this large, domed shrine stands by itself, separated from and dominating the town cemetery. A continual stream of pilgrims go there throughout the year, and during the saint's *hillula* the crowds are enormous – often numbering well over 50,000 participants. In addition, a large *yeshiva* – named after the *zaddik* – is located in the town, and it serves as the focus for the various activities that celebrate the saint's memory and miraculous works. In fact, the local town council has considered changing the town's name from "Netivoth" to "Netivoth Israel", in orer to connect itself even more closely with the saint, Rabbi Israel Abouhatzeira. This small town – a failure as an Israeli development town – may yet prosper as the centre for the ever-expanding activities being promoted in the name of the Baba Sali. It is, indeed, becoming a pilgrimage centre in which the *zaddik*'s son plays the role of the "living saint".

There is, finally, still another way in which the new *zaddikim* have become linked with Israeli politics and culture. The recent attention given to saints and pilgrimages can also be seen as part of a deeper political and cultural trend. To be more specific, what Ben-Ami (1984) calls "saint veneration" is related to broader movements in which significant minorities within Israeli society have become more fundamentalist in outlook, nationalist in ideology, and supportive of right-wing political parties (Cohen 1983). These trends have undoubtedly become more pronounced during the past two decades; indeed, it is fair to state that within the same or overlapping populations a certain mystical religious orientation seems to have grown together with, or close to, what can properly be labelled as right-wing political nationalism. This is a distinctly frothy, unstable mix, and at certain moments it has swung in curious, unexpected directions. *Zaddikim* and *hillulot* have at times been directly interwoven with these currents; for example, some of the pilgrimages provide occasions in which rabbinic figures and right-of-centre political leaders appear together before crowds of believers, and during election campaigns the image of a holy shrine may be flashed upon the television screen. Beyond these particular occasions, the growing popularity of these celebrations has encouraged a certain nationalist–religious sensibility that has grown more pervasive and influential.

Comparisons and conclusions

The short-spanned, volatile bursts of energy that have been described in this chapter point to a number of broader conclusions. The lines of analysis have flowed mainly around belief and ideology, on the one hand, and power and practice, on the other. The theoretical problem is to understand how they are connected – in other words, how culture and politics become intertwined within the particular realities of migration and immigration.

These topics can be seen comparatively: certainly, the examples are reduced to miniature, but they help to illustrate the issues. Of relevance here is Abner Cohen's analysis of the origins and explosive growth of a West Indian carnival in Notting Hill in London. The context and actors studied – West Indian immigrants seeking to find their way in contemporary London – have a great many parallels with Moroccan immigrants in Israel and the emergence of new saints and pilgrimages. Cohen shows how, in a brief span of years, a local interest in organising an "English country fayre" became transformed into a giant Trinidadian-styled carnival replete with steel bands, calypso tunes, and street performances – all set within a working-class section of contemporary London (Cohen 1980, 1982). Political energies were set loose in this event, and so too was creative artistry in organisation, music, and pageantry; at one level, the carnival, like the *hillula*, is a prime example of an ethnic renewal ceremony as thousands of West Indians parade through London streets.

The second example is drawn from the Muslim world – or to be more specific, from Muslims presently engaged in building new lives in a number of western European countries. Turkish *Gastarbeiter* in Germany and Belgium, or Moroccans in France and Holland, are the obvious parallels. Away from their homes "temporarily" (meaning for lengthy, extended periods of time) in what has fast become a Muslim diaspora, these new immigrant minorities are also fashioning novel cultural designs. Ruth Mandel's chapter in this volume suggests some of the cultural-cum-political dimensions of this process. Her depiction of the changes taking place among the Turkish Alevis is particularly apt. A minority group within Sunni Turkey, the Alevis seem to have taken a prominent role within some of the *Gastarbeiter* communities – where, among other things, their distinctive religious rituals (*ayin-i cem*) take on new substance as rival political factions contest over group leadership. Thus, in common with the Beersheba cemetery and London's Notting Hill, new cultural performances designed by Turks in Berlin or Berne also become formats for rapid cultural creativity.

Finally, there is a more general conclusion to be drawn. Abner Cohen's previously cited studies present a useful starting point. Cohen's main theoretical conclusion is that "politics" (as represented in his research by ambitious leaders or in social class conflicts) and "culture" (expressed by steel bands and a syncretic religion) are not properly reducible to one another: each has a different internal dynamic, follows along different tracks, and consequently may merge or interact with the other in ways that are unpredictable and often paradoxical. The processes traced in this study underscore and strengthen this conclusion. For example, the spontaneous, essentially naïve fashion in which new saints and shrines become popularised is only subsequently understood to be linked with the emergence of radical political ideologies. To cite another example, a saintly presence leads, with snowball-like speed, to the development of a religious seminary, schools, and streams of pilgrims and other resources – all of which suggests an Israeli version of a Moroccan shrine-centre. There is, in brief, a kind of "ricochet effect" in which action in one corner of the system will have implications elsewhere.

What this also means is that complex relationships exist between culture and politics which, at least in retrospect, appear to be systematic. This conclusion may not be surprising, but it is intriguing none the less. When they do intersect – while the "ricocheting" takes place – political and cultural currents build a nurturant, supportive set of beliefs and understandings. Hence, once religious nationalist ideologies emerge, they dovetail with belief in the efficacy of saintly powers. This statement is, of course, a version of Weberian theories concerning the relationship between politics and religion, or elites and ideologies. That theory continues to provide useful perspectives upon these endlessly engaging topics.

Notes

1 During the last two decades in particular, North Africa has been a focus for a series of excellent anthropological studies. In regard to relationships between Muslims and Jews, see in particular Abitbol (1986); Rosen (1972); Geertz *et al.* (1979); and Udovitch and Valensi (1984).
2 An exception is the shrine and *hillula* celebrated in memory of Bu-Shaif, a Libyan Jewish female saint. The synagogue built in her memory, which is the site of the pilgrimage, is located in a village close to the large Tel Aviv urban area. The *hillula* attracts crowds of several thousand persons, most of whom apparently are Libyan Jews.
3 The issues are complex: the official rabbinate mainly seems to ignore the shrines and *hillulot*, although some of the North African rabbis in Israel are present on these occasions. The exception is the Baba Sali, where

religious dignitaries join other "celebrities" in a public demonstration of participation.

References

Abitbol, M. (1986) *The Jews of North Africa during World War II* (in Hebrew), Ben Zvi Institute, Jerusalem.

Bar Yosef, R. (1959) 'An analysis of the status of the North African immigrants in Israel' (in Hebrew), *Molad*, 17, no. 131, pp. 247–51.

Ben-Ami, I. (1981) 'Folk veneration of saints among Moroccan Jews', in S. Morag, I. Ben-Ami, and N. Stillman (eds), *Studies in Judaism and Islam*, The Magnes Press, Jerusalem.

—— (1984) *Saint veneration among the Jews of Morocco* (in Hebrew), The Magnes Press, Jerusalem.

Ben-Ari, E. and Bilu, Y. (1987) 'Saints' sanctuaries in Israeli development towns', *Urban Anthropology*, 16, no. 2, pp. 243–72.

Bilu, Y. (1987) 'Dreams and wishes of the saint', in H. Goldberg (ed.), *Judaism viewed from within and without*, SUNY Press, Albany, pp. 285–313.

Brown, P. (1981) *The Cult of the Saints*, University of Chicago Press, Chicago.

Chouraqui, A. (1952) *Les juifs d'Afrique du nord*, Presses Universitaires de France, Paris.

Cohen, A. (1980) 'Drama and politics in the development of a London carnival', *Man*, 15, no. 3, pp. 66–85.

—— (1982) 'A polyethnic London carnival as a contested cultural performance', *Ethnic and Racial Studies*, 5, no. 1, pp. 23–38.

Cohen, E. (1983) 'Ethnicity and legitimation in contemporary Israel', *Jerusalem Quarterly*, no. 24, pp. 21–34.

Deshen, S. (1977) 'Tunisian hillulot', in M. Shokeid and S. Deshen (eds), *The generation of transition* (in Hebrew), Ben Zvi Institute, Jerusalem.

Eickelman, D. (1976) *Moroccan Islam*, University of Texas Press, Austin.

—— (1983) 'Religion and trade in western Morocco', *Research in Economic Anthropology*, 5, pp. 335–48.

Geertz, C. (1968) *Islam Observed*, Yale University Press, New Haven, Conn.

Geertz, C., Geertz, H., and Rosen, L. (1979) *Meaning and Order in Moroccan Society*, Cambridge University Press, Cambridge.

Gellner, E. (1969) *Saints of the Atlas*, University of Chicago Press, Chicago.

—— (1981) *Muslim Society*, Cambridge University Press, Cambridge.

Goldberg, H. (1978) 'The mimouna and the minority status of Moroccan Jews', *Ethnology*, 17, no. 1, pp. 75–88.

—— (1983) 'The mellahs of southern Morocco: report of a survey', *The Maghreb Review*, 9, pp. 61–9.

Goldstein, J. (1985) 'Iranian ethnicity in Israel', in A. Weingrod (ed.), *Studies in Israeli Ethnicity*, Gordon & Breach, New York, pp. 237–58.

Goldziher, I. (1971) *Muslim Studies*, trans. by S.M. Stern, Aldine Publishers, Chicago.

Lewis, B. (1985) *The Jews of Islam*, Princeton University Press, Princeton.

Marx, E. (1976) *The Social Context of Violent Behaviour*, Routledge & Kegan Paul, London.

Peres, Y. (1985) 'Horizontal integration and vertical differentiation among Jewish ethnicities in Israel', in A. Weingrod (ed.), *Studies in Israeli ethnicity*, Gordon & Breach, New York, pp. 39–56.

Rosen, L. (1972) 'Muslim and Jewish relations in a Moroccan city', *International Journal of Middle East Studies*, 3, no. 3, pp. 435–49.

—— (1984) *Bargaining for Reality*, University of Chicago Press, Chicago.

Shokeid, M. (1985a) 'Aggression and social relationships among Moroccan immigrants', in A. Weingrod (ed.), *Studies in Israeli Ethnicity*, Gordon & Breach, New York, pp. 281–96.

—— (1985b) *The Dual Heritage*, Transaction Books, New Brunswick.

Stillman, N. (1982) 'Saddiq and marabout in Morocco', in I. Ben-Ami (ed.), *The Sephardi and Oriental Jewish Heritage*, The Magnes Press, Jerusalem, pp. 489–500.

Udovitch, A.L. and Valensi, L. (1984) *The Last Arab Jews: The Communities of Jerba, Tunisia*, Harwood, New York.

Weingrod, A. (1965) *Israel: Group Relations in a New Society*, Pall Mall Press, London.

—— (1979) 'Recent trends in Israeli ethnicity', *Ethnic and Racial Studies*, 2, no. 2, pp. 55–65.

Westermarck, E. (1926) *Ritual and Belief in Morocco*, Macmillan & Co., London.

Chapter twelve

Ziyaret: gender, movement, and exchange in a Turkish community

Nancy Tapper

This chapter describes the beliefs and practices associated with the notion of *ziyaret* (Arabic, *ziyara*) in a single Muslim community, that of Eğirdir, a provincial town in south-western Turkey. My account is thus tied to a specific ethnographic context. I have incorporated a number of Turkish terms in my text, not only because I feel that readers should consider how key terms have been translated, but also because these terms are in fact widely known and used in the Muslim Middle East and thus can be used to locate my argument cross-culturally. I have also limited my investigation in a second way. The semantic range of the notion of *ziyaret* is considerable and raises many interesting problems. However, I have chosen to address specifically only two related questions of comparative interest: Why are Muslim women, more often than Muslim men, concerned with the shrine visits known as *ziyaret*? Why are such women's *ziyaret* activities often disparaged by men?

In Eğirdir, and indeed elsewhere in the Muslim Middle East, *ziyaret* forms a single category denoting shrines, pilgrimages to shrines, and formal visits in a variety of social contexts. However, I suggest that an understanding of the notion of *ziyaret* depends on several related assumptions.

First, a study of categories of movement, such as *ziyaret*, should be concerned not just with the form of movement *per se*, but with the content of the exchanges and communication which that movement facilitates. Thus, how does the movement associated with *ziyaret* organise interactions both between individuals and between human beings and supernatural entities – greeting rituals, prayers, vows and sacrifices whose returns are material, and spiritual blessings? I suggest that such interactions are structured by the pervasive notion of respect (*saygı*; *hürmet*), a key to understanding the meaning of *ziyaret* in Turkish society and probably elsewhere. In the broadest sense, then, *ziyaret* is voluntary movement for the purpose of paying respect, implicitly to a person or shrine whose

236

authority is thereby acknowledged. Legitimate authority for Muslims is primarily religious, or religiously sanctioned, hence the pervasive religious connotation of *ziyaret*.

Second, I consider that an understanding of the constructions of practised Islam, which include notions such as *ziyaret*, depends upon understanding local standards of orthodoxy and heterodoxy as they are defined and sanctioned by the religious and political establishments. For instance, in the past, the town of Eğirdir and its environment were felt to be permeated with a sanctity that derived from the shrines (*ziyaret*) of the many saints (*evliya*) who were buried there. Many of these sites were destroyed in the zealous secular Republicanism of the 1930s and 1940s and contemporary Turkish Islam continues to devalue the role of saints and to become increasingly mosque-centred. Thus in Eğirdir today, the status of the notion of *ziyaret* as applied to saints and shrines is ambiguous: the religious and political establishment, and indeed virtually all men, scorn shrine visits and consider that faith in the power of the saints is unnecessary and inappropriate.

Third, I suggest that *ziyaret* also derives meaning from its contrasting relations with other categories of movement (*hareket*) or journey (*yolculuk, seyahat, sefer*). Some of these have specifically religious connotations, such as the prescribed *hajj* (Turkish, *hac*) or pilgrimage to Mecca; others, such as picnics (*piknik*) with their paradisical associations, are ambiguous; yet other categories of movement have no explicit religious connotations but are intimately associated with gender constructs, as is the case of the non-purposive movement associated with going for a stroll (*gezi*), a male prerogative *par excellence*.

Finally, in academic studies of Muslim societies, men's ideals, beliefs, and actions have usually been privileged above those of women; typically, this bias confirms and reinforces the bias against women that is intrinsic to Muslim cultural traditions themselves. If questions of gender are to be investigated, it is essential to analyse a notion such as *ziyaret* that has a prominent place in practised Islam, and to consider implicit behaviours that are associated with it. Thus, in this chapter, I examine the relation between movement, gender, and the indigenous notion of *ziyaret* in terms of two analytic categories. One concerns those occasions when women and men move outside the home together, and the other when women without men leave the domestic setting. As we shall see, gender differences are relatively unmarked and women and men participate more or less equally in those occasions associated with the first category, whereas the women's activities of the second category differentiate women from men and reinforce constructions of female inferiority.

Eğirdir[1]

Eğirdir is a market and administrative centre for a region of some forty villages. The town itself has a population of about 9,000 – brought to a total of over 12,000 by two substantial national institutions, the army commando school and an orthopaedic hospital. The town lies on the shores of a large lake, and fishing still brings in a proportion of the income, but nowadays the economy of the town is based on the international export of locally grown apples. All Eğirdir families own orchard land outside the town, and all have benefited to some degree from the apple boom.

In general terms, most townspeople are both committed Republicans and committed Muslims. However, in spite of their self-image as a uniformly "middle-class" community, large differences in wealth are now emerging and there are distinct strata in the town based on differences in socio-economic status and life-style. As we shall see, there is a relation between these "classes" and their differing emphases on Islamic or Republican values, and concepts of gender. In particular, the relationship is suggestive of the meaning that movement and *ziyaret* have in women's lives: all women of the town are involved in *ziyaret* visits to senior kin, while usually only women from the more "traditional"[2] households are involved in *ziyaret* visits to shrines. Although this difference is important to my argument, it should not obscure our understanding of the even greater similarities in the situation of all townswomen when compared to that of men.

Respect and authority

In Eğirdir, and indeed in Turkey generally, the concept of respect (*saygı*; *hürmet*) is of key importance in the ordering of all social relations.[3] Most importantly, the Turks believe that respect for God should guide the actions and belief of all Muslims. Relations between Turkish citizens and the state are also constructed in terms of respect – as are relations between young and old, women and men, the ill-informed and the educated. Indeed, the generic concept of respect, buttressed by a comprehensive social etiquette and a complex symbolic idiom related to bodily control and stasis as opposed to movement, is used to create hierarchies of authority in all areas of social life.

Respectful behaviour in all contexts is associated with religious merit (*sevab*), God's blessing, and reward for piety and meritorious action. Relations of respect are derived by analogy from the respect due from man to God. The analogy is developed in the context of gender in terms of an elaborate theological anthropology which associates men with greater, and women with less, reason (*akıl*) and control of their animal souls (*nefs*). Women, in order to merit God's promise of salvation, must overcome, through discipline and control, the impediments associated with their carnal nature.

These ideas create a fundamental difference between the sexes in the scope that they have for independent voluntary action and movement outside the household. Within certain broad limits, a man is free to determine his own actions within the community, and the respect he is accorded as a manly adult is directly related to his autonomy. By contrast, a woman's autonomy is limited and she is expected to be circumspect in all her actions, particularly those which take her outside the home. Indeed, only the respect accorded to age qualifies women's inferiority to men: men as well as women have an obligation to respect women who are older than themselves, though this is not in fact associated with a greater freedom of movement outside the home for older women.

Women, as well as men, accept their ascribed statuses and the comprehensive hierarchy of authority and control with which they are associated. Yet, to the outsider, the question arises, how do women, who are defined as intrinsically inferior, come to terms with their inferiority? What elements are there in their characterisation and practice of Islam which continue to foster their religious commitment and perhaps offer them compensations or consolation for their subservient position? And, finally, how do women reconcile their temporal disabilties with their potential equality with men in paradise? In what follows I suggest that the complex relation between the ideology of respect and the notion of *ziyaret* serves both to constrain and to facilitate movement and exchange among women, thus allowing women certain areas of action while ultimately reinforcing the ideology of the passive subordination of women to men.

Women and movement

Eğirdir women see themselves as confined to their homes by considerations of propriety and by domestic duties, and they greatly value opportunities for movement outside. Older women remember that not so long ago women never went anywhere except to visit their neighbours, so that *bayram* (or *'Id*) visits and trips to local shrines (all *ziyaret*), and the women's picnics, were very special indeed. Although both women and men agree that attitudes towards movement changed, and became more open (*açık*) during the 1950s – when people realised they could actually leave the town

– in practice, the changes have been limited with regard to women's movements. Women can now shop in the town, and they travel to wedding receptions in Isparta (the provincial capital) and elsewhere by hired coach – either with their husbands or in groups of men and women – but neither these nor other types of movement are undertaken without the express permission of the men of the households in which they live. The contrast between the openness of men's actions, and the closed (*kapalı*) behaviour required of women remains relevant, and the formal occasions for movement continue to be of considerable importance to women.

Today, those occasions which women consider to be the most important opportunities for movement can be divided into two categories. Each category includes a major type of ritual movement, which the townspeople describe in terms of the concept of *ziyaret*. The first of these analytical categories includes women and men acting together as quasi-equals to pay *ziyaret* visits to senior relatives; the second category includes single-sex groups of women who visit local shrines (*ziyaret*). Members of all families in the town are involved in the rituals of the first category, whereas usually only the women of more "traditional" families are involved in the range of activities included in the second.

More generally, the first category concerns the celebration of most of the important religious and secular festivals. These require movement to and from sacred spots or respected individuals. In Eğirdir, these activities involve women and men of a family travelling or visiting together and enjoin their companionship and good-natured attitudes of mutual respect. Predominantly, such occasions comprise the following: the *hajj* and the little pilgrimages (Turkish, *umre hac*) to Mecca; family visits to senior kin and to family graves, on Şeker Bayramı at the end of the Ramazan (Arabic, Ramadan), the month of fasting, and on Kurban Bayramı, the Feast of Sacrifice; and family picnics on occasions such as the third day of Şeker Bayramı, the festival of Hıdrellez, and the civic festivals of Children's Bayram and Youth and Sport Bayram.[4] These occasions allow women significant opportunities for movement in the company of men and are positive in their various associations: they are occasions of explicit joy and thanksgiving. Their symbolism is associated both with the notion of sacrifice and its reward – a blessing (*sevab*) – and with greeting gestures of respect which are reciprocated with sweets and material gifts.

The second category includes those occasions when women alone may leave their houses in the company of other women. Such occasions comprise women's participation in the formal visiting or reception days (*kabul günü*), *mevlûd* recitals, *ziyaret* visits to shrines, the celebration of fulfilment of vows (*adak*); and the women's picnic, Kadın Pazarı, at the end of the harvest period.[5] These occasions offer women particular opportunities to create movement symbolically, by signalling changes of personal status and marking their individual wishes and needs, particularly through the idiom of cooking. However, these types of occasion are considered by many local men and members of the local religious establishment to be of a dubious nature. Men typically dismiss this kind of movement outside of the home as trivial or superstitious, while women themselves are divided in their attitudes.

Women who accept "traditional" gender constructions relating to their work, domestic identity, and relations with men are also those who are most involved in those occasions in which women leave their homes in the company of other women. Others, who subscribe to what they see as more "modern" ideas about gender relations – including, in theory at least, a degree of autonomy and freedom of individual movement – generally ignore the opportunities that these occasions offer, and participate with enthusiasm only in the institution of formal reception day visiting. Thus, somewhat paradoxically, there seems to be an inverse relation between certain "modern" gender constructs and women's interest in, and actual movements outside, the home. Moreover, when "modern" women do meet in the single-sex gatherings of reception days, they often represent the status of their husbands and families and express little of themselves as individuals in their own right. By contrast, the more "traditional" opportunities that women have for movement on their own allow them a degree of autonomous action in settings where they can create and confirm their individuality *vis-à-vis* both other women and God.

Joyful celebrations and the movements of men and women

The hajj

Both the *hajj* and the "little" pilgrimages – in the past and today – provide the most important opportunities for men and older women to travel outside Turkey.[6] Though perhaps only twenty or thirty individuals from the town participate in the pilgimages annually, they have included members of all families in the town. The *hajj* journey is widely celebrated, both during the Feast of Sacrifice when the *hajjis* (Turkish, *hacıs*) themselves make their sacrifice at Mina, and on their return.

Whole families (never men alone) may travel to Konya to greet their returning kinsfolk, the *hajjis*. As the coach caravan approaches the town, townspeople throng to greet the pilgrims and join them in prayers in the main mosque, after which they are led home by close kin, friends, and neighbours. A goat is then sacrificed at their door, and the merit (*sevab*) of the vow which has been fulfilled is shared by all the well-wishers, who are invited to a special meal that ends with the eating of great dishes of sweets and the distribution of presents from Mecca.

Whereas men may make the pilgrimage alone, women must be accompanied by a male member of their family – ideally husbands and wives make the pilgrimage together. Although it is difficult to establish the extent to which this changes the conjugal relationship, women *hajjis* care greatly about the close friendships generated by the pilgrimage, including friendships between women and men, and they hope to make the "little" pilgrimage perhaps several times again.

Ziyarets *and religious* bayrams

There are considerable structural similarities in the rituals associated with the two most important religious festivals celebrated in Eğirdir: Şeker Bayramı at the end of the fast of Ramazan; and Kurban Bayramı, the Feast of Sacrifice. But their differences allow the former to be used as a model for *ziyaret* visiting and the latter as a model for relations created through sacrifice.

Early in the morning of the first day after Ramazan, when the men return from prayers at the main mosque, they are greeted by their children who are given money and sweets in return for a respectful kiss on the hand. Mothers are greeted next, and then each family, clothed in new garments, begins the round of *bayram* visiting, or *ziyaret*: first, to the household of the husband's parents, then to those of the wife, and then to all other kinspeople of the senior generation. Each visit begins with greetings, and juniors kiss the hands of the senior persons of the household who, in return, bless those who have greeted them. The guests are served coffee, sweets, and a plate of baklava. The occasion is usually very formal; conversation is perfunctory and as a new family group of guests arrives, earlier visitors depart. Each family may make ten or more such visits before mid-afternoon. Then the adults, if they have not done so the day before, may visit the cemetery – usually the only occasion when women may do so – and pay respect to their dead kinsfolk through prayer and readings of the Yasin *sûre* (Arabic, *sura*, chapter) of the Qur'an.

On the second day of Şeker Bayramı, the *ziyaret* visits continue – this time families of senior kin visit more junior and collateral

Figure 12.1 For pilgrims, domestic space becomes intricately linked to the Ka'ba, as suggested by this *hajj* mural on a house wall in Imbaba, Cairo. (From Juan E. Campo [1987] 'Shrines and Talismans: Domestic Islam in the Pilgrimage Paintings of Egypt', *Journal of the American Academy of Religion*, 55, no. 2, p. 292. Line drawing by Allan Grapard. Used with permission of the author and publisher.)

kin and neighbours – while on the third day each family organises a picnic meal at some local beauty spot, almost invariably one with a spring. For the three days, each nuclear family becomes a ritual unit: together they walk through the streets to pay respect to kins-people and neighbours and together they join in the fun and relaxation of the picnic. Bayram visits are said to remind people of their roots and the value of respect; the appropriateness of these reminders is confirmed in the pleasure that family members share on the third day.

The Feast of Sacrifice also begins with men's morning prayers in the mosque, after which a man returns home and performs the animal sacrifice that commemorates Abraham's willingness to sacrifice his son, Isma'il, as an expression of his complete submission to God's will. A portion of this meat is used to provide a festive meal for members of the family itself. Then, after they have eaten, the family again makes *ziyaret* visits, whose structure is very similar to the *ziyaret* visits at the end of Ramazan.

Family picnics

I have already mentioned the family picnics held at the end of Ramazan, whose timing, of course, depends on the Islamic lunar calendar. There are, however, other occasions when family picnics occur in association with the annual solar cycle. Of these, the most important are those associated with the festival of Hıdrellez, on the 6th of May, when the Prophet Hızır is expected to visit the world. In the past, this was an especially important time for in-laws or families who had just arranged an engagement between them. They would share in the food preparations and visit a local spring (often one with a nearby shrine) for a picnic and recital of the *mevlûd* poem commemorating the life of the Prophet Muhammad. Although the explicitly religious associations of this day are now tenuous, family picnics at Hıdrellez continue to be a highlight of the spring season. Equally, two national holidays in the same season – Children's Bayram (23 April) and Youth and Sport Bayram (19 May) – have also become, probably only relatively recently, occasions for family picnics.

Picnics in all these contexts have explicitly paradisical associations for the townspeople. Springs are known as "the eyes of the world". The setting of green trees, meadows, and cold, clear flowing water is linked to an atmosphere of informality and good-natured fun, when women and men stroll (*gezi*) together and may join in traditional games and competitions. Even the picnic meals, although often lavish, are deemed by women to be effortless by comparison with the elaborate, oven-baked dishes of everyday fare and, uniquely, they involve both men and women in food preparation.

Though neither women nor men mention it, it is nevertheless clear to the outsider that these joyous occasions – the pilgrimages, Bayram *ziyarets*, and family picnics – share a common characteristic: all involve expressions of practical gender equality. As we have seen, the ideology of respect informs participation in both the pilgrimage and the *bayram* greeting rituals in which women and men, equally, are given their due respect as *hajjis* or senior relatives. Equally, women and men can recognise and reward such respect on the part of their juniors – who may also be both women and men. The case of family picnics is rather different, for the essence of the picnic ritual as a whole is not hierarchical but egalitarian; yet the consequences, from the point of view of women, are similar. On picnics, gender distinctions are relatively unmarked and the women and men of a family are all more or less equal participants. Moreover, in all of these contexts, practised gender equality – through the ritual associations with the sacred centres of Mecca, the family, and springs, and through the idiom of sacrifice – offers women and men together a chance to experience a little of heaven on earth; it also confirms that all Muslims are equal before God and that women, as well as men, may achieve salvation after death.

The multivocality of the rituals on these occasions, and the variety of ways in which they support a construction of gender equality, could be explored much further, but the data I have presented suggests the ways in which they differ from the second category of occasions when women, without men, may move outside of the domestic domain.

Women's journeys alone

Women may leave their homes to join other women in four contexts: domestic visits to other households on formal reception days; *mevlûd* recitals; *ziyaret* visits to shrines; and women's picnics.

Visiting days and mevlûd *recitals*

These two kinds of women's gatherings have been described at length elsewhere (see Tapper 1983; Tapper and Tapper 1987a), and I will only summarise their main characteristics here. In Tapper (1983), I treated them as a contrasting set. They are similar in the way that they mobilise women's networks and in the extent to which they are disparaged and dismissed by men; they differ, however, in the ambiance that they create.

Visiting or reception days (*kabul günü*) are a type of formal visiting among women which has come relatively recently to Eğirdir. They are associated particularly with younger, educated, married women and the women of more affluent "secular" households, among whom such formal visiting is directly related to the ideals of individuality and consumer capitalism fostered by the Turkish state. Formal visiting is by invitation and is reciprocal, and the visiting circles thus created may meet regularly in the afternoons at the houses of the various participants. The ambiance of these gatherings, while ostensibly companionable, is often highly competitive. The hostess displays the cleanliness of the house, and its luxury goods, in much the same way as she displays her own gracious manners, good dress sense, and domestic skills in producing elaborate savouries and cakes. The structure of reception-day gatherings thus depends on the perception of equality among women participants, but their content is about inequality among wives.

Structurally, women's participation in *mevlûd* recitals is comparable to their involvement in formal visiting days, since invited women meet in private homes for this religious service. By contrast to visiting days, however, the stucture of *mevlûds* accepts differentiation among women as wives, while the content of *mevlûds* – as intense religious experiences that focus on birth and motherhood – is about the equality of women.

Each *mevlûd* is a commemoration of the life of the Prophet Muhammad in prayers, hymns, and the recital of the *mevlûd* poem itself. *Mevlûd* recitals are sponsored by women as intercessionary rituals held to gain religious merit (*sevab*) for the souls of the family's dead. Indeed, *mevlûds* are regarded as presents for the souls of the dead, while those who participate in the services are themselves believed to gain merit (*sevab*) from their gifts. The sense of female solidarity, and the special relation between women of the congregation and the Prophet and the Islamic promise of salvation, are particularly evident in the more "traditional" *mevlûds* – those in which women most commonly participate, and which are sponsored and preferred by those women who accept what are felt to be more "traditional" gender constructions.

However, some women, whose education, economic, and/or marital status links them closely to the secular ideals of the Turkish Republic, do not seek the opportunities for self-expression or consolation and support offered by the elaborate, "traditional"

246

women's *mevlûds*. Such women (often those who participate in formal reception-day circles) are most likely to sponsor *mevlûds* that replicate the short, unemotional *mevlûds* held by and for men (cf. Tapper and Tapper 1987a: 82).

The variation between different types of *mevlûds* sponsored by women is particularly revealing of three things: the effect of more "modern" notions of gender on female solidarity; the import of the contrast between formal visiting days and *mevlûd* gatherings; and the distaste that some more "modern" women express for the various kinds of exclusively female activities included in the second category of movement that I have distinguished. Only women who accept the more "traditional" ideas of gender participate regularly in the other activities in this category.

Ziyaret *visits to shrines*[7]

The saints whose shrines remain to be visited are seen as active personalities (*zat*), to whom respect is due because of the greater respect which they showed to God. Miracle stories tell of the saints' extraordinary qualities and it is believed that they have the power not only to punish disrespect but also to make positive interventions in the world of the living.

Most women say a fixed liturgy of Qur'anic prayers whenever they pass one of the town shrines, and in this (and in the regular prayers they utter when passing a graveyard) they show themselves to be more conscious than men of the sacred geography of the town and the opportunities for religious contact that it provides. Though men may on occasion visit shrines with the women of their own family, they do not visit shrines on their own; single-sex shrine visiting is an activity exclusively reserved for women. In general, men treat the women's shrine *ziyarets* as verging on heresy and they invariably describe them in terms of the women's desire for children. Women, by contrast, insist that the fundamental intention of their visits is to show respect, and only secondly will a saint be asked to intercede with God in response to a vow (*adak*).

Individual women may sometimes visit one of the remaining house-shrines in the town. Such visits are essentially private, as is the sorrow or heartache which the vows made on such visits seek to relieve. However, when women speak of *ziyaret* visits, they usually refer to the relaxed occasions when they visit a shrine with a group of kinswomen, friends, and neighbours. The shrines that are visited in this way are most often those on the periphery of the town and the walk there provides women with one of the few opportunities for strolling (*gezi*) by themselves – an occupation usually held to be appropriate only for men.

At the shrine a woman will vow that, should her request be fulfilled, she will make a return gift: she may undertake to say special prayers, make some charitable offering, or sponsor a *mevlûd* service. Most often however, she may undertake to cook and share "hot" foods especially associated with religious merit (*sevab*); it is said in such contexts that food, like the rags and strings attached to shrines, "ties up the prayers". Thus, if the woman's request has been substantial, she may hold a special service known as a "vow prayer" (*adak duası*). She will invite a few of her closest kin and friends to her home at a time when there are likely to be no men in the house. Then one of the women, or a woman religious teacher (*hoca*), will read the Yasin *sûre* of the Qur'an seven times while all the other women, in total silence, will take turns stirring a pot of *irmik helvası*, a sweet pudding associated with all traditional formal meals. Together the women then eat a substantial meal followed by the *helva* (Arabic, *hilwa*).

In their *ziyaret* visits to shrines women have a considerable degree of autonomy – to choose their company, to manage the outing, and to construct a personal relationship with God via the saint. Women in Eğirdir, as elsewhere, are not allowed to take a creature's life. However, the substitution of a cooked, vegetable food offering in lieu of an animal sacrifice – which is the usual idiom of thanksgiving – makes it possible for women to perform the complete ritual sequence of a shrine visit without recourse to men. This kind of substitution is imitated on other occasions when women alone seek to adjust their own or their families' ritual condition.

Women's picnics

In the past in Eğirdir, women's picnics were important events of the annual cycle, which had their counterparts in single-sex parties for men, in the winter and at Hıdrellez. Although the most important of the women's picnics, Sekibag, which was held in early May, ceased to be observed some two decades ago, it remains a model for the one women's picnic, Kadın Pazarı, which continues to be celebrated today.

Kadın Pazarı was, in the past, a three-day celebration held each autumn. Groups of women left their orchard homes together to meet on the first day at the river outlet of the lake, then on the next at a nearby spring, and on the third at a yet larger spring which was also the site of the autumn food market where women would buy great quantities of meat, vegetables, and fruit to be preserved for the coming winter. On the third day, young betrothed girls were given new clothes by women of their fiancé's family, and other young girls and young married women dressed in their most up-to-date clothes. The women ate, sang, danced, played traditional games, and took the opportunity to explore – strolling along the surrounding lanes and clambering up nearby hillsides.

Today, although the need to buy foodstuffs for winter preserves has largely passed, a single day of Kadın Pazarı, held on a Sunday at the large market-site by the largest of the springs outside town, continues. Though new brides are no longer dressed at the picnic spot, women no longer dance, and men are no longer so rigorously excluded (newly married couples now may come together), the women's picnic day remains an impressive event. Hundreds of women, in groups of ten or fifteen, don smart clothes and prepare elaborate picnic dishes. The effort and display is for the picnickers themselves, an indulgence the women thoroughly enjoy. The picnickers stroll around the stalls and young and old alike will join traditional running games that demand cunning and swiftness of foot. The day comes to an end with a scramble to catch the last buses back to town before night falls.

Traditionally, the women's picnics were a celebration of female sexuality and fertility and of the friendship, solidarity, and support among women, both kin and affines, young and old. The Kadın Pazarı outing continues to create and confirm the women's sense of identity and worth as women, while its timing and watery associations link it explicitly to general notions of fertility and abundance.

Ziyaret, gender, movement, and exchange

I have distinguished for analysis two categories of occasions which afford women valuable opportunities to move outside their domestic environment. This analytic division of opportunities for movement according to the criterion of gender offers insights into the relationship of gender and religion. Among these, perhaps the most important is a recognition of the extent to which, through opportunities for movement, women's inherent subordination to men in the Islamic tradition is modified and alleviated.

Women's and men's *ziyaret* visits on the occasions of the two major Islamic festivals make them more or less equal in their subordination to senior kinfolk. By the same token, gender equality is a dominant message of those other ritual occasions (such as the *hajj* and family picnics) when women leave their households in the company of men.

By contrast, when women make *ziyaret* visits to shrines, they travel alone outside the household. On these occasions which, according to men, only confirm the gender stereotypes of women's inferiority, women are none the less able to construct an identity for themselves as women that is validated by the supernatural context in which it occurs. The possibility that women may have a relationship with the supernatural which is unmediated by men and unlike the other kinds of relationship that women and men have in common, such as that based on daily prayer, is most clearly seen in the women's visits to shrines, but it is also an important aspect of the women's *mevlûd* services and their annual picnic. However, there still remain contrasting attitudes between more or less "modern" and "traditional" women to formal visiting days and *mevlûd* recitals. Those "modern" women who, in theory if not in practice, reject gender constructions which entail women's subordination to men also devalue and dismiss those occasions when women may separate themselves from men and emphasise their shared, positive identity as women *per se* and as women *vis-à-vis* God.

From the Eğirdir material, is it possible to construct a more general hypothesis concerning the relation between gender and movement in the Islamic tradition? It seems possible that women's institutionalised movements outside their homes are everywhere likely to be construed, by women at least, in a positive way. However, the extent and frequency of such movements, and the degree to which they are emphasised in any particular society, vary considerably. It is this variation which requires explanation. I suggest that, in part at least, the answer may lie in differing ideological constructions of relations between the sexes.

If women and men subscribe to the idea that the sexes are different in kind and that men are superior to women (as is the case in the more or less "traditional" notions of gender in Eğirdir), women's theoretical equality with men as Muslims becomes paradoxical and problematic, particularly for the women themselves. However, in so far as certain occasions for movement allow women to act as men's equals, and others validate special dimensions of women's nature, the paradox is partially obscured and partially denied.

If, on the other hand, women and men subscribe to the idea that the sexes are different in kind but essentially complementary in nature, or that the sexes are of similar human natures (both emphases occur in the more "modern" constructions of gender relations in Egirdir), then men's and women's equality as Muslims is not an issue. In these cases, women are likely to make journeys outside the house as men's equals, but there is little need for them to move in single-sex groups to recreate a special religious identity for themselves. *Ziyaret* visits to shrines, and other single-sex gatherings that have no counterpart in the activities of men, are likely to play little part in women's lives.

In my discussion of the notion of *ziyaret*, among many possible themes, I have concentrated on the differences between those occasions when women and men travel together outside the household and when women travel alone. As we have seen, these latter occasions are often much valued by women, not least because of the opportunities that they offer to create personal identities by contrast with each other and with supernatural entities that are independent of their ascribed domestic circumstances. Such women's movements, including reception-day visiting and picnicking activities on the one hand and women's religious services and shrine visits on the other, would hardly seem to constitute a threat to men's practical dominance of women's lives. Yet these occasions when women travel and meet in single-sex groups are often disparaged and discouraged by men and by the religious establishment. Following Parry's elegant discussion of theories of reciprocity (1986), I shall argue that the content of the women's exchanges on these occasions may explain why they are derided by men with such dismissive hostility.

Parry makes a clear distinction between two extreme ideologies of reciprocity, which, he suggests, define each other. The first is the ideology of the "pure gift" given to a supernatural entity as part of a quest for salvation. The second, and related, ideology is that associated with the self-interest of market exchange. Here nothing is ventured without the expectation of at least an equivalent return. Parry suggests that the notion of the "pure gift" is stressed particularly in the traditions of the ancient literate civilisations of Europe and Asia and that it contrasts with the kind of reciprocity involved in market relations. He writes: "the ideology of the 'pure gift' is most likely to arise in highly differentiated societies with an advanced division of labour . . . and a significant commercial sector" (Parry 1986: 467). The "pure gift" is defined as what market relations are not: "altruistic, moral and loaded with emotion" (Parry 1986: 466).

Though he does not use Islamic material, there can be no doubt that Parry's insights are as relevant to the Islamic tradition as they are to other world religious traditions of the Indian sub-continent and Europe. More specifically, the Turkish material that I have presented seems particularly fertile ground for exploring the implications of his ideas with regard to the concept of *ziyaret*

251

and women's movement (cf. Betteridge 1980; 1985).

Richard Tapper and I have described in detail elsewhere (1987b) how in Eğirdir the paired ideologies of modern Turkish Islam and Republicanism are, each in its own sphere, highly valued orthodoxies, supported by the religious establishment and the state respectively. In practice, they also govern all aspects of the townspeoples' lives. Within each of these ideologies, we find notions of both "pure gift" (the stress on self-sacrifice and subservience of the individual) and "market mentality" (calculations of personal merit and advancement and the values of consumer capitalism) combined.

With respect to both ideologies it is clear that women suffer particular disadvantages compared with men. Women cannot participate as men do in the "pure gift" economy of salvation – as expressed in public prayers, in military service, and in the notions of sacrifice which inform the concept of responsibility in religious and civic contexts. Nor do women have the same facility of access or degree of control over political and economic resources: they are thus excluded from many forms of charitable work and achievement in the market economy. In all these various secular and religious contexts, gender constructions preclude women's full participation; their involvement in the range of valued activities is vicarious and dependent on or mediated by men. In this way, the relationship of women to the dominant ideologies and culture of the town is clearly secondary to that of men.

When women are involved in travel outside the home in the company of other women, however, the rituals of reciprocity in which they engage have a quite distinct character and are unlike those of men. The women's exchanges are not expressions of the extreme ideological forms of the "pure gift" or the market. Rather, they combine muted elements of both: social and temporal aspects of the exchanges are emphasised in what amounts to a give-and-take kind of reciprocity in which offerings are made for favours (cf. Parry 1986: 462).

I shall illustrate this by two quite different examples. First, in the case of women's vows made at *ziyaret* shrines, although the women insist that the intention (*niyet*) is of paramount importance, the vow that they make is a contingent promise – an "offering for a boon" not a "pure gift". Second, by way of thanksgiving should the vow be fulfilled, the women, who cannot themselves follow the model of Abraham and sacrifice a beast, perform an act which is "superstitious" (because it is not validated by establishment traditions), and cook *helva* to be shared and eaten among themselves. Equally, the self-defined "modern" women, who reject most single-sex activities in favour of secular definitions of their equality with men, nevertheless meet for formal receptions days. When they do, it is not as full participants in the market economy, but as conspicuous consumers whose consumption, and thus relative social power, derive from their dependent relationship upon the men of their household.

The social and psychological compensations which women gain in their contacts with other women outside the home can be considerable, not least because the women's own activities form systems of exchange that modify elements of the two dominant ideologies of reciprocity while at the same time avoiding the logical disjunction of the two. Ironically, precisely because the women's activities blur the kinds of exchanges which are well-defined and prestigious in terms of orthodox religion or the Turkish state, women confirm, to men and themselves, their distance from the sources of both supernatural and secular power. In each case the exchanges associated with women's movements outside the home become a further expression of women's marginality and dubious orthodoxy, while their inferior gender status becomes a self-fulfilling ideology in itself.

Acknowledgements

Following the Social Science Research Council conference on Movement and Exchange in Muslim Societies, a draft of this chapter was presented at the Middle East Center, University of Pennsylvannia, and at the 1987 Middle East Studies Association meeting in Baltimore. I would like to thank my colleagues on those occasions, including Dale Eickelman and James Piscatori, for their helpful comments and suggestions.

Notes

1 Anthropological fieldwork in Turkey was done over a period of fifteen months between 1980 and 1984 and was sponsored by the Social Science Research Council (UK), Project HR 7410. The fieldwork was done jointly with Richard Tapper, whom I thank for his incisive comments on the present paper. Further discussion of the Turkish ethnography can be found in Tapper (1983, 1985) and in Tapper and Tapper (1987a, 1987b).
2 The townspeople themselves use the contrasting notions of "tradition" and "modernity" to classify many aspects of social organisation and structure, as well as to characterise the life-style and degree of religious commitment of various Eğirdirli families. The indigenous use of these ideas is explored in detail with respect to wedding customs in Tapper (1985 and unpublished manuscript).

3 The two words, which are often used synonymously, convey notions of esteem, thoughtfulness, consideration, honour, reverence, and veneration (cf. Redhouse 1968: 498, 990; cf. also Beeman's (1986) discussion of *ta'arof* and *ziarat kardan* in Iran.

4 In the past this category would also have included the great collective migration of all the families of the town to their orchard houses at harvest time in September.

5 Traditionally, this category would also have included the three other women's "picnics": the first in early spring; the second – and most important – in May (Sekibag); and a third in late autumn. However, such past occasions, which the townspeople now term *piknik*, were not known by a single generic term but rather by their special local names.

6 Military service, traditionally and today, obliges local men to leave the town, but such service has always been compulsory. In the past, local men were also involved in seasonal labour migration to the provinces of the Aegean coast. Today, in spite of the importance of labour migration from Turkey to Arab countries and Western Europe, very few men from Eğirdir are involved in this process.

7 See also the detailed account of women's shrine visits in Turkey given by Olson (1987 and forthcoming).

References

Beeman, W.O. (1986) *Language, Status and Power in Iran*, Indiana University Press, Bloomington.

Betteridge, A.H. (1980) 'The controversial vows of urban Muslim women in Iran', in N.A. Falk and R.M. Gross (eds) *Unspoken Worlds*, Harper & Row, San Francisco.

—— (1985) 'Gift exchange in Iran: the locus of self-identity in social interaction', *Anthropological Quarterly*, 58, no. 4, pp. 190–202.

Olson, E.A. (1987) 'The use of religious symbol systems and ritual in Turkey', unpublished paper presented at the Second International Conference in Turkic Studies, Indiana University, Bloomington, May 1987.

—— (forthcoming) 'Of *turbe* and *evliyalari*: the creation and manipulation of symbol systems and ritual exchange as coping strategies', in M. Kiray (ed.) *Women and Change in Turkey*, Indiana University Press, Bloomington.

Parry, J. (1986) 'The gift, the Indian gift and the "Indian gift"', *Man* (N.S.), 21, no. 3, pp. 453–73.

Redhouse Turkish–English dictionary (1968) Celtut, Istanbul.

Tapper, N. (1983) 'Gender and religion in a Turkish town: a comparison of two types of formal women's gathering', in P. Holden (ed.) *Women's Religious Experience*, Croom Helm, London, pp. 71–88.

—— (1985) 'Changing wedding rituals in a Turkish town', *Journal of Turkish Studies*, 9, pp. 305–13.

—— ' "Traditional" and "modern" wedding rituals in a Turkish town', unpublished manuscript.

—— and R. Tapper (1987a) 'The birth of the Prophet: ritual and gender in Turkish Islam', *Man* (N.S.), 21, no. 1, pp., 69–92.

R. Tapper and N. Tapper (1987b) ' "Thank God we're secular": aspects of fundamentalism in a Turkish town', in L. Caplan (ed.) *Studies in Religious Fundamentalism*, Macmillan, London, pp. 51–78.

Annotated bibliography of related studies

Martin's (1987) "Muslim Pilgrimage" provides an excellent concise introduction to the topic. The articles "Ha*djdj*" and "Hi*dj*ra" in both editions of the *Encylcopaedia of Islam* (1st edn, 1913–38; 2nd edn, 1960– [EI²]) remain useful, but narrowly interpret their respective topics. Thus the EI² article on the *hajj* (pp. 31–8) is divided into sections on the pre-Islamic era, the origins of the Muslim *hajj*, the stages in the *hajj* to Mecca, 'Arafat, and Mina, and general notes on the *hajj* in modern times. All but the last section of the article primarily update the treatment of the topic in the earlier edition. W. Montgomery Watt's EI² article on the *hijra* (pp. 366–7) deals exclusively with the topic in seventh-century Arabia.

Metcalf (Chapter 5 of this volume) provides an accessible guide to *hajj* accounts written by pilgrims from the Indian sub-continent. Matheson and Milner (1984), whose work in part inspired Metcalf's, deal with South-east Asian texts. Esin (1963) offers a particularly sensitive, beautifully illustrated account of the *hajj*. Abdul-Rauf (1978) also provides an extensive bibliography. Iranian novelist Al-e Ahmed's (1985) day-to-day account of his pilgrimage will dispel the notion that this genre of literature is only devotional.

On the medieval *rihla*, Dunn's (1986) account of the great Muslim traveller Ibn Battuta (1304–68) is both comprehensive and entertaining. The chapters by Gellens and El Moudden (Chapters 3 and 4 of this volume), dealing with the medieval and late medieval periods, are usefully complemented by Harvey (1988) on the role of the *hajj* among Muslims in Spain under Christian domination. His discussion of the religious leadership provided by women merits particular attention. Much work remains to be done in understanding the roles of movement and travel in the religious imagination in medieval Muslim societies. Studies such as those of Gellens, El Moudden, and Harvey suggest that the topic is beginning to receive appropriate attention. For the modern period, the account of the *rihlas* of Muhammad Rashid Rida' (1865–1935) to the Hijaz as well as to Europe indicates the importance of travel for learning in the modern period and suggests how it led to the development of modernist Islam (Rida' 1971).

Of the numerous nineteenth-century European accounts of the pilgrimage, two merit particular attention. Burton (1964 [orig. 1893]) is self-important but never dull and conveys much useful information. Snouck Hurgronje (1931 [orig. 1888–9]) provides an unusual ethnographic account of Mecca with important information on the organisation of the pilgrimage. Muslim accounts are particularly fascinating for this period because European economic and political domination had an increasing influence upon the conduct of the pilgrimage itself (McDonnell, Chapter 6 of this volume) and upon the *hajj* accounts as a literary *genre* (Metcalf, this volume). Bezzaz (1982–3) analyses the perils of the pilgrimage from nineteenth-century Morocco, based upon contemporary Moroccan accounts and early efforts by Morocco's rulers to curtail the exploitation of pilgrims. Gallagher (1983) describes how "health" considerations provided a rationale for the growing regulation of the pilgrimage by European powers. For the twentieth century, Zainuddin (1978), the first Malaysian Pilgrimage Control Officer for Malaysia, provides valuable insights into growing governmental control of the pilgrimage, a trend perhaps even intensified in the post-colonial era. The fact that he was also a Special Branch officer suggests the political significance imputed to the *hajj* by colonial authorities.

Among contemporary studies of the pilgrimage, Birks (1978; also see Naqar 1972), one of the first studies by a social scientist to cross disciplinary lines in the study of the *hajj*, focuses upon the present-day overland pilgrimage routes from West Africa. Long (1979), who describes the practical organisation of the contemporary pilgrimage, is now complemented by the ongoing studies of the Hajj Research Centre in Jidda. The first volume of the Centre's *Hajj Studies*, co-edited by Ziauddin Sardar and M.A. Zaki Badawi, appeared in 1978. A related bibliography (Sardar 1982), dealing with the *hajj* in all its aspects, includes dissertations and unpublished studies conducted by the Hajj Research Centre itself. Kramer (1987), who provides abundant references, reviews current efforts to politicise the *hajj*.

For the purposes of this volume, the chapter by Peters (1986) on "The pilgrimage network' (pp. 27–59) is especially relevant. His concern is to "translate" the "high tradition of ideology and institutions" of Christianity, Judaism, and Islam in Jerusalem and Mecca "into the earthly vernacular of places, buildings, and streets, of buying and selling, and finding bed and board" (p. ix), including discussions of the linkages between primary and secondary religious centres and shrines, and between sacred and secular (particularly mercantile) activities. Roff (1985) outlines the theoretical implications of studies of the *hajj*.

Although Turner (1973; also Turner and Turner 1978) deals only incidentally with the Muslim pilgrimage, his account is useful for comparative purposes and is a point of critical reference for later studies (e.g. Bowman 1988). Also useful for comparison are Werbner (1977), who deals with regional shrines and visits (*ziyaras*) in both Muslim and non-Muslim societies, and Abélès (1988), who describes a secular counterpart to pilgrimage with a "religious dimension".

Recent studies of the pilgrimage, as Werbner (in Bowman 1988: 22) and others note, place emphasis on how "the pilgrimage experience is effectively a construct of the people using it rather than something that itself gives form". In this regard, Maeda (1975) represents an early empirical study of the consequences of undertaking the pilgrimage for social status in the pilgrim's home community in Malaysia. In a more recent study, Campo (1987) explores the multiple levels of significance of the *hajj* for Egyptian pilgrims. He analyses the murals commissioned to decorate the facades of the homes and shops of returned pilgrims. Campo argues that these murals are collective enterprises that reflect the expectations of the pilgrim, his family, and neighbours. Campo (1987: 293) argues that the iconography and epigraphy of the murals are highly structured forms of expression, "like that of certain types of myth, epic, poetry, and ritual". They demonstrate a complex relationship between the two "homes" of the pilgrim – Mecca and his dwelling of origin. Unlike the "discursive" formulations of Islam of both rulers and militant opposition groups, *hajj* murals "testify to a concern for linking mundane domestic space and its realm of familial values with Islamically formulated definitions of sacred power and space" (Campo 1987: 302; 1990). A more recent essay by Campo (forthcoming) examines "the interrelationships between political authority, ritual, and spatial order in the context of the history of Islam", showing how pilgrimage rituals "embody and validate configurations of power, of dominance and submission".

If Campo deals with the links between domestic space and the pilgrimage to Mecca, Peters (1986) and others suggest the equally intricate links between the pilgrimage to Mecca and regional shrines. Algar (1971) is useful as a case study. He writes: "The convergence of the pilgrimage routes at the Ka'ba mirrors the meeting of the Sufi paths at that central point – *haqiqat* – to which they all lead" (Algar 1971: 197). Eickelman (1976) discusses a regional Moroccan shrine, and elsewhere (1989: 288–304) provides key references to discussions of Sufi orders and shrines throughout the Muslim Middle East. Shinar (1980) discusses the politics, rivalry, and shifting audiences of North African regional religious leaders during the colonial era, and Stillman (1982) compares Jewish and Muslim shrines and saints in North Africa.

The classical points of reference for doctrinal thought on emigration (*hijra*) are the early years of Islam and medieval Islamic jurisprudence (Masud, this volume). Contemporary interpretations of *hijra* show a range of variation. Some activists (e.g. Faruqi 1985) go so far as to say that the only legitimate reason for Muslims to remain in the west is the call to Islam (*da'wa*), proselytisation. The fact that the Egyptian extremist organisation responsible for the assassination of Sadat was called, at least by those hostile to it, the "Society of Excommunication and Emigration" (*hijra*) has inspired chronicles of religious extremism linked loosely to the concept (for Egypt, see Hammuda 1987). The exposition of *hijra* by 'Uthman dan Fodio (1978) in the early nineteenth century, available in English, provides a complex discussion of the relationship between *hijra* and *jihad* and also offers insight into the relationship between the doctrine and the reformist movement that he inspired. In Wahhabi doctrine, the notion applies to the settlement of bedouin and their formation into a military force to achieve Wahhabi goals (Habib 1978).

Ferré (1985) focuses upon how migration and travel influence proselytisation in various historical epochs, while Oded (1986) deals with modern migration to the Arab "centre" from Africa for educational purposes. Qureshi (1979) deals with the Khilafat movement (1918–24) in British India, in which between 10,000 to 60,000 Indian Muslims, in spite of adverse economic and political realities, were encouraged by their leaders to interpret doctrine literally and emigrate to Afghanistan in 1920.

Until quite recently, studies of migration in the social sciences, however valuable in other respects, have tended to neglect its implications for religious experience (e.g. Bourgey, Gorokhoff, Nancy *et al* 1985; Owen 1985; Seccombe 1985; Serageldin *et al.* 1984; Weiner 1985). However, Ahmed (1986) presents a case study of a contemporary religious movement in Pakistan primarily associated with Pakistani workers returned from the Arabian Peninsula. Some Muslims point ironically to the fact that Muslims in western countries, freed from the political restraints of their countries of origin, can be more creative and open in religious expression and practice. "Western" countries increasingly serve

259

both as a meeting place for Muslim activists from throughout the Muslim world and as the primary residence of an increasing number of Muslims. Whatever one's literary (and political) judgement on the merits of Rushdie (1988), he is surely accurate in depicting his novel as "an attempt to write about migration, its stresses and transformations, from the point of view of migrants from the Indian sub-continent to Britain" (Rushdie 1989). As one commentator wrote:

> Just as the immigrant speaks his new language with an accent, his vision will acquire an accent. It seems that a different light, a different color, has been cast on everything he has known before . . . So the immigrant's task is to struggle for some kind of peaceful coexistence between the old value system and the new one.
>
> (Modaressi 1989)

If Rushdie's experience indicates the strength, and limits, of the immigrant's experience in challenging and shaping the religious imagination, more standard academic accounts indicate the significance of the experience of migration for the religious imagination, a situation increasingly recognised by Muslim activists (see *Hijra* 1986). By early in the next century, current projections indicate that adherents to Islam will constitute, after Christianity, the second largest religious grouping in the United States (Haddad and Lummis 1987: 3). Studies by Kepel (1987), Kepel and Leveau (1987), Alia (1989), and the French polling organisation IFOP (1989) — the first public opinion polls of Muslims in France — are particularly effective in tracing the changing religious sensibilities and practices of France's Muslim communities, which as of 1987 comprised between 2.5 and 3 million persons. For Islam in Europe as a whole, the essays in Gerholm and Lithman (1988) and by Halliday (1989) offer a useful point of departure. Elsewhere, Fisher (1986) deals with immigration to towns in West Africa.

References

Abélès, Marc (1988) 'Modern political ritual: ethnography of an inauguration and pilgrimage by President Mitterand', *Current Anthropology*, 29, no. 3, pp. 391–404.

Abdul-Rauf, Muhammad (1978) 'Pilgrimage to Mecca', *National Geographic*, 154, no. 5, pp. 581–607.

Ahmed, Akbar S. (1986) 'Death in Islam: the Hawkes Bay case', *Man*, 21, no. 1, pp. 120–34.

Al-e Ahmad (1985) *Lost in the Crowd*, trans. J. Green, A. Alizadeh, and F. Yazdanfar, Three Continents Press, Washington.

Algar, H. (1971) 'Some notes on the Naqshbandi Tariqat in Bosnia', *Die Welt des Islams*, 13, pp. 168–203.

Alia, Josette (1989) 'Que veulent les musulmans de France?', *Le Nouvel Observateur*, 23–29 March, pp. 50–3.

el-Bezzaz, Mohammed Amine (1982–83) 'La chronique scandaleuse du pèlerinage marocain à la Mecque au XIXème siècle', *Hespéris-Tamuda*, 20–1, pp. 319–32.

Birks, J.S. (1978) *Across the Savannas to Mecca: The Overland Pilgrimage Route from West Africa*, Frank Cass, Totowa, N.J.

Bourgey, André, Gorokhoff, Philippe, Nancy, Michel *et al.* (1985) *Migrations et changements sociaux dans l'Orient arabe*, Centre d'Études et de Recherches sur le Moyen-Orient contemporain, Beirut.

Bowman, Glenn (1988) 'Pilgrimage Conference', *Anthropology Today*, 4, no. 6, pp. 20–3.

Burton, Richard F. (1964) *Personal Narrative of a Pilgrimage to Al-Madinah and Meccah*, Dover Publications, New York.

Campo, Juan E. (1987) 'Shrines and talismans: domestic Islam in the pilgrimage paintings of Egypt', *Journal of the American Academy of Religion*, 55, no. 2, pp. 285–305.

—— (1990) *The Other Sides of Paradise: The Religious Meanings of Domestic Space in Islam*, University of South Carolina Press, Columbia.

—— (forthcoming) 'Authority, ritual, and spatial order in Islam: the pilgrimage to Mecca', *Journal of Ritual Studies*.

Dan Fodio, Uthman (1978) *Bayan wujub al-hijra 'ala 'l-'Ibad*, ed. and trans. F.H. El Masri, Khartoum University Press, Khartoum.

Dunn, Ross E. (1986) *The Adventures of Ibn Battuta: A Muslim Traveler of the 14th Century*, University of California Press, Berkeley and Los Angeles.

Eickelman, Dale F. (1976) *Moroccan Islam: Tradition and Society in a Pilgrimage Center*, University of Texas Press, Austin.

—— (1989) *The Middle East: An Anthropological Approach*, 2nd edn, Prentice-Hall, Englewood Cliffs.

Esin, Emel (1963) *Mecca the Blessed, Madinah the Radiant*, Elek Books, London.

Faruqi, Ismail R. (1985) *The Hijrah: The Necessity of Its Iqamat or Vergegenw' Artigung*, National Islamic Council, Islamabad.

Ferré, A. (1985) 'The role of migration in the expansion of the Muslim faith', *Encounter: Documents for Muslim–Christian Understanding*, no. 111. Pontifico Istituto di Studi Arabi e d'Islamista, Rome.

Fisher, Humphrey J. (1986) 'Liminality, *Hijra* and the City', *Asian and African Studies*, 20, pp. 153–77.

Gallagher, Nancy (1983) *Medicine and Power in Tunisia, 1780–1900*, Cambridge University Press, New York.

Gerholm, Tomas, and Lithman, Yngve Georg (eds) (1988) *The New Islamic Presence in Western Europe*, Mansell, London.

Habib, John S. (1978) *Ibn Sa'ud's Warriors of Islam: The Ikhwan of Najd and Their Role in the Creation of the Sa'udi Kingdom, 1910–1930*, E.J. Brill, Leiden.

Haddad, Yvonne Yazbeck and Lummis, Adair T. (1987) *Islamic Values in the United States*, Oxford University Press, New York.

Hajj Studies (1978–   ) published by Croom Helm for the Hajj Research Centre, King Abdul Aziz University (Jidda), London.

Halliday, Fred (1989) 'The struggle for the migrant soul', *Times Literary Supplement* (London), 14–29 April, pp. 387–8.

Hammuda, 'Adil (1987) *Al-Mahjaza ila al-'unf: al-tatarruf al-dini min hazima yunyo ila ightilal uktubir* [Emigration towards Violence: Religious Extremism from the June Crisis to the October Assassination], Atlas Press, Cairo.

Harvey, L.P. (1988) 'The Moriscos and the Hajj', *British Society for Middle East Studies Bulletin*, 14, no. 1, pp. 11–24.

Hijra: la publication de l'émigration et de l'immigration musulmanes en France, no. 1.

IFOP (Institut Français de l'Opinion Publique) poll (1989), published in *Le Monde*, 30 November, 1, 2 December.

Kepel, Gilles (1987) *Les banlieues de l'Islam*, Editions du Seuil, Paris.

—— and Leveau, Rémy (1987) 'Les Musulmanes dans la société Française' (special issue), *Revue Française de Science Politique*, 37, no. 6.

Kramer, Martin (1987) 'Behind the riot in Mecca', *Policy Focus*, Research Memorandum 5, Washington Institute for Near East Policy, Washington.

Long, David (1979) *The Hajj Today: A Survey of the Contemporary Makkah Pilgrimage*, The Middle East Institute, Washington.

Maeda, Narifumi (1975) 'The Aftereffects of Hajj and Kaan Buat', *Journal of Southeast Asian Studies*, 6, no. 2, pp. 178–89.

Martin, Richard C. (1987) 'Muslim Pilgrimage', in *Encyclopaedia of Religion*, vol. 11, Macmillan, New York, pp. 338–46.

Matheson, V. and Milner, A.C. (1984) *Perceptions of the Hajj: Five Malay Texts*, Institute of South Asian Studies, Singapore.

Modaressi, Taghi (1989) 'Salman Rushdie and the immigrant's dilemma', *The Washington Post*, 12 March.

Naqar, Umar Abd al-Razzaq (1972) *The Pilgrimage Tradition in West Africa: An Historical Study with Special Reference to the Nineteenth Century*, Khartoum University Press, Khartoum.

Oded, Arye (1986) 'The Islamic Factor in Afro-Arab Relations', *Middle East Review* (special issue on 'Migration in the Islamic World'), 18, no. 3, pp. 15–23.

Owen, Roger (1985) *Migrant Workers in the Gulf*, Report no. 68, The Minority Rights Group, London.

Peters, F.E. (1986) *Jerusalem and Mecca: The Typology of the Holy City in the Near East*, New York University Press, New York.

Qureshi, M. Naeem (1979) 'The 'Ulama' of British India and the Hijrat of 1920', *Modern Asian Studies*, 13, no. 1, pp. 41–59.

Rida', Muhammad Rashid (1971) *Rihlat al-Imam Muhammad Rashid Rida'*, ed. Y. Ibish, Al-Mu'assasat al-'Arabiyya li-l-dirasat wa-l-nashr, Beirut.

Roff, W.R. (1985) 'Pilgrimage and the history of religions: theoretical approaches to the hajj', in Richard C. Martin (ed.) *Approaches to Islam* in Religious Studies, The University of Arizona Press, Tucson, pp. 78–86.

Rushdie, Salman (1988) *The Satanic Verses*, Viking, New York.

—— (1989) 'War of the word: faiths, languages and the art of the novel', *The New York Review of Books*, 2 March, p. 26.

Sardar, Ziauddin (1982) 'The Hajj – a select bibliography', *Muslim World Book Review*, 3, no. 1, pp. 57–66.

Seccombe, Ian J. (1985) 'International labor migration in the Middle East: a review of literature and research', *International Migration Review*, 19, no. 2, pp. 335–52.

Serageldin, I., Socknat, J., Birks, J.S., and Sinclair, C. (1984) 'Some issues related to labor migration in the Middle East and North Africa', *The Middle East Journal*, 38, no. 4, pp. 615–42.

Shinar, Pessah (1980) ' 'Ulama, marabouts and government: an overview of their relationships in the French Colonial Maghrib', *Israel Oriental Studies*, 10, pp. 211–29.

Snouck Hurgronje, Christaan (1931) *Mekka in the Later Part of the Nineteenth Century*, trans. J.H. Monahan, E.J. Brill, Leiden.

Stillman, Norman A. (1982) 'Saddiq and marabout in Morocco', in Issachar Ben-Ami (ed.) *The Sephardi and Oriental Jewish Heritage*, The Magnes Press, Jerusalem, pp. 489–500.

Turner, Victor W. (1973) 'The center out there: pilgrim's goal', *History of Religions*, 12, no. 3, pp. 191–230.

—— with Edith Turner (1978) *Image and Pilgrimage in Christian Culture: Anthropological Perspectives*, Columbia University Press, New York.

Weiner, Myron (1985) 'On international migration and international relations: suggestions for future research', *Population and Development Review*, 11, no. 3, pp. 441–55.

Werbner, Richard P. (ed.) (1977) *Regional Cults*, Academic Press, New York and London.

Zainuddin, Haji Abdul Majid bin (1978) in William R. Roff (ed.) *The Wandering Thoughts of a Dying Man*, Oxford University Press, Kuala Lumpur.

Glossary*

adhān (A) Muslim call to prayer.

akıl (T from the Arabic *'aql*) reason, reasoning, intelligence.

alamancı, almancı (T) Turkish worker in Germany; lit. "German-ish/like".

alamanya (T) Germany.

'ālim (A, pl. *'ulamā'*) learned man; in particular one learned in Islamic legal and religious studies.

'allāma (A) honorific title for a learned person.

alman (T) German.

'āmma (A) the "masses".

anavatan (T) mother country, homeland.

anṣār (A, sing. *nāṣir*) supporters; companions of the Prophet Muhammed who accompanied him from Mecca to Medina.

'arab (A) Arabs; bedouin.

'arifīn (sing. *'ārif*) (A) mystics.

âyîn-i cem, cem (T) Central Asian communal ritual, led by *pir* or *dede*. Both men and women participate.

bakal haji (Malay) a person preparing to perform the *ḥajj*.

baraka (A) supernatural blessing; quality of divine grace; abundance.

bay'a (A) pact, pledge.

bay'at al-hijra (A) the pledge to emigrate.

bay'at al-nisā' (A) the women's pledge.

bayram (T) religious or national holiday or festivity.

begum (Urdu) lady, queen, title used for Mughal women.

berkat (Malay, from the Arabic *baraka*) blessing.

bey (T) Turkish military title for official in charge of a beylik or Ottoman administrative division.

bomoh (Malay) traditional Malay medical man or practitioner or curer.

---

* *Abbreviations*: (A) = Arabic; (T) = Turkish; (P) = Persian.

cennet (T, from the Arabic *janna*) paradise, heaven.

communitas sense of community or fellowship.

dakwah (Malay, from the Arabic *da'wa*) call, propagation; a generic term for Islamic missionary activity in Malaysia and elsewhere.

dār al-'ahd (A) the land of the pact; *dār al-amān* (A) "the land of peace"; *dār al-ḥarb* (A) the "land of war", enemy territory; *dār al-hudna* (A) the "land of peace"; *dār al-imān* (A) the "land of faith"; *dār al-Islam* (A) the "land of Islam", the Islamic World; *dār al-kufr* (A) the "land of disbelief"; *dār al-ṣulḥ* (A) the land of "settlement" or truce.

dato, datok (Malay) honorific title granted by the king.

dede (T) Alevi holy man; also grandfather, shaykh of a dervish order.

dey (T) Turkish or Algerian Ottoman military title, generally an office superior to that held by a *bey*.

dhimmī (A) non-Muslim "protected" person.

dīnār (A) unit of currency.

dirhām (A) unit of currency.

dünya (T, from the Arabic *dunyā*) world (*bu dünyā* this world, *öbür dünyā* other world).

ehl al-dünya (T, from the Arabic *ahl al-dunyā*) worldly people.

evliya (T sing., from Arabic plural *awliya'*) Muslim saint or saint-like person.

faḍā'il (A, sing. *faḍīla*) merits or special qualities of people or places.

faqīh (A, pl. *fuquhā*) Islamic legal scholar; jurist.

farḍ (A, pl. *farā'iḍ*) fundamental Muslim obligation.

farḍ kifaya (A) collective duty in Islam.

fatāwā (A, sing. *fatwā*) formal legal opinions or advice issued by a recognised Muslim scholar.

fiqh (A) Muslim jurisprudence.

Gastarbeiter (German) "guestworker".

gâvur (T) infidel, unbeliever.

gâvuristan (T) land of infidels.

gecekondu (T) lit. "built at night"; shanty or squatter towns.

gezi (T) stroll, excursion, outing.

ghanīma (A) spoils of war.

ghurabā' (A, sing. *gharīb*) foreigners or non-natives.

gurbet (T) exile, state of being away from home.

gurbetçi (T) one who is in *gurbet*.

ḥadīth (A, pl. *aḥādīth*) reported words of the Prophet Muḥammad, based on the authority of a chain of reliable transmitters.

ḥajj (A) (T *hac*, Malay *haj*) the Meccan pilgrimage, and the rites there; *ḥajj, ḥājjī, ḥājja,* one who has performed the pilgrimage.

ḥanafī (A) one of the four major "schools" of Sunni legal doctrines; the official school of the Ottoman Empire.

ḥaqīqa (A) reality; mystical truth.

ḥarām (A) forbidden.

ḥaramayn (A) the two sacred places of Mecca and Medina.

hareket (T, from the Arabic *ḥaraka*) movement, act, deed.

harman (T) heap of grain; colloq. threshing place.

Hıdrellez (T) 6 May, the 40th day after the spring equinox, often thought to be the beginning of summer; associated with legends of the prophets Hızır and Ilyas (Elias).

helâl (T, from the Arabic *ḥalāl*) approved.

Ḥijāz (A) the Arabian province which includes Mecca and Medina.

hijra (Urdu *hijrat*) migration.

ḥillula (H and A) festival for a Jewish saint.

Hızır (T, from the Arabic *al-Khiḍr*) legendary prophet who attained immortality by drinking from the water of life.

hoşaf (T) cold drink of stewed fruit.

ḥubus in North Africa, a religious bequest, synonymous with *waqf.*

hürmet (T, from the Arabic *ḥurma*) respect, honour, sacredness.

'ibādāt (A, sing. *'ibāda*) ritual duties, including ablutions, prayer, almsgiving, fasting, pilgrimage to Mecca, reading the Qur'ān, and recollection of God.

'īd (A) festival; *'Īd al-Adhā,* Feast of Sacrifice (during *ḥajj*), *'Īd al-Fiṭr,* festival marking the end of the fasting month.

ihrām (A) seamless garment worn by pilgrims in Mecca.

ikinci kuşak (T) second generation (foreign children born or raised in Germany).

imām (A) prayer leader.

isnād (A) the chain of transmitters of authentic tradition (*hadīth*).

izin (T) leave, permission, consent.

izinli (T) one who is on leave.

jamā'a (A) organisation.

jawa (A) members of the Malayo-Polynesian language group resident in Mecca.

jihād (A) striving, effort; *jihād fī sabīl Allāh,* striving in the way of God, if necessary, war in this cause.

Ka'ba (A) the square building in the sanctuary in Mecca which contains the Black Stone and is the focus of the *ḥajj.*

kabul günü (T) women's formal visiting or reception days.

kadın pazarı (T) women's autumn picnics.

kāfir (A, pl. *kuffār*) unbeliever in the Islamic revelation.

kalām (A) scholastics.

kampong (Malay) village.

kapalı (T) covered, closed.

karamogo (Manding) a scholar, a person learned in the Islamic faith and qualified to teach at an advanced level.

kathi (Malay, from the Arabic qāḍī) religious magistrate.

kerajaan (Malay) government, symbolic nationhood or kingdom.

kesin dönüş (T) permanent return (to Turkey from Germany), repatriation.

ketua (Malay) a village headman.

kharaja (A) to go out.

khāṣṣa (A) elite, distinguished.

khaṭīb (A) preacher, the person who delivers the Friday sermon (*khuṭba*) at the noon prayer of assembly.

khenduri (Malay) a village headman.

khirqa (A) a ritual garment symbolising a Sufi follower's obedience to the rule of his *ṭarīqa*; the tattered woollen mantle of the Sufi worn to symbolise poverty.

kufr (A) disbelief.

kurban (T) sacrifice; *Kurban Bayramı* (T, Arabic *'Īd al Aḍḥā*) feast of sacrifice.

kutsal (T) sacred, holy.

lahu riḥlatun (A) lit. "he made a journey"; typical sentence in the biography of an *'ālim*.

lira unit of currency.

lo (Manding) initiation societies among the Dyula.

ma'dān (A) greenhouse, place where things are grown.

madrasa (A) school, often associated with a mosque.

mahdī (A) the expected, divinely guided leader.

maḥshasha (A) a café or popular urban gathering place.

makhzan (A) in North Africa, the central government of the tribes in its service.

malikī (A) one of the four major schools of Islamic jurisprudence, predominant in North Africa.

masjid (A) mosque.

mawsim, mūsim (A) "season" for a celebration; in North Africa, a rural or tribal fair, often held under the auspices of a patron saint.

mevlûd (T, from the Arabic *mawlid*) a religious service commemorating the birth of the Prophet Muhammad.

milla (A and P; *millet* T) religious community or, in some contemporary contexts, "people" or "nation".

misbaḥa (A) a rosary.

mory (Manding) a hereditary category of Dyula Muslims who were expected to conform religiously to the strictures of the *shari'a*.

mu'ākhāt (A) brotherhood.

muezzin (A, *mu'adhdhin*) prayer-caller.

muftī (A) a jurisconsult; an issuer of *fatwa*.

muhājir (A, pl. *muhājirūn*) emigrant, Meccans who emigrated to Medina in the early period of Islam.

muhtar (T, from the Arabic *mukhtār*) headman.

muqaddam (A) a circle or sectional leader in a Sufi order; in North Africa, a Sufi representative capable of formally initiating followers into a *tarīqa*.

murābiṭ (A) often rendered in French as "marabout"; a person living or dead believed to enjoy a special relationship with God which enables him or her to channel God's graces or blessings.

mushrik (A) believer in more than one God.

mustaḍ'afīn (A) weak, oppressed.

muṭawwif (A) pilgrims' guide in Mecca.

muwālāt (A) friendship.

namaz (T) prayer ritual.

nasta'liq (A) the distinctive writing style for Urdu and Persian.

nefs (T) from the Arabic *nafs*) personality, soul, flesh, and bodily desires.

niyet (T, from the Arabic *nīya*) intention, formal resolve to perform a religious act.

penghulu (Malay) traditional title for a lesser chief; district-level state bureaucrat.

piknik (T, from the English) picnic.

pir (T) Alevi holy man, from a holy lineage; leader of a dervish order.

qadama (A) to reach, arrive, get to.

qāḍī (A) Muslim judge, magistrate.

Qādiriyya (A) a Sufi order, tracing its origins to 'Abd al-Qādir al Jīlānī (d. 1166). *Qādirī*, an adherent of the order.

qanūn (A) law; state law.

qirā'a (A) recitation of the Qur'ān.

qubba (A) a dome; a domed building or memorial shrine.

rafidī (A) member of a heretical group.

Ramaḍān (A) Islamic month of fasting.

rībā (A) usurious interest.

rihla (A) travel, often for religious knowledge; *rihla hijāzyya* (A) the pilgrimage trip, travel account of the pilgrimage; *rihla sifāriyya* (A), travel account of, for instance, an embassy mission.

riwāq (A) cloisters around a court; living quarters, dormitories and workrooms of the students of al-Azhar University in Cairo

sam' (A) attention.

saraka (Manding, from the Arabic *saḍaqa*) voluntary charity among the Dyula refers to a variety of prestations, including those obligatory prestations made during life-cycle rituals.

şart (T) condition; stipulation.

saygı (T) respect, esteem, consideration.

sefer (T, from the Arabic *safar*) journey, voyage, travel.

Şeker Bayramı (T, Arabic *'Īd al-Fiṭr*) the feast following *Ramaḍān*.

sevap, sevab (T) religious merit acquired by good action.

seyahat (T, from the Arabic *sayāḥa*) journey, trip, expedition.

sharī'a (A) the laws and practices of Islam, "the straight path".

sharīf (pl. *shurafā, ashrāf*) someone who is distinguished or highborn; Turkish provincial ruler; descendant of the Prophet Muhammad.

shaykh (A) a tribal leader, scholar, or elderly man.

silsila (A) "chain"; lineage, chain of spiritual descent.

Şūfī (A) Muslim mystic.

Sufism Islamic mysticism.

sünnet (T) ritual circumcision; more broadly, from the Arabic *sunna*, the practices derived from the Prophet Muhammad's example.

Sunnī (A) a Muslim who belongs to the majority Muslim community (as distinct from the Shi'a) which accepts the authority and validity of the actions of the early Muslim community and its jurists.

sūra (A, T *sûre*) a chapter of the Qur'an.

sürgün (T) deportation.

ṭabaqāt (A) lit. "classes" or "generations"; Islamic biographical literature.

Tabaski (West African) annual festival, involving the slaughter of sheep, coinciding with the *hajj* season.

ṭā'a (A) obedience.

tafsīr (A) Qur'anic commentary.

tajdid (A) religious reform and renewal.

ṭalab al-'ilm (A) the seeking of religious knowledge, mainly through travel.

ṭālib (A) a (religious) student or scholar; *talip* (T) followers or clients of a holy man, e.g. *dede* or *pir*.

taqiyya (A) dissimulation of one's religion (in the face of a perceived threat).

ṭarīqa (A, pl. *ṭuruq*, T *tarikat*) Sufi brotherhood or order.

taṣawwuf (A) Islamic mysticism; Sufism; the Sufi way of life.

tek (T) single, singleness.

Tijaniyya (A) a North African Sufi order.

toyol (Malay) a type of spirit believed to come from Malaysia via the *hajj*.

tun tigi (Manding) hereditary category of Dyula Muslims who participated in *lo* initiation society rituals and who were not expected to conform rigorously to the strictures of the *sharīʿa*; see also *mory*.

umma (A) the Islamic community.

ʿumra (A), *umre hac* (T) "minor" pilgrimage to Mecca at any time of year. Often understood in Turkey as a commemorative pilgrimage made after the *hajj*.

vatan (T, from the Arabic *watan*) fatherland, homeland.

Wahhābiyya (A) an Islamic reform movement founded in the Arabian Peninsula by Ibn ʿAbd al-Wahhab in the eighteenth century. More properly known as al-Muwaḥḥidūn, or "the Unitarians"; *Wahhābī*, a follower of this movement. Also used loosely to denote a strict fundamentalist.

wali (A) saint.

yerli (T) native, indigenous.

yeshivot (Hebrew, sing. *yeshiva*) Jewish schools of higher religious instruction and learning.

yolculuk (T) travel, journey.

zaddik (H, from the Arabic *saḍīq*) Jewish saint.

zāhidīn (A) ascetics.

zāʾir (A) a visitor; a pilgrim who visits a shrine.

zat (T, from the Arabic *dhat*) personality, individual essence or substance.

zāwīya (A) shrine, usually associated with a saint's tomb.

ziyāra (A, T *ziyaret*) a visit or voluntary pilgrimage; a shrine.

Zweite Generation (German) second generation.

Index

orthodoxy xv, 12, 76, 123, 127,
132, 138, 139, 145, 146, 147,
201, 205, 221, 237, 252, 253
orthopraxy 19, 118, 124, 125, 126
"other" xv, xx, 5, 154, 158
Ottoman Empire xix, xx, 76, 77,
78, 79, 80, 81–2, 131–51, 132,
133, 134, 135, 136, 137, 138,
139, 140, 141, 142, 143, 144,
145, 146, 147, 148, 150, 151,
165, 169, 170, 203, 205 (*see also*
government)

"paganism" 134, 175, 176, 180,
181, 196
Pakistan 10, 11, 12, 29, 30, 41,
46, 104, 112, 259; Ahmadi riots
16; Family Laws Ordinance 29,
46; Munir commission 16 (*see
also* government)
Palestine 138, 221, 222
Parry, John 251
patriarchy 164
patronage 169, 204
peasants 115, 116, 122, 123, 125,
128, 132, 134, 135, 142
periphery xviii, xix, xx, 3, 8,
12–14, 16, 21, 56, 59, 60, 61,
63, 112, 126, 133, 138, 146,
153–70, 185, 205–8, 219, 221,
229, 247
piety 53, 88, 90, 177, 179, 180,
183, 184, 200, 201, 210, 211,
212, 221, 238
pilgrimage xii, xiv, xv, xvi, xviii,
xix, 3, 5, 6, 8, 12, 14, 15, 17,
18, 22, 51, 52, 69, 70, 73, 74,
75, 76, 82, 85–104, 111–29,
139, 180, 184, 185, 200, 201,
206, 208, 211, 217, 218, 220,
221, 222, 223, 226, 227, 228,
229, 230, 231, 232, 233, 236,
237, 240, 241, 242, 243, 244,
256, 257, 258; management of
112, (*see also hajj*)
Piscatori, James 3–22, 122, 153,
253
Pletch, Carl 169

poetry 14, 86, 88, 92, 103, 159,
170, 246, 258
politics 41, 85, 93, 122, 124, 135,
149, 155, 165, 166, 169, 170,
176, 179, 181, 182, 186, 196,
197, 201, 202, 205, 207, 208,
210, 212, 213, 217–33, 237,
252, 257, 258, 259, 260;
participation in 156 (*see also*
change; consciousness;
leadership)
population 111, 112, 114, 117,
125, 131, 132, 136, 139, 147,
155, 158, 161, 202, 203, 208,
213, 220, 229, 230, 231, 238
Porte (*see* government; Ottoman
Empire)
power 120, 123, 124, 125, 140,
141, 142, 163, 176, 180, 202,
218, 219, 220, 221, 223, 225,
226, 227, 230, 232, 233, 237,
247, 253, 257, 258
prayer 18, 55, 78, 79, 100, 116,
118, 119, 121, 175, 176, 177,
183, 186, 192, 198, 221, 223,
228, 236, 242, 244, 246, 247,
248, 250, 252
preaching 144, 163, 170, 183, 188,
192, 203, 205, 207
prestige 111, 121, 123, 124, 125,
158, 160, 175, 194, 198, 203,
204, 253
proselytisation 8, 179, 203, 204,
259

qadi [religious judge] 37, 54, 61,
78, 148
Qadiriyya (Sufi order) 145, 180
al-Qarawiyyin (Morocco) 12, 72
Qayrawan (Tunisia) 72, 178
al-Qayrawani, Shaykh Salim 72
qira [recitation of the Qur'an] 55
Qum (Iran) 12
Qur'an 7, 8, 10, 14, 19, 29, 31,
32, 33, 36, 38, 39, 42, 46, 51,
53, 54, 55, 56, 95, 122, 139,
160, 164, 170, 175, 186, 189,
190, 207, 242, 247, 248

unbelief (*see kufr*)
unemployment 142
United States xvii, 42, 43, 91, 150, 260
Urdu 86, 90, 92, 102, 103

Ibn 'Abd al-Wahhab, Muhammad 206
Wahhabiyya 11, 15, 16, 70, 116, 117, 125, 181–8, 189, 190, 192, 193, 195, 196, 198, 206, 259
wali [saint] xii, 64, 70, 74, 88, 185, 200, 201, 202, 204, 205, 206, 207, 208, 209, 210, 211, 212, 213, 217–33, 237, 247, 259
warfare 30, 31, 176, 178, 182
wealth 18, 115, 123, 159, 186, 187, 189, 193, 196, 198, 238
Weber, Max 20, 233
Weingrod, Alex xii, xv, xxi, 5, 17, 211, 217–33
West Berlin (*see* Berlin)
women xii, xiv, 188, 189, 196; and migration 81, 86, 115, 116, 119;
participation in *hajj* xix, xxi, 17, 31; in Turkey 236–54

Yemen 53, 55
Yochai, Rabbi Simeon bar 222, 228, 229
"Young Turks" 146, 148

Zabid (Yemen) 55
zaddik [Jewish saint] 222, 223, 224, 226, 227, 228, 229, 230, 231
Zaheer, Allama Ihsan Ilahi 29, 46
Abu Zahra, Muhammad bin Ahmad 43
zakat [almsgiving] 8, 10, 18
Zardar, Muhammad 92, 93, 94
Zaydi 16, 35
za'ir [shrine visitor] 87
Bin Zainuddin, Hj. Abdul Majid 120
zawiya [shrine] 72, 76, 204, 205, 206, 210, 211
ziyara [visit to shrine] xii, 5, 204, 206, 208, 210, 236–54, 258